The changing politics of sport

The changing politics of sport

Edited by
LINCOLN ALLISON

Manchester University Press

Manchester and New York

distributed exclusively in the USA and Canada by St Martin's Press

Copyright © Manchester University Press 1993

Published by Manchester University Press
Oxford Road, Manchester M13 9PL, UK
and Room 400, 175 Fifth Avenue,
New York, NY 10010, USA

Distributed exclusively in the USA and Canada
by St Martin's Press, Inc.,
175 Fifth Avenue, New York, NY 10010, USA

British Library Cataloguing-in-Publication Data

A catalogue record for this book is available from the British Library

Library of Congress Cataloguing-in-Publication Data applied for
The Changing politics of sport / edited by Lincoln Allison.
p. cm.
Includes bibliographical references and index.
ISBN 0–7190–3670–4.   ISBN 0–7190–3671–2 (pbk.)
1. Sports and state. I. Allison, Lincoln.
GV706.35.C46   1993
796—dc20   92–26931   CIP

ISBN 0–7190–3670–4 *cased*
ISBN 0–7190–3671–2 *paperback*

Typeset by The Electronic Book Factory Ltd, Fife, Scotland
Printed in Great Britain
by Bell & Bain Limited, Glasgow

Contents

Contributors

Lincoln Allison was educated at University and Nuffield Colleges, Oxford and is currently Senior Lecturer in the Department of Politics and International Studies at the University of Warwick. His books include *Right Principles, A Conservative Philosophy of Politics* and *Ecology and Utility, The Philosophical Dilemmas of Planetary Management.* He has written numerous articles, including series of articles for *New Society, The Countryman* and *The World & I,* the magazine of the *Washington Times.* He has played a variety of games and supported Burnley Football Club all his life. Since 1987 he has been captain of the University of Warwick Staff Cricket Club.

Alan Bairner was educated at the universities of Edinburgh and Hull and is Lecturer in Politics at the University of Ulster at Jordanstown. His research interests include the history of political ideas, Marxism and Northern Ireland and he is the co-author (with John Sugden) of *Games of Two Halves: Sport, Politics and National Identity in Northern Ireland.* He has contributed to a number of magazines and journals and is a fervent supporter of Dunfermline Football Club.

Ken Foster was educated at Manchester University and currently teaches in the Law School at the University of Warwick, where he offers an option in Sport and the Law. His other research interests are mainly in the field of legal theory. He is still an occasional cricketer, and follows the fortunes of Middlesbrough Football Club.

Adrian Guelke lectures in the Department of Politics at Queen's University, Belfast. He was born in Pretoria and grew up in Cape

Town. As a schoolboy he witnessed the All Blacks' victory over the Springboks in the second rugby test at Newlands in 1960 and the different reactions of White and Black spectators to the outcome. His principal research interest is the politics of deeply divided societies. He is author of *Northern Ireland: The International Perspective*. He enjoys canoeing as a summertime leisure activity.

Christopher R. Hill worked in the City, the Diplomatic Service and the Institute of Race Relations (London) before taking up an academic appointment in 1965. He spent a year at the (then) University College at Rhodesia before moving to the University of York where he is Senior Lecturer in Politics. He was director of the Centre for Southern African Studies at York from 1972 to 1982 and wrote extensively on Southern Africa. More recently he has published *Horse Power: The Politics of the Turf*. His personal sporting interests are principally in horse racing and he is Senior Consultant to the Jockey Club Education Trust.

John Hoberman was educated at Haverford College and at the University of California at Berkeley. He is professor of Germanic Languages at the University of Texas at Austin. His books include *Sport and Political Ideology* and *Mortal Engines: Scientific Ambition and the Dehumanisation of Sport*. His main sporting interests, active and passive, are in running.

Grant Jarvie was educated at the universities of Exeter, Queen's (Canada) and Leicester, and currently teaches at the University of Warwick. He is author of several books, including *Sport, Racism and Ethnicity* (1991), *Highland Games: The Making of the Myth* (1991) and *Class, Race and Sport in South Africa's Political Economy* (1985). Born in Scotland, he is a fervent supporter of Motherwell Football Club and enjoys the odd game of squash and football.

Terry Monnington was educated at the University of Birmingham and at Loughborough College of Physical Education and is currently Lecturer in Physical Education at the University of Warwick. His principle research interests have ranged across such areas as politics and sport, sport and the environment and the provision of sports opportunities in British industry. He has played rugby for Moseley and North Midlands and coaches both rugby and volleyball.

Jim Riordan is Professor of Russian Studies and head of the Department of Linguistic and International Studies at the University of Surrey. He was born in Portsmouth in 1936, learned Russian in national service, studied at Birmingham, London and Moscow universities and worked in Moscow for five years. He is author of numerous books and articles; his most recent book is *Sport, Politics and Communism*. He was a crude, but effective soccer player, representing Moscow Spartak, *inter alia*. He is a marathon runner now in his dotage and is an avid follower of Portsmouth Football Club.

John Sugden was educated at the universities of Essex, Liverpool and Connecticut and is Senior Lecturer in Sport and Leisure Studies at the University of Ulster at Jordanstown. His main areas of research are in the sociology of sport, leisure and popular culture. He is co-author (with Alan Bairner) of *Games of Two Halves: Sport, Politics and National Identity in Northern Ireland*. He has played a number of sports, including football in the Irish League 'B' Division. He is Chairman of the University of Ulster Football Club, manager of the Northern Ireland Colleges football team and a life-long supporter of Everton Football Club.

Preface

This book is a sequel or successor to the volume which I previously edited, *The Politics of Sport*; a mere new edition would have been out of the question given the pace of events since the original was published. The themes of this volume are change and the direction of change in aspects of contemporary sport and politics and the relationship between them. The issues aroused by a consideration of these themes are some of the most interesting and challenging in world politics: the consequences of the end of the Cold War, the phenomenon of contemporary nationalism and the prospects for and constraints on a global commercial society.

The quality of individual chapters of this book and the coherence of the whole were much augmented by the authors being able to assemble and to discuss their material thoroughly. The money for doing this came from three individual departments at the University of Warwick: most of it was provided by the Department of Politics & International Studies, substantially aided by the School of Law and the Department of Physical Education. Thanks are due to all of these institutions. I should also like to thank Dorothy Foster of the Department of Politics & International Studies for her invaluable help in the preparation of this manuscript and my wife, Ann, for her encouragement and assistance in bringing the contributors together for what I believe were very valuable discussions.

Lincoln Allison
University of Warwick, 1992

I

The changing context of sporting life

LINCOLN ALLISON

It has been less than six years from the publication of *The Politics of Sport*, the predecessor to this volume, to the time of writing. But that volume is now, in many respects, thoroughly out of date. There are dangers in trying to compute change, but it is *roughly* the case that the six years in question have contained as much change to sport and its political context as the previous generation, perhaps as much as any generation since the period from 1860 to 1890. These changes can be divided into two main categories: the dramatic shifts in world politics, revolutionary in Eastern Europe and radical in Southern Africa, and the acceleration in the endemic trends in the development of sport itself and in the part it plays in society. The second kind of change has been a great deal more predictable than the first.

Eastern Europe during the last six years has experienced the breakdown of an entire system of social, political and economic organisation. Comecon and the Warsaw Pact have collapsed; nowhere has the Communist Party retained its old 'leading role'. In 1989 the Berlin Wall came down, to be followed by the unification of Germany as an unashamedly capitalist country. In the same year nearly all of the regimes in the Communist Countries collapsed, most spectacularly in Romania where the head of state and his wife, Nicolae and Elena Ceausescu, were executed on Christmas Day. In 1991, following an abortive coup by 'conservatives', the regime in the Soviet Union finally collapsed, to be replaced by the Russian State and the ill-defined Commonwealth of Independent States. In none of these cases, except for the former East Germany, is it clear what kind of regime, if any, will replace the old order. In South

Africa the changes in the same period have been only marginally less dramatic: the old regime, the Nationalist Party government which has been in power since 1948, is still in power, but it has demolished the formal structure of *apartheid*, released Nelson Mandela and is moving inexorably towards a multiracial regime.

Nobody could have predicted the timing and pace of these events, but their nature was, I think, predictable; indeed, I would claim to have predicted it.[1] What you needed to predict these changes was to abandon a power model of politics and to replace it by a model of politics whose key concepts are authority and legitimacy. Power models, in this distinction, are those which see the possession of power and the existence of power structures as the causal dynamic in politics. If you make these assumptions, you would expect the political beliefs of the mass of the population to be controllable by the government and the ruling class: the idea of totalitarianism was an extreme version of this model. If, on the other hand, you assume that authority is the key to the stability of regimes and that it exists in the minds of its objects, as an acceptance of the right to command, then political beliefs are crucial and autonomous. They change at the grass roots in ways which are not controllable from above; regimes cannot indefinitely survive an unsuitable structure of belief and ruling classes and military enforcers are necessarily permeated and undermined by attacks on the belief-systems which legitimise their regimes. According to this theory the important processes at work in the Soviet Union were first the steady erosion of any pretence that the Soviet Union was the head of an international communist movement and then the erosion of Marxism–Leninism by western ideas, transmitted by television and radio, by photocopies and by video and audio tapes, culminating in the refusal of Soviet troops to attack the Russian parliament in August 1991. A key change in South Africa was the abandonment of a formal doctrine of racism which made it improper for people of different races to play sport together in favour of a disingenuously naive official liberalism which said it wasn't the government's business whether they did or they did not. A parallel, and even more important, change was the formal abandonment by the Dutch Reformed Church of the doctrine that the Bible prescribed racial separation and hierarchy.

Both of these areas of change have had important sporting dimensions. These are covered in this volume primarily by the chapters by Adrian Guelke on South Africa and Jim Riordan on Eastern Europe, but there are aspects and implications of these events in many other parts of the book. In the South African case, the most interesting questions concern the role of sport as a cause or catalyst of change. To what extent was an ideology of racial distinction and separation rendered untenable by the sporting boycott of South Africa and the perception of a glamorous and commercially attractive multi-racial world of sport outside state borders? Certainly the sporting boycott played a direct part in changing the Nationalist government's official doctrine on race and sport. That it had broader and deeper effects can be judged from the intensity of the current debate in South Africa about the abandonment of the Springbok sporting symbol, a debate which is more intensely conducted in many quarters than is the debate about constitutional reform.

In Eastern Europe, the more interesting questions concern the consequences, rather than the causes, of political change. The Soviet and East German sporting systems were overtly intended to proselytise the superiority of the political regimes which produced them, though their most effective role, in Russia at least, may well have been to legitimise the regime internally. The sports establishment was wholly associated with the *ancien régime*, the demise of which has brought about a new situation in which sport is politically reviled and the system of providing resources for sport has collapsed. That has consequences for the Olympic movement and for international sport which will be discussed later and which may be profound.

A framework for understanding sporting change

It would have been justifiable to publish this volume, or its predecessor, simply as a set of stories, interesting and important in themselves, about Ireland, South Africa, the Soviet Union and so on. After all, many of the chapters in this book are about subjects on which their authors have written books or are going to write books. The politics of sport does not require any overarching theory to justify its interest to readers. But there were general underlying themes which emerged in the discussions surrounding the original volume and which have persistently offered insight since. They remain the best vehicles for understanding the second kind of change, the endemic forces for change in sport:

The inherent politics of sport

When *The Politics of Sport* was published it was still necessary to challenge existing preconceptions about politics and explore alternative definitions. The problem was that politics was still seen principally in terms of a materialist paradigm which lay at the basis of the political thinking of both Marxists and their apparent ideological opponents, the behavourists and positivists. Politics was about 'Who gets What, When, How' in Harold Lasswell's immortal phrase.[2] Real politics was about class, about 'left' and 'right', about the haggle over the distribution of resources. A politics of culture, religion, the arts or sport was a mere superstructure or periphery to this reality. Religious conflicts, even ethnic and national conflicts, were really a kind of class conflict, a matter of privilege, 'under-privilege' and demand for privilege.

It is no longer so necessary to attack this materialist paradigm. The recognition has grown throughout the humanities and social studies that culture and symbolism are important and real in themselves, irrespective of their relations to struggles for resources. For Marxists and former Marxists the greatest influence on the road away from materialism has been Antonio Gramsci, whose explanations in terms of culture and cultural hegemony have helped establish the autonomy of cultural symbolism. Politics can now be seen to be about 'Who care about What, Where and Why' or about 'Who believes What and with What effect'.

Once materialism is denied, the cultural significance of sport is revealed and undeniable. Sport is about prowess; it is one of the most potent of human activities in its capacity to give meaning to life, to create and interconnect senses of achievement and identity. This capacity affects not only participants, but also partisans. Therefore there is a sporting dimension of many political activities. Sport has legitimised regimes from Imperial Rome to Soviet Russia though legitimisation may have backfired in the latter case. It has been used by a wide range of individual politicians to establish credibility and develop an image, a phenomenon discussed in the chapter by Terry Monnington which follows. Above all, and increasingly, sport has a complex and important interaction with nationality and the phenomenon of nationalism. In the chapters which follow Grant Jarvie discusses this phenomenon in general and the Scottish case in particular, John Hoberman looks at the increase in 'sportive nationalism' in the period of the decline and disappearnace of the Cold War while John Sugden and Alan Bairner discuss the sporting scene in Northern Ireland. In that instance every variety of the complex relationship between sport, nationality and nationalism can be found in one small province. There are three rival nationalities: British, Irish and Ulster. There are teams representing all of these and teams which overlap and combine them. There are individuals who represent national teams whose citizenship they do not have and, in some cases, eschew. There is nationalist competition not only within sports, but also between sports. Even in politics, few complexities can rival the world of Irish sport.

The myth of autonomy

What we described in *The Politics of Sport* as 'the myth of autonomy' was the persistent assertion (and sometimes belief) that sport was somehow separate from society, that it transcended or had 'nothing to do with' politics and social conflict. It ought to have been quite difficult to believe these propositions *per se*, but they were often put and perhaps held at least in the weaker form that sport was trivial and therefore had no significant effects or, in the purely ethical version, that sport ought to be treated as if it had nothing to do with anything else.

The specific invocation that sport should not be used for boycotts and that sportsmen should be allowed to pursue their sporting careers without regard to the political significance or consequence of their play was naturally the most common form of the idea of sporting autonomy. But this rested on some very general perceptions about the status of sport in society, which included the belief that sport could not be a serious subject for academic study. It is difficult to specify with any precision the conditions which allowed these beliefs to persist. I believe that, paradoxically, they were supported by two opposite assumptions, that sport was both 'above' and 'below' the political dimensions of social life. For some people, sport was an ideal, not to be tainted by the corrupt and divisive elements of society. The ideal could approach the status of a religion, particularly when applied to a favourite sport: I have particular memories of an Irish rugby union coach preaching, with all the style of a baptist evangelist, the virtues of mini-rugby, for both sexes, as a prophylactic for delinquency, moral decay and sectarian conflict. For others, sport was a trivial diversion from any serious human purpose, pursued by 'muddied oafs on flannelled fools' in Kipling's famous phrase.

These perceptions of sport are by no means dead: in 1992 I was involved in a conversation on an Oxford high table in which a fellow assumed that sport was an entirely separate form of human activity and asserted that having a minister for sport and a Sports Council were absurd gimmicks. (He did not know my views or connection with the subject and was not trying to provoke.) But the myth has retreated steadily, its general form battered by the increasing weight of the serious study of sport by historians, sociologists and some political scientists and its specific, practical form by the demonstration that sport could be used to cause political pain, that the recipients of sporting pressure (white popular culture in South Africa, Communist elite strategy in the case of the 1980 American-led boycott of the Moscow Olympics) *were* affected. By 1990, when Mike Gatting led the last of the 'rebel' cricket tours to South Africa, his protestations that he was just a professional cricketer and that had nothing to do with politics in general and *apartheid* in particular, sounded risibly thin to the vast majority of those who heard them.

An important dimension of the decline of the autonomy of sport and sporting institutions is covered in the chapter by Ken Foster. In the previous volume he outlined the ways in which sporting issues were increasingly being resolved within a legal framework rather than within the traditional and informal institutions which sports themselves had evolved. This process has accelerated and raises complex questions in a number of legal fields; of course, it is connected not only with the decline of beliefs about the autonomy of sport, but also with the increased importance of sport and the greater commercial pressures within it.

The onward march of commercialism

The central theme of the internal politics of sport has been the conflict between a commercial-professional ethos and an amateur-elite ethos. This is markedly true of the history of British sport and true only to a slightly lesser extent of the history of world sport on which the British influence, taking the last century as a whole, has been the greatest single national influence. The commercial-professional ethos exploits and legitimises the market possibilities of mass audiences for sport in industrial society and creates and maintains a class of paid, specialist players. The amateur-elite ethos has always, to a greater or lesser extent, held that such commercialisation debases the nobility and purity of sport as an activity and opens the road to corruption, gambling, fixing and exploitation. Of course, the context of the issue was always the class system: if one is an Oxford or Cambridge graduate, with a potential career in the church, the army, the university or public service, then the idea of being paid to play the games one loves seems demeaning. One might have an intuitive understanding of how the 'commercialisation effect' reduces the worth of action and consumption, in sport as in sex, without having to read the brilliantly clear account of the nature of the effect in the works of the late Fred Hirsch.[3] If, on the other hand, one's most likely source of employment is manual work in the coal mine or the steel mill, pay for play seems far from demeaning.

Between 1860 and 1900, as modern sport evolved in Britain, the conflict between the two views resulted in a series of compromises, schisms and impasses. The amateurs pointed to the grotesque corruption which had existed in pre-modern British professional sport, in horse racing, pugilism and even cricket, and were generally successful in putting strict regulative constitutions in place. In racing and boxing the existence of professionalism was never really in doubt, but the amateurs were able to secure separate statuses and separate competitions which persist to this day. Rowing made itself an overtly class-based sport by excluding manual workers. Rugby experienced total schism: two separate games with the amateur excluding and persecuting the professional with all the zeal of a religious sect. Association Football allowed professional players, but contained the commercial ethos with tight restrictions on dividends and a strict system of limiting players' earnings which lasted from 1885 to 1961. The cricket compromise, made possible only by the distinction between batsmen and bowlers, was the most bizarre: professional and amateurs played together, but the professionals used separate changing facilities and modes of address to their social superiors.

In *The Politics of Sport*, we recorded the steady advance of the commercial ethos and Kate Brasher described the capitulation of tennis since the All-England championships became open to professionals in 1968. Since then, the advance has accelerated and become more of a rout. All serious pretensions to amateurism have been abandoned in the Olympic movement; the nature of this process and the enormous magnitude of the commercial pressures on Olympic sport is covered by Christopher Hill's chapter in this volume. The appearance of highly paid professional tennis players in the 1988 Olympics and, *inter alia*, professional basketball players in the 1992 Games as well as the unashamed professionalism of contemporary track athletes represents a complete reversal of the original spirit of the modern Games. If ever the cliché about dead men turning in their graves was appropriate it must apply to the hypothetical attitude of Avery Brundage, President of the International Olympic Committee from 1952 to 1972, to the concessions made by his current successor, Juan Samaranch. To Brundage, professional sportsmen were no better than 'performing monkeys' and Samaranch's tolerance of professionalism would be a betrayal parallel to the first French revolution's metamorphosis into an empire. To most of Samaranch's contemporaries his policy has been a form of practical reason which has removed massive sources of hypocrisy and unfairness from world sport, the most pernicious of those sources being the pastiche form of amateurism invented by the Soviet Union in 1945.

The last great bastion amateurism outside the Olympic movement, Rugby Union, has also begun to crumble dramatically. When the predecessor volume to this was published the (English) Rugby Union was still enforcing its code of amateurism with fanatical rigour: if the wife of the England coach stayed with him during the period around an international match he was asked to pay half his hotel bill! (And this in relation to a match whose takings were over £1 million.) Rugby has since changed enormously. It has held two world cups, the second of which, in 1991, was televised to seventy countries; its final was watched in England by nearly fourteen million people, the third largest sports television audience of the year. The English and Welsh Rugby Union have started national leagues: the games in those leagues attract big crowds and have entirely eclipsed the traditional club 'friendlies' which were, in the minds of old-fashioned Rugby

Union followers, the real essence of the game. The 'shamateurism' of players in the southern hemisphere and in France and Italy has reached Olympic proportions; this, combined with the pressures of competition for players from Rugby League, has made most of the leading national unions favour a relaxation of amateur regulations. In 1990 the International Rugby Board, following the surprising defection of Scotland, allowed players to make money from off-the-field activities related to the game. In 1991, the principal opponent of relaxation, the English Rugby Union, were put under severe pressure from their own national team following their first win in Cardiff since 1963 when the players refused to talk to the press because they could not charge for interviews. The way is now open to a quasi-professionalisation of the game in which a limited number of players will be able to make a living from books, television, personal appearances and so on and all players will receive compensation for lost earnings, without anybody formally being paid for actually playing.

Even association football in England has taken further important steps towards total commercialisation. When the last volume was produced the game had still made few concessions to television: only special events like FA and European cup finals and major international competitions were televised live. Since then, games have become routinely televised, in the context of a fierce competition between state and independent television companies. Of course, television reaches a different and much larger audience: for instance, the English television audience for the 1990 World Cup was 44 per cent female whereas most estimates for the proportion of women among those who attend matches are in the range of 7–10 per cent. A group of the biggest and most successful clubs, anxious to retain for themselves their full potential earnings from football rather than see them diffused throughout the professional game, constantly threatened to break away from the Football League and finally did so in 1992 in the form of a Football Association Premier League. At the heart of this dispute is a conflict of interest between true football fans and a much larger, casual following and a conflict of principle within the game as to which group's interests should predominate. Once again, as it was with the abolition of the maximum wage in 1961, a major impetus to change has been the pressure of international competition and the desire of major English clubs to compete with their Italian and Spanish rivals who are potentially wealthier.

Post-modern sport?

There is a fairly well agreed developmental model which applies to the history of sport:

Vernacular or *traditional* sport existed for centuries in predominantly rural societies. It was based on local terrain and traditions and was therefore very diffuse. It was highly participatory and used the extensive holidays and big spaces available in a rural society.

Modern or *industrial* sport was developed for the conditions of the urban working class. It required standardised rules overseen by national organisations and was confined to precise, small slices of time and space. Typically, spectators far outnumbered participants. It evolved an international dimension.

Transitional sport occurred in the British Isles in the period of flux from 1850 to 1900 (to give its maximum extent) during which alternative forms of modern sport, mainly developed from traditional models, were created and competed for popularity and establishment.

Post-industrial sport has developed as disurbanisation and the breakdown of a predominantly manufacturing economy have occurred. A newly mobile population increasingly participates in a vast range of sporting and quasi-sporting activities, most of which take them out of the city to the country, the wilderness, the sea, the waterways or the snow.

There is a case for calling the post-industrial phase 'post-modern'. The case against is that post-modernism, even if it was clear in its origins in the discussion of art and architecture in the 1970s, has become a promiscuous and mystical term which is high on fashionability and low on clarity. But the current diffusion of sporting activity seems to have as many of the features of the 'post-modern' as any of the phenomena to which the phrase is applied in other genres: there is the breakdown of a unified, rationalised pattern and a return to aspects of the pre-modern; no longer is there consensus on the direction of progress; developments are very diffused. Paradoxically, the rapid development of post-modern sport also includes the revival of aspects of the modern: Football League and Rugby

League attendances have gone up since the last volume was published.

My own chapter later in this book concerns the post-modern clash between sport and environmentalism. Do we want the countryside, the wilderness *et al.* as an efficient playground? Or is there a case for treating them more reverently than one treats a playground? These questions raise, yet again, further questions about the meaning and value of sport.

A complex system of change

In this chapter I have described two distinct kinds of change: political revolution, which has been rapid, explosive and unpredictable and a range of slow, evolutionary, inexorable changes in the relations between sport and social structure. Of course, they are related, even in their origins and their consequences intertwined, so the result is a complex, systematic pattern of change. The demise of the Soviet Union has a great deal to do with the resurgent victory of commercial values (to use Adam Smith's terminology; 'capitalist values' if you prefer Marx). The same resurgence which penetrated the USSR also puts pressure on South African employers to favour a more competitive labour market and a fuller incorporation into the world economy and on England rugby players to get their own slice of the financial action. The Stalinist push on the Olympics put enormous stress, in the long term, on their amateur status; the demise of the Soviet Union ends the Cold War and removes the *raison d'être* of much investment in Olympic sport. As a result of these changes, the Olympic movement is cut off from much of its original spirit and purpose, but dragged into new territory by its immense financial successes and even greater potential in the age of commercial television.

The old amateur ethos declines to extinction; nobody any more believes in the separateness of sport from politics and commerce; the ideological struggle for the globe is over. Sport comes under the sway of the immense pressures of nationalism and corruption. Above all, in the kind of account that John Hoberman gives, it becomes permeated by drugs, as the techniques developed by both sides in the Cold War are spread throughout the world. In the English-speaking world we perhaps underestimate the use of drugs in sport: they are far more widely discussed in Germany. We tend to regard the drugs issue as a technical, criminological one whose arguments are about techniques of detection and enforcement. We are unaware that there is a continental tradition of thinking about athletics which seeks a perfection of human physical performance through science and regards drugs as an inevitable means, perhaps even a legitimate means, to that end.

Sport is entering a period of change in which it is becoming more important and entering new fields of controversy. It is going to be much less easy to curb the excesses of the performance principle and to maintain the kind of idealistic illusion which has given modern sport part of its special glamour. Perhaps the most immune sports to these trends will be the fully established professional sports where technique and tactical judgement are at least as important as athletic ability, sports like cricket and baseball.

Of course, in some respects these tendencies can be seen as a case of *plus ça change*: the eternal war between corruption and regulation which was the main concern of the Victorian administrators of the transitional phase.

Sport and gender

In this account of the pattern of change affecting sport, there is one unmentioned subject, a dog which didn't bark more noticeably than the others: the role of women in sport. In *The Politics of Sport* I suggested that the key concepts in understanding sport were skill and prowess. Skill concerns technique, craft, ability and practical knowledge. Prowess is 'valour, bravery, gallantry, martial daring, manly courage, active fortitude': the word is out-dated, but the concept is clearly represented in modern English by such words as 'guts' and 'bottle'. The unavoidable implication of these assertions is that sport is associated with ideas of masculinity; the cultural roots of sporting practices and our appreciation of sporting prowess are laced with specifically masculine images and virtues.

In preparing both this volume and its predecessor I tried to solicit a feminist perspective on this analysis and its implications, but the result on both occasions was failure and disappointment. Feminism has become extremely diffuse since, a quarter of a century ago, it was taken as a straightforward demand for equal rights and treatment for women with those accorded to men. 'Post-feminism' is now thought to exist, though the term is as difficult as 'post-modernism' and seems to cover a range of forms, opponents and successors of feminism. As far as sport is concerned, contemporary feminism offers two entirely divergent strains:

Anti-patriarchalism. There is a large and coherent body of ideas which analyses the specifically masculine structure of thought which long ago came to dominate human institutions: a male god; domination over the earth rather than harmony with it as the purpose of labour; ambition and acquisition as virtues. This is contrasted with the culture of earth-goddesses and the ethics of harmony, stability and acquiescence. It is an important strain of our thinking about nature and there are many male writers, as diverse as Robert Graves and Jonathan Porritt, who have embraced aspects of this analysis. A minor theme of it is that competitive games are a specifically patriarchal institution; even in simple forms they are a socialisation into patriarchy while, *in extremis*, modern American sport is an instructive metaphor for the brutally aggressive and acquisitive ways of modern American capitalism. I have no quarrel with this analysis as such; the problem for its proponents is that it is so radical (and reactionary) that it has no *practical* content. We cannot be expected to reject meanings and institutions hundreds of thousands of years old and embedded in most cultures.

Sports feminism. This reformist approach concentrates on equal opportunities for women in sport and an equal status to parallel and reaffirm movements for equal status in society generally. Women can find self-development through sport in the same ways as men can. Much of the academic writing tends to concentrate on banalities like the existence of structural male power in sport.

The difficulty is a profound one for pro-sports feminists. The role and nature of prowess-concepts can change, but we should expect them to change only slowly and with the constant threat of reactions and reaffirmations of old values (parallels, perhaps, to the renaissance of fundamentalist Islam). The brute facts are that men are better at sport than women and like it more. It is true that many women's performances are catching up on men's in measurable terms, but it has become increasingly clear (given the circumstances described in the chapter by John Hoberman) that it is male hormones which allows this to happen: the performance principle demands that females become more male. For what it is worth, my (non-feminist) argument suggests that anti-sport feminism is far more capable of coherent development than is pro-sport feminism.

I should add, lest this argument is interpreted simplistically, that there is nothing here which implies opposition to women getting the full benefits of sport if that is what they wish. But you don't have to be a feminist to be in favour of that, nor to have any principle of male–female equality or inequality, homogeneity or hetereogeneity. All you have to be (as I am) is a Utilitarian who believes in female emanicipation to the degree that it is to the aggregate benefit of our actual society in the foreseeable future.

Notes

1 See Lincoln Allison, 'Down in the old USSR', *New Society*, vol. 65, no. 1087, 15 September 1983. In the South African case I can only quote my paper, 'Sport and South Africa: what is to be done?', given at the conference on sport held at Queen's University, Belfast in June–July 1989.
2 Harold Lasswell, *Politics: Who Gets What, When How*, McGraw-Hill, 1936. The phrase is a materialist slogan, but Lasswell's own range of views was more eclectic.
3 Fred Hirsch, *Social Limits to Growth*, Routledge and Kegan Paul, 1976, pp. 71–113.

2

Sport and ideology in the post-Communist age

JOHN HOBERMAN

The collapse of Eastern European Communism and its vaunted sports systems raises the question of whether the familiar left–right bipolar model of the ideological spectrum is still relevant to political life in general or to international sport in particular. If the traditional bipolar model has somehow survived the end of the Cold War, then precisely where have the old ideological tensions been preserved?[1] Alternatively, if the old bipolar model has become irrelevant, then is ideological bipolarity a thing of the past or has a new bipolar model, representing a new axis of political contention, succeeded it?

My response to these questions takes the form of four major arguments: (1) that the traditional ideological spectrum is essentially moribund following the collapse of Communism and the attendant triumph of capitalist ideology; (2) that the ideological interpretation and exploitation of sport, while of historical significance, have always been subordinate to a generic phenomenon I call sportive nationalism and its unquestioning acceptance of the high-performance ideal and the competitive ethos; (3) that the old ideological tensions between left and right have been succeeded by new tensions between advocates and opponents of scientific techniques that aim to boost athletic performance; and (4) that sportive nationalism is, in fact, only one form of national self-assertion among others that promote the high-performance ideal and any techniques that might serve it.

The end of the Cold War

The virtual disappearance of classic ideological tensions between East and West marks a major historical shift that has brought about epochal readjustments in foreign policy. The disintegration of the Soviet Union and the absorption of the East German state by the Federal Republic have dissolved long-standing and potentially deadly rivalries. But the impact of this revolution on the theory and practice of elite sport has been negligible, since the relaxation of political tensions has not reduced the intensity of international sports competition. On the contrary, the pressures that fuel international sports rivalries have not abated and even show signs of intensifying, as in the case of the sports build-up by the People's Republic of China (see below).

These rivalries continue because they are essentially independent of what we think of as the political process in the familiar sense, including the superpower dynamics of the Cold War period. The independence of world-class sport *vis-à-vis* the changing political landscape is rooted in three important sociological phenomena that belong to the political dimension but transcend its familiar ideological divisions. The first of these forces is sportive nationalism. This ambition to see a nation's athletes excel in the international arena may be promoted by a political elite or it may be felt by many citizens without the promptings of national leaders. Sportive nationalism has appeared in a variety of political cultures, and the use of this generic term should not obscure the diversity it represents (see below). The second factor is the international sports system, prominently including the Olympic movement, which survives by accommodating sportive nationalism while dressing it in the pseudo-cosmopolitan ethos of the 'Olympic idea' or other variations on the theme of internationalist fraternalism. If sportive nationalism is the energy that drives athletic rivalries, then the international sports system is the framework in which these contests occur. The third dimension of this system is the commercialisation of certain Olympic sports such as track and field and, indeed, of the Olympic movement as a whole during the tenure of Juan Antonio Samaranch, who assumed the presidency of the International Olympic Committee in 1980.[2] The point here is that the nationalist, international and commercial aspects of this total sports system exist largely independent of the political interests that, having clashed during the Cold War era, have now entered an age of co-operation. Indeed, the major question addressed in this chapter is why an analogous reconciliation has not occurred in the realm of sport.

A short answer to this question is that the competitive impulse is a basic human drive that is more durable than the political regimes that channel and exploit it. All kinds of governments, representing every type of political ideology, have endorsed international sporting competition as a testing ground for the nation or for a political 'system'. German Nazis, Italian Fascists, Soviet and Cuban Communists, Chinese Maoists, western capitalist democrats, Latin American juntas – all have played this game and believed in it. Indeed, a once-familiar phenomenon like 'socialist competition' – a Soviet term intended to rescue the competitive impulse from its decadent capitalist motives – reminds us that ideological arguments about the nature of competition have left the ideal of the contest itself quite intact. Yet the idea of 'socialist competition' also shows that political ideologists have differed on the subject of competition. Fascists, for example, have always exalted the most merciless competitions, e.g. wars, as crucibles in which (male) character was both tested and forged, while less fanatical versions of this doctrine are found in many societies. The left, by contrast, has traditionally adopted internationalist (and, therefore, anti-war) doctrines that stress co-operation over competition.[3] Similarly, humanitarian ideals, whether real or merely rhetorical, are basically contrary to a competitive ethos. A capitalist democracy such as the United States has steered a middle course by hailing competition as the engine of economic progress while also endorsing internationalist schemes designed to hold competing nations within certain limits. In the last analysis, however, these 'ideological' differences have had little impact on the practice of international sport. In fact, the competitive ethos has been in the ascendancy throughout the twentieth century. Since the the late 1980s, for example, it has become politically difficult if not impossible for schoolteachers to oppose competitive sport in British schools – a revival of the *Tom Brown*-style approach to character-building that we remember as one of the distinctive features of Victorian England.[4] Our own century has adopted this competitive principle as a way of life, and we may predict that sportive nationalism will remain a prominent feature of the political landscape for the foreseeable future.

Sportive nationalism

Sportive nationalism is not a single generic phenomenon; on the contrary, it is a complicated socio-political response to challenges and events, both sportive and non-sportive, that must be understood in terms of the varying national contexts in which it appears. Sportive nationalism is poorly understood for two basic reasons. First, we still do not understand the symbolic potency of the athlete for modern societies, a symbolic role that always survives changes in official ideology. Why do these people achieve such popularity in a wide variety of societies? Which psychological processes make it possible for black athletes to 'represent' predominantly white societies? How is athletic prowess converted into other kinds of prowess in our minds? Do any of these processes vary in quality or intensity from one society to another? These questions address sportive nationalism as a mass psychological phenomenon. What is more, they tend to suggest that the feelings that are involved in sportive nationalism are too diffuse and intangible to be understood.

While these feelings may, indeed, be finally indefinable, we can also study sportive nationalism as the more tangible behaviour of empowered individuals and institutions. In this sense, sportive nationalism exists, not as an inchoate mass emotional condition, but as the product of specific choices and decisions made by identifiable political actors.

This political process has taken different forms in different political cultures. In the Soviet Union, the official promotion of competitive sport began during the 1930s, in conjunction with feverish industrialisation and the Stalinist cult of the Stakhanovite superworker who broke records like an athlete. This rehabilitation of sport was, of course, achieved under the aegis of an official ideology.[5] In the United States, the Amateur Sports Act passed by Congress in 1978 aimed at promoting American success in international sports competitions but offered no accompanying ideological strictures.[6] Smaller states have practised an even more intense sportive nationalism as a deliberate and carefully managed policy. The former East German state created an unparalleled high-performance sports establishment for the purpose of winning international stature and domestic political credibility for the Communist regime.[7] It is now known that East German authorities mobilised over a thousand scientists, physicians and trainers in its programme to develop successful athletes by means of anabolic steroids.[8] Canada presents a similar, if less extreme, example of a small state administered by a government with specific political needs – national unity above all – that could be addressed (if not solved) through a self-assertive sports policy that included 'direct, forceful involvement in the development of elite athletes'.[9] *A Proposed Sports Policy for Canadians*, a document presented to the Canadian Amateur Sports Federation in 1970, clearly emphasised the development of elite athletes.[10] Indeed, for years after its triumph at the 1978 Edmonton Commonwealth Games, Canada was frequently referred to as 'the East Germany of the Commonwealth', a sobriquet that inevitably reappeared during the Ben Johnson scandal of 1988.[11]

For the Canadian government of Prime Minister Brian Mulroney the Ben Johnson affair was deadly serious political business – a public relations disaster that threatened to dismantle an official policy that linked Canadian state identity quite explicitly to international success in high-performance sport.[12] Here, as in East Germany, steroids became nothing less than a national security issue. Consequently, the Dubin Commission of Inquiry, appointed by the federal government itself to investigate doping in Canadian sport, was in large measure an exercise in political damage control – a wholly unintended consequence of sportive nationalism and the drugs it requires to be successful in the steroid age.[13]

There are many examples of sportive nationalism and its improbably extreme effects on otherwise sober people. We are all familiar with the extravagant fantasies of national grandeur that have often taken the form of athletic ambition. During the 1986 World Cup soccer matches in Mexico City, for example, the Argentine footballer Diego Maradona described as 'crazy' those Argentine legislators who had demanded a boycott of the game against England out of residual bitterness over the Falklands Islands war. The Argentine players even went so far as to present gifts to the members of the British team on the field.[14]

Is there, one might ask, a connection between such fantasies of national grandeur and socio-political instability? It is tempting to assume that the hysterical element one detects in the national football mania of Argentina or Brazil is related in some way to their precarious political structures, to hyperinflation, to crushing foreign debts, and to the military-sponsored terror of their recent pasts. The frequent association of sportive nationalism and domestic political tensions might even reflect a societal need for occasional cathartic outbursts to relieve feelings of anger and frustration. We might thus assume that politically stable and prosperous societies are likely to be immune to the aggressive mass psychology of sportive nationalism.

But that is not necessarily the case. In fact, exaggerated, even sinister, outbreaks of sportive nationalism can occur in societies that are both stable and wealthy. A case in point is the wave of chauvinism that swept over Switzerland in February 1987 after its skiers achieved a staggering series of victories at the world championships – a surge of popular emotion that included an ugly streak of xenophobic scorn for the foreign athletes who could not match the native champions. The writer Peter Bichsel commented: 'I am horrified by these victories and by the national frenzy they have unleashed. This has nothing to do with sport, but rather with Switzerland. We are anything but a peaceful people.'

But not all Swiss saw this episode of national delirium in the same way. Adolf Ogi, president of the agrarian-conservative Swiss People's Party and himself a former manager of the Swiss Skiing Federation, offered the following explanation: 'Erika and Pirmin, but also Maria Walliser, come close to an ideal image of the youthful Swiss: modest, as we all are to some extent, and successful, as we would all like to be.' At the same time, as Ogi pointed out himself, these idealised figures are something more than quiet bucolic youths who have done well in the wider world. 'In business and in politics,' he says, 'there are only a few people who, in critical situations, are capable of responding in two short minutes to the command "On your marks, get set!" and make the most fateful kinds of decisions.' In short, for this observer the high-performance athlete symbolised nothing less than national survival in the unforgiving environment of international economic competition. Muscular strength and co-ordination fuse with economic strength and co-ordination into a metaphorical relationship, so that each of these twin dynamisms implies the other.

Does this metaphor play a role in the real world? Many newspaper and magazine advertisements that equate corporate and athletic achievement suggest that it does. The recent triumphalist response of the Norwegian prime minister to the gold medals won by her country's skiers at the 1992 Albertville Winter Olympic Games is a particularly suggestive case study of this metaphorical sportive nationalism. Indeed, her painstaking attempts to convince her countrymen that Olympic victories could actually be translated into success in the larger World Capitalist Games illustrate the underlying pathos of all small-country sportive nationalism (see below).

This theory does not account, however, for the timing of the Swiss incident. Indeed, constant demands on the Swiss economy would, according to this model, produce constant eruptions of nationalist feeling. According to the Swiss journalist Jürg Bürgi, this episode had its roots in Swiss dissatisfaction with the modern world and the plagues it has visited upon the once-sheltered society that has not known war for five hundred years. Environmental disasters and the endless stream of refugees seeking safety and employment in Switzerland had poisoned the national mood to the bursting point. Given this national state of mind, sportive nationalism could assume its classic function of hurling a combination of megalomania and resentment against the outside world.[15]

All of the anecdotal evidence considered up to this point links sportive nationalism to political pathology. But we might also speculate that sportive nationalism plays a 'normal' symbolic role for smaller nations that have few opportunities to assert themselves against much larger states. If this is the case, then the more civilised forms of sportive nationalism may have to be recognised as an inherent right of the 'minor' nations that participate in international sport.

The idea that some national communities actually have a psychological need to assert themselves through sportive achievement is intriguing. The ideal test case would be a small and culturally homogenous national community, economically productive and politically stable, displaying no unusual need for the emotional compensations of sporting success in the international arena.

Let us use Norway as a good approximation to the ideal test case. In 1985, after a considerable amount of public discussion regarding government financing of sport, the parliamentary leader of the conservative (Høyre) party, Jo Benkow, stated that sport should not be a special priority for state funding and that social welfare measures were more important. What is more, he was prepared to defend this position even if it cost him political support.

This call for restraints on state funding for sport is especially interesting because it came from a conservative politician. For reasons I do not have time to analyse in this context, conservatives will generally support sportive nationalism – indeed, virtually all nationalist initiatives – more often and with greater fervour than centrists or leftists. And yet an independent Christian (and, there-fore, conservative) newspaper that supported Benkow's position noted that 'a number of ardent souls on the right' should heed his message on sport funding.[16]

Jo Benkow's provocative moderation in the area of sport confirms the broad political consensus behind Norway's traditional welfare policies. But it would be misleading to suggest that Norwegian society is immune to concerns about its competitiveness in high-performance sport. English and Norwegian soccer fans, for exam-ple, are likely to remember the famous outburst in 1981 by a Norwegian television commentator, Bjœrge Lillelien. Follow-ing Norway's 2–1 upset victory over the English team, Lillelien seemed to go berserk, screaming 'William Shakespeare, Francis Drake, Winston Churchill . . . we've beaten you all!'[17] This most un-Norwegian display of naked chauvinist passion confirmed that sportive nationalism could breach even the famous self-containment of the Scandinavians.

In fact, Norwegian sportive nationalism is usually tempered by a sober practicality, irrespective of whether it is responding to victory or defeat. In February 1988, for example, Norway's Olympic athletes returned from the Calgary Winter Olympic Games after a dismal performance. Never before had a Norwegian team come home without a gold medal. The significance of this failure was discussed in an editorial that appeared in the conservative Oslo newspaper *Aftenposten*. The purpose of this editorial was not to lament a dark day in the history of Norwegian sport, but rather to determine whether sporting success is of authentic value to the national community. One conclusion was that, although gold medals do not rank with economic performance and educational achievement as foundations of national security, they have played a role in building national self-respect. What is more, Norwegian anxieties about doing conspicuously well in the winter sports is rooted in a long tradition that teaches virtually all children to ski and skate because these practical skills are a way of life. This commentary concludes by noting that a limited, focused programme to develop high-performance athletes in certain traditional disciplines answers an authentic psychological need of the nation; and that the mass media should reduce the indiscriminate pressure exerted on many athletes to perform at the highest level.[18]

Four years later this situation had utterly reversed itself. The 1992 Albertville Winter Games witnessed the greatest Norwegian Olympic performance in history – nine gold, six silver and five bronze medals. Even before the Games, Prime Minister Gro Harlem Brundtland had welcomed in the New Year by declaring that 'Excellence is typically Norwegian'. citing the achievements of successful (women) handball players, skiers and the Oslo Philharmonic.[19] Now she immediately seized the opportunity to address the topic of high performance on the editorial page of Norway's largest and most respectable newspaper. Gold-medal victories, she declared, had provided a windfall of positive publicity for Norway, and only two years before the opening of the 1994 Winter Olympic Games in Lillehammer. Norwegian athletes had done valuable service as 'ambassadors of Norwegian initiative', reinforcing self-confidence at home while convincing potential customers abroad that Norwegian companies, like Norwegian athletes, had to be taken seriously. The finely tuned co-operative effort and 'team spirit' of the Norwegian Olympic team, the prime minister wrote, must be emulated by the economic sector. 'In the years ahead, we must do a better job of asserting ourselves internationally in arenas other than sports and culture,' she warned. She went on to imply that athletes and business people were really playing the same game, whether inside or outside the stadium: 'Large sectors of our export industry have been competing hard in both the European Cup and the World Cup' – an effective metaphorical strategem for a sports-minded body politic with the prospect of European Community membership on its mind. Indeed, with impressive political legerdemain, Prime Minister Brundtland managed to deliver this blunt warning about international economic competitiveness without once mentioning her hard-driving campaign to persuade Norwegians that they should enter the EC – an economic major league naturally feared by people accustomed to a less Darwinian existence and the creature comforts of deeply rooted local economies[20] Nor was this an 'ideological' issue of left and right. The only 'ideology' (or *Weltanschauung*) left standing in this debate was the competitive ethos itself.

In short, Norwegian responses to national Olympc performance in both 1988 and 1992 included some impressively sober assessments by leading politicians. Here was sportive nationalism at its calculating best, first looking inward for the historical foundations of national character (Benkow), then looking outward to the markets that could ensure national survival (Brundtland). The Norwegian experience shows that it is simply irresponsible to approach sportive nationalism as though it were a kind of mass psychosis beyond our understanding. On the contrary, it is sport's legendary effects in the political world that have prompted us to overestimate the irrational factor. 'We must invest in sport because it contributes to the identification of the citizen with the state,' a West German sports official stated after the 1988 Seoul Olympiad.[21] While the ultimate basis of this identification may well be 'irrational', planning to create it is not.

A different version of the rational approach to sportive nationalism was once proposed by the president of Finland, Mauno Koivisto. When Finland's Olympic athletes returned from the 1984 Sarajevo Winter Games, they had won more medals than ever before and President Koivisto did not hesitate to express pride in their accomplishments. But he went on to suggest that the nationalistic character of the Games should be de-emphasized and even proposed the elimination of national anthems from the medal ceremonies at major international competitions. These comments produced a public controversy, and one opinion poll showed that fully 70 per cent of the Finnish population disagreed with their president and that 50 per cent felt his political popularity had diminished.[22] A year later Koivisto made another public comment that showed how committed he was to the antinationalist point of view. On this occasion he provoked a second debate by complaining of an anti-Soviet 'sports mentality' among the Finnish population.[23]

The very idea of applying a 'rational' approach to the management of sportive nationalism is intriguing. (One might add that the historical evidence suggests it is also quixotic.) Only the Maoist regime of the People's Republic of China made a serious effort to curb such feelings, and it is important to note that these ideologically-based behavioral norms have been eroding since the death of Mao Zedong in 1976. Prior to this date Maoist sport 'specialized in an etiquette based on the eradication of hostile or aggressive feelings toward an opponent'.[24] and this fraternal ethos ('friendship first, competition second') prescribed correct behaviour for spectators as well as athletes and referees. It is also significant that only these most rigid and doctrinaire ideologists imagined that they could control such emotions, and for some years this improbable experiment in psychological engineering actually worked. Foreign athletes and spectators were awed by the exquisite *politesse* of Chinese athletes and the emotional self-control of Chinese audiences. Now that the Communist edifice has collapsed in all but a few hardline states, the artificiality of these emotional restraints is more evident than it was in the heyday of Maoist enthusiasm in China and in the West.

But sport doctrine in Communist China has another, and very different, lesson to teach us about the relationship between ideology and Marxist–Leninist sport. Upon closer inspection, the developmental process whereby 'Maoist' sport became 'post-Maoist' sport turns out to have been somewhat illusory. Contrary to appearances, the ideological content of Maoist sport doctrine has actually been retained during the post-Maoist period. What changed was the relative degree of emphasis accorded specific ideological elements, so that these two doctrinal phases may be analysed in terms of dominant and recessive traits. While the official ideology changed in this manner, allegiance to the modernisation process and the performance principle – so effectively camouflaged while Mao Zedong was alive – remained constant. Our conclusion is that the Maoist defection from the high-performance ideal was partial at best – a propaganda tactic that amazed, and misled, many outsiders. From this perspective, it becomes clear that allegiance to the performance principle – not Maoist principle – is the real ideological constant. This confirms the thesis that there is a great deal of continuity linking the sport cultures of the pre- and post-Communist eras in China and elsewhere.[25]

The decay of Maoist sports ideology raises the larger question of how important Communist ideology was to the practice of sport in the Marxist–Leninist states. Was Marxism–Leninism an important factor in the formation of the major Communist sports establishments? Did Communist ideology really motivate athletes to perform better? Did Marxism–Leninism expedite the scientific approach to boosting athletic achievement?

In response to the first question, let us first note the role of personal idiosyncrasy in the cases of Walter Ulbricht and Fidel Castro, both former athletes who decided that high-performance sport would make an ideal showcase subculture in East Germany and Cuba, respectively. Indeed, as I have suggested elsewhere, the traditional Marxist emphasis on intellectualism tended to produce indifference or even hostility to sport.[26] Nevertheless, the global view of labour that is peculiar to Marxism–Leninism certainly promoted the Stalinist appropriation of sport and the resulting exploitation of athletes; this ideological view of labour also promoted the scientisation of sport by rationalising the athlete's exposure to risk and stress, a line of thinking perfected by the East German authorities. For example, the former East German swimmer Raik Hannemann recounted the fervent admonition delivered to a group of elite athletes in 1987 by the one-time sport czar Manfred Ewald: 'In the capitalist countries doping is being practised in an increasingly unpredictable manner. For that reason our own sports medicine must also make its contribution. And from the athletes I expect both creativity and a willingness to take risks.'[27] Ewald's evident meaning was that he expected athletes to participate in experiments with anabolic steroids, and that is exactly what happened on a massive scale.[28]

As for the second question, Communist ideology did motivate some, but certainly not all, East German and Soviet athletes to perform well against their 'capitalist' adversaries. The persisting effects of this indoctrination were evident in 1989 as the GDR began to fall apart and the elite sport system came under public attack. Petra Felke, the world record-holder in the javelin, stated that the only proper response to the many doping allegations appearing at this time was an even greater level of performance.[29] Kristin Otto, winner of six gold medals in swimming at the 1988 Seoul Olympic Games, replied to the resentment of ordinary East Germans by invoking the 'performance principle' (Leistungsprinzip) by name. 'I believe', she said, 'that in no other field of endeavour was it better realized than in elite sport. And that, in my opinion, is the secret of our success.' Otto's ideological schooling also prompted her to draw an invidious comparison between the achievements of East German athletes and their counterparts in the world of art and literature, confirming the postwar Marxist–Leninist line that ascribed equal status to sport and art.[30] This sport–art synthesis can be traced in turn to the rejection of mind–body dualism that was characteristic of Soviet psychology and the East German sports psychology derived from it (see below).[31]

Otto's invocation of the performance principle rather than a specifically Marxist–Leninist formula is of real significance. Her claim, in effect, was that a Communist society had given unlimited reign to the performance principle in a way that other societies could not. But careful scrutiny of this claim suggests that it is far too categorical. For while it is true that the East German regime did create an optimal (if also perverse) environment for the development of high-performance athletes, it is hardly the case that East German communism represented a fulfilment of the performance principle in its wider sense, as the backward state of the former East German economy amply demonstrates. In short, the East German sports system fascinated the western world, not because it was alien, but because it represented a perfect expression of the performance principle that rules us all. Indeed, technological civilisation celebrates high-performance sport precisely because sport is the faithful image of its own deepest impulse.

From this perspective, the idea that Communism enjoys a special affinity with the performance principle or the technological ethos that serves it appears highly problematic. It would be more accurate to say that the high-performance sports science of the East Germans was compatible, but not synonymous, with Marxist–Leninist doctrine. As Dieter Voigt pointed out in 1975, the East German method 'is not inherent in the system in an a priori sense, but is also possible in other societies'.[32] In other words, the mobilisation of the human organism on behalf of athletic achievement is not a specifically Communist theme. It is possible, however, that ideological factors did make Communist regimes more eager than others to develop high-performance athletes with the available methods. This possibility leads in turn to the question of whether Marxism–Leninism gave special encouragement to the scientific development of high-performance athletes.

The answer to this question is somewhat ambiguous. Marxist–Leninist scientism put special emphasis on the power of science and technology to bring about social change and the transformation of man. As the Soviet physicist Sergei Kapitza noted in 1991, the

Soviet Union was 'a society that until recently was purportedly pro-scientific, rational and even "scientifically" designed'.[33] But the prioritising of science and technology by Communists does not make these disciplines and techniques inherently Communist in an ideological sense.[34] (The fraudulent genetic doctrine of Trofim Lysenko – a Stalinist neo-Lamarckianism – was, indeed, ideologically motivated, but 'Lysenko's views on genetics were a chapter in the history of pseudoscience rather than the history of science.'[35] Similarly, the ideological dimension of Communist sports science was a prioritising of (often illicit) scientific attempts to boost athletic performance, but not the methods themselves. These caveats notwithstanding, there are in fact certain ideological factors that may well have contributed to promoting a scientific approach to athletic performance.

The crucial theme in this regard is the environmentalist dogma that goes back to the earliest years of the Soviet Union, and the key figure is the physiologist Ivan Pavlov. It is well known that Communist regimes have resolved the nature–nuture debate in favour of the doctrine of human malleability, emphasising the power of environmental shaping over the power of the genes to shape human nature. (Indeed, the study of human genetics was banned in the Soviet Union from the early 1930s until the early 1970s.[36]) Pavlov's importance derives from the fact that, despite his lack of interest in the official Soviet ideology of dialectical materialism, Soviet ideologists valued his work on conditioned reflexes for its tendency to assimilate psychology to physiology and its emphasis on the environmental conditioning of the human organism. Pavlovian man, as he became known to Soviet ideologists and the western public, was a crudely decomplexified type of man who could be presented in the charismatic figure of the high-performance athlete – a conveniently mute and self-disciplined hero whose body acted out a dramatic version of the Stalinist cult of labour. In addition, a seldom-noted corollary of the Pavlovian conflation of mind and body was an analogous conflation of muscular and intellectual skills. In summary, this sort of vulgar Pavlovianism was entirely compatible with both the idealising of and scientific experimentation on athletes, even if it is difficult at this point to give an accurate assessment of its impact on Soviet practices in this area.

The import of this discussion can be summed up in one question:

Does the end of the Communist era mean the end of this conceptual approach to boosting athletic performance? I believe the answer to this question is no, because once again one cannot simply equate the 'Pavlovian' mind-set with Soviet ideology. Pavlovian reflex theory is one form of behaviourism, a school of psychology that insists on confining the study of human beings to objectively observable phenomena and that emphasises the role of environmental factors in determining behaviour. Behaviourism appeared independently in the United States in 1914, and as a philosophy or mind-set it transcends the familiar ideological divide separating Communists and capitalists. In fact, the behaviouristic fusion of mind and muscle – and the use of sports images to express the importance of muscular skills and sensations – appears most eloquently in the work of the pioneering American behaviourist John B. Watson and the British psychologist T. H. Pear, both of whom were aware that their ideas had a 'bolshevist' flavour.[37] Today the question is whether western athletes or the practitioners of western sports science – for what it is worth[38] – are any less ambitious or more restrained by outside forces than their Communist counterparts were before the era of *glasnost* and the fall of the Berlin Wall. In fact, the only major difference between these two worlds was state-sponsored doping in East Germany and the USSR. At the same time, the universality of the doping epidemic that began in the 1960s and continues today strongly suggests that the end of Communist sport does not portend the end of doping. On the contrary, the absorption of East German doping experts by the West German sports establishment points to the existence of a vigorous pro-doping lobby that is by no means confined to Germany.[39] In addition, the migration of East German doping experts to China and possibly other countries will further internationalise the use of anabolic steroids.[40]

The new tensions

Let us now address the question of whether or not 'ideological' tensions in the world of elite sport will survive the passing of the major Communist regimes. We have in fact already entered a new era in which the traditional ideological spectrum of left and right has been replaced by largely unacknowledged tensions between pro- and anti-doping factions within the ranks of athletes, sports officials, sports physicians and trainers. The conventional

dichotomy that sets drug-testing sports bureaucracies against the
(potentially dishonest) athletes they are supposed to regulate is,
therefore, both incomplete and misleading. In Germany today, for
example, the truly fateful struggle is between some track-and-field
athletes who are demanding stricter drug testing and a caste
of sports bureaucrats whose opposition to doping has been at
best inconsistent and at worst a sham.[41] The general lack of
interest in taking drastic steps against doping is due to a profound
ambivalence towards giving up the use of drugs that have enabled
German athletes to compete on an equal basis with their foreign
competitors in, for example, weightlifting and the throwing events
in track and field.[42] I would argue that the German situation is a
useful case study for understanding the social-political dynamics of
doping in most if not all developed societies.

Careful observation of the struggle over doping in Germany
reveals that certain of the old ideological divisions have played a
role in shaping the contending positions. That political ideology
plays a role in this issue at all is due to the fact that elite
sport in Germany is funding by the Bundestag, creating a federal
responsibility for the doping practices of federally-funded athletes,
trainers and physicians. The history of Bundestag debates on
this issue show that conservative politicians have tended to be
less eager to oppose doping, since the use of drugs to improve
athletic performance can be rationalised on nationalistic grounds.
On the other side, some members of the left-of-centre SPD and, in
particular, representatives of the Green Party have constituted the
militant anti-doping faction. It is, in fact, the Greens who have been
the driving force behind the Bundestag's episodic and unenthusiastic
engagement with the doping problem. By 1984 they had begun
to revive the radical critique of sport developed by West German
neo-Marxists during the late 1960s and early 1970s. The Green
critique of high-performance sport attacked medically hazardous
training regimens, the biochemical manipulation of athletes, the
'Darwinistic' selection of national teams, the athletic exploitation
of children, and the 'ruthless violation of the inherent limits of
human nature'.[43] Their uncompromising position against doping
should thus be understood as one part of a critique of technology
in general and technological interventions into the human organism
in particular.

As the citizens of all the developed societies become more

aware of these bioethical issues, and especially genetic engineering, it is likely that 'ideological' tensions between pro- and anti-interventionist factions will further displace the traditional left – right divisions. Genetic engineering poses an even graver danger than doping to the future of sport, since it could lead to the selective development of human types that are functionally adapted to specific sports disciplines – in effect, a range of athletic monsters.[44] It is certain, then, that sport will play a role in the great struggle over genetic biotechnology and reproductive biology that has already begun. This struggle will feature an ambitious and uninhibited scientific faction bent on circumventing the conservative instincts of the general public. As one editorialist pointed out in 1991 in *Nature*, 'questions that seem cut and dried to professional people may be deeply worrying for the more general public.' 'The politically correct position,' this commentator adds, 'often defined without prompting by molecular geneticists, is that the human genome must not as such be interfered with, and *should* not be interfered with directly, even if that could be done safely (or without substantial risk of introducing genetic mutations).[45] Unfortunately, this impatient critic of bioethical political correctness fails to note the crucial distinction between therapeutic intervention that corrects or prevents disease and the eugenic ambitions this biotechnology will both serve and stimulate in a dialectical fashion. In summary, bioethical issues are likely to be the most important 'ideological variables' of the coming age.

Consequences of the performance principle

The athletic ambitions of nations have never been explained by social psychologists. A neglected analytical approach to this hunger for status recognises that elite sport belongs to a larger group of international competitions that compares a range of human performances, including some that cannot be quantified in the manner of Olympic competitions. At least two developing nations, for example, have recently seen literature as an outlet for competitive energies within the context of modernising (and westernising) themselves. In December 1984, for example, the Chinese Writers' Association issued a declaration combining a demand for artistic freedom with a clarion call for high performance: 'We need works that can compare with the magnificent literary creations of our people in the past, and with the most famous works of mankind', said Ba Jin, the 80-year-old chairman. He called for 'epic master-pieces' that would put Chinese writers alongside Chinese athletes and musicians 'in the front ranks of the world.'[46] In a similar vein, the South Korean government's propaganda campaign on behalf of the 1988 Seoul Olympic Games employed 'a holistic idea of "culture"' that combines sport and the arts into a vaguely homogeneous commodity that can be imported, exported, produced in bulk, and whose various forms – books, films, musical groups, art works, athletic teams – can compete in the global marketplace.'[47] One consequence of this integrated and agonistic notion of 'culture' was the so-called 'Nobel fever' that swept through the South Korean publishing industry prior to the Seoul Olympiad. In 1982, shortly after the Games were given to Seoul, a Korean publisher stated that South Korea had to produce a Nobel prizewinner in literature before 1988. In 1985 it was reported that the Korean Culture and Arts Foundation 'is now targeting a Nobel Prize in literature.'[48]

Intellectual competitions between nations are necessarily more subtle contests than athletic competitions.[49] There is a *de facto* competition among many nations regarding the collective educa-tional achievements of their children, but this rivalry cannot be dramatised like a sporting event.[50] The ideal vehicle for dramatising mental competition is rather the 'sport' of chess, and it is interesting to note that the massive Chinese campaign to become a world sports power[51] has been matched by an equivalent effort in chess – including collectivistic training camps – that recently produced a 21-year-old women's world champion, Xie Jun.[52] As chess competitions between humans and computers become more sharply contested[53], and as computer software for high-performance chess players becomes even more indispensable than it already is[54], international competitions between man – machine partnerships will make perfect sense. In this new era the most important function of sport will be to insist on the importance of the human body in a world that is increasingly filled and managed by artificial intelligence.

Notes

1 In a book published five years before the collapse of the East German state, I attempted to produce a study that 'interprets the major sport ideologies of the twentieth century as distinct expressions of political doctrine', and further

'interprets the political cultures of sport as proxy warriors in a larger ideological conflict'. My basic thesis was that political ideologies 'have distinct political anthropologies or idealized models of the exemplary citizen which constitute complex answers to the fundamental question of philosophical anthropology: 'What is a human being?' Departing from this premise, I tried to describe how, in particular, the various types of Marxism – Leninism and fascism prescribed official roles for sport in these highly disciplined social-political orders. See John M. Hoberman, *Sport and Political Ideology*, University of Texas Press, 1984, p. 262.

2 On the causes of consequences of Olympic commercialisation, see 'Olympia ist Coca-Colarisiert, *Der Spiegel*, 24 September 1990, 250–3; 'Immer mehr Geld scheffeln', *Der Spiegel*, 8 April 1991 212–19; 'Bett voller Geschenke', *Der Spiegel*, 4 November 1991, 256–60; 'Wie im Bundestag', *Der Spiegel*, 10 February 1992, 218–21; 'These Olympic Games are brought to you by', *New York Times*, 13 February 1992; 'A few winners in the Olympic slush', *New York Times*, 25 February 1992.

3 On ideological resistance to sports competition during the early years of the Soviet Union, see James Riordan, *Sport in Soviet Society: Development of Sport and Physical Education in Russia and the USSR*, Cambridge University Press, 1977, pp. 51, 53, 74, 95–8, 100–1.

4 I am indebted to Lincoln Allison for this observation.

5 Hoberman, *Sport and Political Ideology*, pp. 193–4.

6 Roy A. Clumpner, 'Pragmatic coercion: the role of government in sport in the United States', in Gerald Redmond, ed., *Sport and Politics* [The 1984 Olympic Scientific Congress Proceedings, vol. 71, Human Kinetics, 1986, 7.]

7 See, for example, Hoberman, *Sport and Political Ideology*, pp. 201–18.

8 See, for example, Steven Dickman, 'East Germany: science in the disservice of the state', *Science*, 254, 4 October 1991, 26–7.

9 Donald Macintosh and C. E. S. Franks, 'Canadian government involvement in sport: Some consequences and issues', in Redmond, ed., *Sport and Politics*, p. 21.

10 G. A. Olafson and C. Lloyd Brown-John, 'Canadian international sport policy: a public policy analysis,' in Redmond, ed., *Sport and Politics*, p. 71.

11 I am indebted to Bruce Kidd for explaining to me the origins of this phrase.

12 For an elegant analysis of the Canadian government's predicament during the Johnson affair see John J. MacAloon, 'Steroids and the state: Dubin, melodrama and the accomplishment of innocence', *Public Culture*, 2, spring 1990, 41–64.

13 The authors of the Dubin report note that 'since the mid-1970s [government support of sport] has increasingly been channeled towards the narrow objectives of winning medals in international competition'. See *Commission of Inquiry into the Use of Drugs and Banned Practices Intended to Increase Athletic Performance*, Canadian Government Publishing Centre, 1990, p. 43.

14 'Rowdyism mars Argentine win,' *Boston Globe*, 23 June 1986.

15 Jürg Bürgi, 'Sie spinnen, diese Schweizer', *Der Spiegel*, 23 February 1987.

16 'Hoyre og idrettspengene', *Ukens nytt* [Oslo], 20 April 1985.

17 This quotation is not a verbatim, but rather a more or less accurate, version of Lillelien's outburst.

18 'Et norsk nederlag', *Ukens nytt* 3 March 1988.
19 'Gro: 'Det er typisk norsk å være god', *Ukens nytt*, 7 January 1992, 8.
20 Gro Harlem Brundtland, 'Vi kan hvis vi vil', *Aftenposten*, 22 February 1992, 2.
   Not long after making this pitch on competitiveness to the Norwegian nation,
   Prime Minister Brundtland provoked a domestic political storm by suggesting
   that Norway's gold medals at the Albertville Games were due to the policies
   of her own Labour Party (Arbeiderpartiet). At least two gold-medal winners,
   the skiers Vegard Ulvang and Finn Chr. Jagge, objected to this use of Olympic
   athletes for political purposes. See 'Storm rundt Gro etter uttalelser om OL-gull',
   Ukens nytt, 3 March 1992, 5.
21 This statement was made by Professor Klaus Heinemann, Professor of Sociology
   at the University of Hamburg and chairman of the Scientific Council of the
   German Sports Association (DSB). See 'Industrie läßt sich nicht von Effekten
   leiten', *Süddeutsche Zeitung*, 11 October 1988.
22 'OL-kritisk Koivisto upopulær', *Ukens nytt*, 13 March 1984.
23 'Näolsting österut oroar i Finland', *Svenska Dagbladet* [Stockholm], 12 April
   1985. Koivisto's unusual critique of sportive nationalism must be understood
   in the context of Finland's highly successful neutralist foreign policy since the
   end of World War II. Prior to the end of the Soviet empire, every postwar
   Finnish leader took neutralism – based on a profound caution regarding
   Soviet sensitivities – as an article of faith. While many western conservatives
   have used the term 'Finlandisation' as a political epithet of contempt, a
   majority of Finns have equated Finnish-style neutralism with national survival.
   Koivisto's cosmopolitan approach to sport was thus a logical extension of his
   foreign policy.
24 Hoberman, *Sport and Political Ideology*, p. 222.
25 See John M. Hoberman, 'Sport and social change: the transformation of Maoist
   sport', *Sociology of Sport Journal* 4, 1987, 156–70.
26 Hoberman, *Sport and Political Ideology*, 109–14.
27 'Muskelpillen als Waffe im Klassenkampf', *Süddeutsche Zeitung*, 5 December
   1990, 55.
28 The standard account of the East German doping system is Brigitte Berendonk,
   Doping-Dokumente: Von der Forschung zum Betrug, Springer-Verlag, 1991.
29 'DDR braucht kleine Geheimnisse', *Süddeutsche Zeitung*, 7 July, 1989.
30 'Das Ende einer Karriere', *Frankfurter Allgemeine Zeitung*, 20 November
   1989. On the Marxist–Leninist sport–art comparison, see John Hoberman,
   The Olympic Crisis: Sport, Politics, and the Moral Order, Aristide D. Caratzas,
   1986, pp. 113–16.
31 See John M. Hoberman, 'Ideological foundations of East German sports
   science', presented at the annual meeting of the American Political Science
   Association, Washington, DC, 3 September 1988.
32 Dieter Voigt, *Soziologie in der DDR*, Verlag Wissenschaft und Politik,
   1975, p. 83.
33 Sergei Kapitza, 'Antiscience trends in the USSR', *Scientific American*, August
   1991, 32.
34 On the relationship between Nazi ideology and technology see Jeffrey Herf,
   *Reactionary Modernism: Technology, Culture, and Politics in Weimar and the
   Third Reich*, Cambridge University Press, 1984.

35 Loren R. Graham, *Science, Philosophy, and Human Behavior in the Soviet Union*, Columbia University Press, 1987, p. 102.

36 *Ibid.*, p. 221.

37 See John B. Watson, *Behaviorism* [1930], The Norton Library, 1970; T. H. Pear, 'The intellectual respectability of muscular skill', *British Journal of Psychology*, 1922, 163–80.

38 On the difficulties involved in applying exercise physiology as it is carried out in the laboratory to high-performance athletics, see Carl Foster, 'Physiologic testing: does it help the athlete?', *The Physician and Sportsmedicine*, 17, 1989, 103–10.

39 The migration of East German sports physicians who participated in state-sponsored doping projects into positions of responsibility in West Germany has been extensively described in the West German press. In addition to Brigitte Berendonk's *Doping-Dokumente*, see *inter alia* 'Sportärzte ohne Berührungsängste', *Süddeutsche Zeitung*, 22 October 1990; 'Neue Freiheit als Chance für das Institut Kreischa', *Frankfurter Allgemeine Zeitung*, 3 March 1990; 'Das muß man nehmen', *Der Spiegel*, 10 December 1990, 258–64; 'Schicksalsstunde des Sportes,' *Der Spiegel*, 10 December 1990, 266–7; 'Der große Knall kommt', *Der Spiegel*, 1 July 1991, 160–1. An important sign of the convergence of East and West German sports medicine was a symposium on the significance of 'hormonal regulation' (read: anabolic steroids) for high-performance sport that was held in Leipzig in May 1990. The proceedings of this conference were published in R. Häcker and H. de Marées, eds, *Hormonelle Regulation und psychophysische Belastung im Leistungssport*, Deutsche Ärzte-Verlag, 1991. For an honest insider's account of the American doping scene in Olympic sport, see Robert Voy, *Drugs, Sport and Politics*, Leisure Press, 1991. The pro-doping lobby is, in a word, international.

40 'Es werden Wunder geschehen', *Der Spiegel*, 7 October 1991, 255, 258. For documentation of the sudden appearance of female Chinese athletes in the world rankings in the shotput, the javelin and the discus throw see *Track & Field News*, November 1991, 56, 58, 63.

41 See, for example, 'Aus einer anderen Welt', *Der Spiegel*, 24 December 1990, 140–1.

42 I have attempted to describe the sociology of doping in Germany in Chapter 7 of *Mortal Engines: Olympic Sport and the Great Experiment on the Human Organism*, The Free Press, 1992.

43 'Krieg der Körper', *Süddeutsche Zeitung*, 28 August 1985, 35.

44 See Claude Bouchard, 'Quelques réflexions sur l'avènement des biotechnologies dans le sport', in F. Landry, M. Landry, and M. Yerlès, eds, *Sport . . . The Third Millenium* [Proceedings of the International Symposium, Quebec City, Canada, 21–5 May 1990], Les Presses de l'Université Laval, 1991, pp. 455–64.

45 John Maddox, 'The case for the human genome', *Nature*, 352, 4 July 1991, 12, 11.

46 'Writers' congress in China demands artistic freedom', *New York Times*, 1 January 1985.

47 John M. Hoberman, 'Olympic internationalism and *The Korea Herald*', in *The Olympic Movement and the Mass Media: Past, Present and Future Issues*, Hurford Enterprises Ltd., 1989, pp. 11–37.

48 'The Nobel epidemic', *Korea Herald*, 10 October 1982, 2; 'World to read more Korean prose', *Korea Herald*, 29 September 1985, 5.

49 Nor should we assume that such competitions in the future will always be between nations. Prior to his disgrace, Ben Johnson and his track club in Canada were being supported by a Japanese corporation (Mazda). Similarly, the recently disgraced German sprinter Katrin Krabbe and her team-mates at the Neubrandenburg Sports Club have been supported in recent years by a million-dollar subsidy from the Nike shoe company, which is headquartered in Oregon. In a word, the internationalization of marketable competitive athletes – or computer-based chess teams – could eventually undermine sportive nationalism itself. It is the advertising market, not national chauvinism, that appears to be in charge.

50 See 'Are US students the worst? Comparisons seen as flawed', *New York Times*, 24 December 1991.

51 See Trip Gabriel, 'China strains for Olympic glory', *New York Times Magazine*, 24 April 1988.

52 In addition, three of the eight women who have qualified for the 1993 Women's World Chess Championship are Chinese. See 'Listig wie die alten Krieger', *Der Spiegel*, 9 December 1991, 236.

53 See, for example, Brad Leithauser, 'Kasparov beats Deep Thought', *New York Times Magazine*, 14 January 1990.

54 'Gezielte Hilfe von Genosse Computer', *Süddeutsche Zeitung*, 29 November 1990.

3

Soviet-style sport in Eastern Europe: the end of an era

JIM RIORDAN

Preface

The sporting success, especially in the Olympic Games, of all East European nations (save Albania) drew considerable attention and admiration. The Soviet Union and East Germany provided good sport with the USA and West Germany, as did other East v. West, communist v. capitalist sports confrontations.

A less remarkable, though in the long run perhaps more far-reaching, aspect of Communist sport, however, was the evolution of a model of sport or 'physical culture' for a developing society, using sport to promote health and hygiene, defence, productivity, and the integration of ethnically diverse peoples into a unified state. It was also instrumental in seeking international recognition and prestige; in general, it was part of a strategy of 'nation building'. After all, with the exception of East Germany and parts of Czechoslovakia, Communist development in Eastern Europe was initially based on illiterate rural majorities.

Now the rapid collapse of Soviet-style Communism throughout Eastern Europe and of the nine nations that subscribed to it (with variations in Albania and Yugoslavia on the totalitarian or 'barracks socialism' model) provides an opportunity to examine the 'Communist sports systems' and to seek answers to a number of salient questions. Why was sport considered so important by Communist leaders? To what extent did Communist ideology motivate athletes and Marxist–Leninist 'scientific socialism' contribute to their achievements? Will sports nationalism and international rivalries survive now that the pressures which fuelled them have abated?

Did Olympic success produce pride, resentment or apathy in the general public? Why is there evidently such haste to dismantle the old sports structures and distance the new regimes from the past?

It is answers to such questions that this chapter attempts to discover. In no other region of the world are the changing politics of sport so cataclysmic.

Impact of the revolutions of 1989

A noteworthy feature of the revolutions that swept across Eastern Europe in late 1989 was the intense debate about sport. Far from being at the periphery of politics, sport was right at the centre. In Romania, athletes manned the barricades, with Dinamo Club members defending their patrons, the Securitate, in opposition to the army athletes of Steaua whose gold medalists in shooting were among those firing on the secret police. Romanian rugby captain, Florica Murariu, and team-mate, Radu Dadac, were just two of the sports heroes who fell in battle. In East Germany, sports stars like Katarina Witt, Roland Matthes and Kornelia Ender all complained of having their homes and cars vandalised by erstwhile 'fans' angry at the privileges of the stars and their close identification with the old regime. Officials of the East German umbrella sports organisation, the DTSB, resigned en masse; its finance director, Franz Rydz, drowned himself.

The events of 1989 and subsequently in the one-time Communist states have demonstrated that to many people sport, particularly elite, Olympic sport, has been identified in the popular consciousness with privilege, paramilitary coercion, hypocrisy, distorted priorities and, in the case of the non-Soviet, non-Russian, nations, with an alien, Soviet-imposed institution.

Some in the West have admired, even tried to copy, the successful talent-spotting and nurturing system developed in the Communist states. It has indeed brought considerable acclaim in world sport – as we shall see below, the USSR and East Germany dominated both Summer and Winter Olympic Games in recent years. Yet many people, East and West of the Oder–Neisse, have abhorred the flag-waving razzmatazz accompanying sporting victories, which were perceived as being more for the purposes of bringing prestige to the regime and its ideology than of bringing benefits to the people.

The elite sports system, moreover, producing medal winners to demonstrate the superiority of Communist society, was apparently popularly felt to be a diversion from the realities of living 'under Communism', a sort of 'red circuses'. As John Hoberman has put it, the events of 1989 were 'a response to the discipline and dehumanising limitations inflicted on athletes by the requirements of high-performance sport.'[1]

In the heat of battle, it is tempting to blame Stalinists and 'stagnators' for neglecting 'sport for all' in their race for glory. In fairness, much effort was exerted over the years to involve the public in some form of exercise and recreation that was completely free of charge – whether through the ubiquitous Soviet-style fitness programme ('Prepared for Work and Defence'), work-based facilities, or compulsory sports lessons for all students in their first years at college and university. But it was the quasi-*coercive* nature of sporting activities, their being part of the plan-fulfilment system (every school, factory, farm and region received a sports quota and incurred penalities if they fell short in the number of registered participants or fitness achievers) that turned people off. The system tended to highlight the custodial role of the state, the power to shape and control the lives of its citizens.

Sporting supremacy

The Olympic record of many Communist states has been remarkable. Since it made its debut at the Summer Olympic Games in Helsinki in 1952 and the Winter Olympics at Cortina d'Ampezzo in 1956, the USSR 'won' every Olympics, Summer and Winter, for which it entered, with the sole exception of 1968, and the Winter Games of 1980 and 1984. It won a quarter of all the medals at the Seoul Olympics in 1988, and it is the most versatile nation in Olympic history, competing in all summer and winter sports, and winning medals in twenty-one of the twenty-three sports represented at the 1988 Olympics.

Table 3.1 shows medals won by the top six Olympic teams, 1952–88, illustrating the Soviet supremacy, but also showing that Communist states have provided two of the top three nations in the Summer Olympics since 1968 (except 1984, when they provided two of the top four despite the overwhelming Communist boycott of the Los Angeles Games) and in the Winter Games since 1972.

Table 3.1: Medals won by the top six Olympic teams, 1952–88

Year and venues of Olympic Games	National Olympic teams	Medals			National Olympic teams	Medals		
1	2	3	4	5	6	7	8	9
1952	USSR	22	30	19	Norway	7	3	6
	USA	40	19	17	USA	4	6	1
Helsinki	Hungary	16	10	16	Finland	3	4	2
	Sweden	12	13	10	Austria	2	4	2
Oslo	West Germany	10	7	17	West Germany	3	2	2
	Finland	6	3	13	Sweden	0	0	4
1956	USSR	37	29	32	USSR	7	3	6
	USA	32	25	17	Austria	4	3	4
Melbourne	Austria	13	8	14	Finland	3	3	1
	Germany	6	13	7	Sweden	2	4	4
Cortina	Hungary	9	10	7	USA	2	3	2
d'Ampezzo	Great Britain	6	7	11	Switzerland	3	2	1
1960	USSR	43	29	31	USSR	7	5	9
	USA	34	21	16	USA	3	4	3
Rome	Germany	12	19	11	Sweden	3	2	2
	Italy	13	10	13	Germany	4	3	1
Squaw	Hungary	6	8	7	Finland	2	3	3
Valley	Poland	4	6	11	Norway	3	3	0
1964	USSR	30	31	35	USSR	11	8	6
	USA	36	26	28	Norway	3	6	6
Tokyo	Germany	10	22	18	Austria	4	5	3
	Japan	16	5	8	Germany	3	2	3
Innsbruck	Italy	10	10	7	Finland	3	4	3
	Hungary	10	7	5	Sweden	3	3	1
1968	USA	45	28	34	Norway	6	6	2
	USSR	29	32	30	USSR	5	5	3
Mexico City	GDR	9	9	7	Austria	3	4	4
	Hungary	10	10	12	Sweden	3	2	3
Grenoble	Japan	11	7	7	France	4	3	2
	West Germany	5	10	10	Holland	3	3	3
1972	USSR	50	27	22	USSR	8	5	3
	USA	33	31	30	GDR	4	3	7
Munich	GDR	20	23	23	Norway	2	5	5

	West Germany	13	11	16	Holland	4	3	2
Sapporo	Hungary	6	13	16	Switzerland	4	3	3
	Japan	13	8	8	West Germany	3	1	1
1976	USSR	49	41	35	USSR	13	6	8
	GDR	40	25	25	GDR	7	5	7
Montreal	USA	34	35	25	USA	3	3	4
	West Germany	10	12	17	West Germany	2	5	3
Innsbruck	Poland	7	6	13	Austria	2	2	2
	Romania	4	9	14	Finland	2	4	1
1980	USSR	80	69	46	GDR	9	7	7
	GDR	47	37	42	USSR	10	6	6
Moscow	Bulgaria	8	16	17	USA	6	4	2
	Poland	3	14	15	Norway	1	3	6
Lake	Hungary	7	10	15	Austria	3	3	2
Placid	Romania	6	6	13	Finland	1	5	3
1984	USA	83	61	31	GDR	9	9	6
Los Angeles	Romania	20	16	17	USSR	6	10	9
	West Germany	17	19	23	USA	4	4	0
	China	15	8	9	Finland	4	3	6
Sarajevo	Italy	14	6	12	Sweden	4	2	2
	Canada	10	18	16	Norway	3	2	4
1988	USSR	55	31	46	USSR	11	9	9
Seoul	GDR	37	35	30	GDR	9	10	6
	USA	36	31	27	Switzerland	5	5	5
	South Korea	12	10	11	Finland	4	1	2
Calgary	West Germany	11	14	15	Sweden	4	0	2
	Hungary	11	6	6	Austria	3	5	2

East Germany advanced from fifteenth medal place in 1956 to second in 1976 and again in 1988, overtaking the USA; and in the Winter Olympics it progressed from sixteenth in 1956 to first in 1980 and again in 1984, overtaking the USSR. It is worth recalling that East Germany had a population of under 17 million (compare 293 million in the USSR and 236 million in the USA in 1990) and was considerably poorer than the most advanced western nations. In Olympic and world championship terms, calculated in per capita medals, East Germany in the last decade won one gold medal for every 425,000 citizens, by contrast with roughly one gold per 6,500,000 in the USA and USSR. That meant that an East German with sports talent was sixteen times more likely to reach the top and gain an Olympic or world gold medal than a US or Soviet citizen.

It is worth mentioning briefly that Cuba was placed fourth in

1980, the last Summer Olympics in which it competed before 1992, and has consistently won more medals than all the countries of South America put together. China was placed fourth in 1984 in the Summer Games, but came behind Japan and South Korea in 1988, although it has dominated the Asian Games of recent years.

The principal reason for this targeting of the Olympics for world supremacy would seem to be an attempt to gain recognition and prestige for the Communist states and their brand of Communism, and thereby to advertise that brand, especially in the Third World, as being superior to the capitalist system. A leading Soviet sports official made this point when the Soviet 'world sports supremacy' policy was launched following World War II:

> The increasing number of successes achieved by Soviet athletes . ... is a victory for the Soviet form of society and the socialist sports system; it provides irrefutable proof of the superiority of socialist culture over the moribund culture of capitalism.[2]

It ought to be pointed out that sport was virtually the only arena (apart from space conquest) in which the USSR was able to demonstrate superiority over the world's most advanced capitalist nations.

An overriding problem facing East Germany after its establishment in 1949 was that of gaining international acceptance as an independent nation. Its leaders, further, had to contend with attempts to impose Soviet values and institutions upon the country, on the one hand, and western hostility, subversion and boycott, on the other. A similar dilemma faced Cuba later. The East German rivalry with West Germany was evidently to become a testing ground for the viability of either socialism or capitalism in all spheres, including that of sport. Success in sport was seen by East German leaders as one means, perhaps the most 'popular' and accessible, of gaining the regime's acceptance and enhancing its image at home and abroad while other channels were closed. It was not easy. In the Winter Olympics of 1960, for example, the USA refused entry visas to East German athletes to travel to Squaw Valley where the Games were being held. Such a denial of visas was made thirty-five times by the USA and its NATO allies between 1957 and 1967. In other instances, when East German athletes won competitions, the awards ceremony was cancelled, and often western officials refused permission for the East German flag and emblem to be displayed at victory ceremonies.

Although the International Olympic Committee had recognised the National Olympic Committee of East Germany in October 1965 and granted it the right to enter a team separately from West Germany in the Mexico Olympics of 1968, it was only in Munich in 1972 that the country possessed its own national team, flag and anthem. This sporting autonomy and success led to mounting diplomatic recognition throughout the world. To quote a West German source:

> Sport played a vital role in breaching the blockade which, at the time of the Cold War, kept East Germany out of vitually all international relations outside the communist states. Because East German sport attained international standards and, in many areas, actually set those standards, world sports organisations were unable to ignore the country.[3]

This was an important step towards helping the German Democratic Republic break out of its political isolation, gain credibility for the government with its own people, and be recognised as an independent German state. Hence the high priority that the authorities accorded the development of sport and international sports performance.

Although the circumstances and degree of sports success differed in other East European states, the priority given to elite sport and their inordinate Olympic success (in relation to their populations) were explicitly used to promote the regime's prestige.

Rejection of the sports supremacy policy

Paradoxically, the sporting success of East European nations, particularly in the Olympic Games and particularly the USSR and GDR, increasingly undermined the ideological basis of the sports supremacy policy among the populations of those countries. Some foreigners may have been impressed by the efficient sports system behind the success; some overseas fans may well have been inspired by the possibilities evidently opened up by socialism. But at home there were many who were sceptical of, even hostile to, the world domination policy, especially through the Olympic Games. This may be puzzling to some westerners brought up on the 'noble principles of Olympism'; in fact, one might construct a paradigm

of traditional western and popular East European perceptions of
the Olympic movement (see Table 3.2).

Table 3.2: Traditional western and East European perceptions of Olympism

West	East
Non-political	Political/ideological
Amateur/voluntary	Shamateur/coercive
Independent clubs/amateur federations	Security & armed forces/the state
Universal/autonomous	Soviet–Russian diktat
Fair play/open participation	Win at all costs/drug abuse, child exploitation
Sport for all/self-financing	Elitist/distorted priorities

It may be justifiably argued that Olympic realities never matched
the noble aims set for Olympism by Baron Pierre de Coubertin and,
in any case, have in recent years turned from largely amateur-elitism
to mainly professional-commercialism. But it is the traditional and
popular perceptions of Olympism that are referred to here. In the
case of Eastern Europe, it will help us to comprehend why the
new leaderships are rapidly switching resources from Olympic
commitment to commercial sport and to sport for all and for fun,
and are dismantling institutions specifically intended for 'breeding'
champions.

To many ordinary people and the new political leaderships, the
Olympic Games and Olympism represent all that is bad in the
old regime's policies: politics and ideology, hypocrisy and sham,
paramilitary coercion, Russian diktat, drug abuse, exploitation
of children, and grossly and immorally distorted priorities in
the dispensation of national resources. A caveat ought to be
entered here: in the present-day societies of Eastern Europe, the
popular mood encourages a tendency 'to cast the baby out with
the bathwater' in all areas – in people's haste to distance themselves
from the past – which exhibits a peculiar propensity to swing from
one extreme to another. So with sport and Olympism.

Let us look more closely at each of the East European perceptions
of the Olympics mentioned above.

1. Politics and ideology

The striving for world supremacy in Olympic sport for political purposes – to demonstrate (largely to the Third World) the superiority
of Soviet-style communism over US-style capitalism – is now utterly

discredited. As the World Chess Champion Garri Kasparov has said of the policy,

> International victories and titles won by Soviet athletes were supposed to prove 'yet again' the advantages of socialism over capitalism ... A world chess champion was nothing short of a political post.[4]

As an example of political interference in sport, the one-time Soviet international goalkeeper and now sports commentator Vladimir Maslachenko recounts an occasion before leaving for the 1982 World (Soccer) Cup in Spain, when he and other journalists were summoned before the then Sports Minister, Marat Gramov,

> Opening a leather-bound folder emblazoned with the gold letters CCCPSU (Central Committee of the Communist Party of the Soviet Union), he told us exactly what we could and could not say in public.[5]

What no one could openly say, owing to strict censorship, was that Dinamo was the sports society sponsored and financed by the security forces, that athletes of Master of Sport ranking and above devoted themselves full-time to sport and were paid accordingly, that athletes received bonuses for winning (including dollars), that the NOC was a government-run institution and that its chairman had to be a member of the Communist Party, that Soviet athletes used drugs, etc., etc.

The last Soviet Sports Minister, Nikolai Rusak, admitted that 'Our sports ministry was oriented primarily on attaining prestigious victories in international tournaments'. In response to pressure, he promised that

> Concern for promoting both sport for all and high-performance sport will steadily shift to independent federations. In time the sports Committee will focus its efforts on training personnel, on the social protection of athletes and the provision of sports facilities.[6]

Time ran out for Rusak and his ministry (Rusak backed the 'wrong' side in the attempted coup of 19–21 August 1991), and the government cut off all funds to it, making it completely self-financing.[7] It was wound up in late 1991.

2. *Hypocrisy and sham*

Communist Party manipulation of sport also involved a great deal of enforced hypocrisy. All athletes, coaches, sports medical personnel, officials and journalists had to toe the line and, not infrequently, 'lie through their teeth' if they wanted to keep their jobs and not fall foul of the law enforcement agencies. They had to assert that Soviet athletes were amateurs, instead of having army officer or KGB sinecures, eternal student status or false registration at a workplace. The Soviet leadership introduced 'state amateur' status into Soviet sport only in the early 1950s as a ploy to join the Olympic movement. From then on the appearance had to be given that performers received no remuneration from their sports performance, nor did they devote themselves fully to sport. The public, of course, knew differently, but it was part of the double-think of the 1950–85 period never to mention it in public. In fact, all athletes, once they attained Master of Sport ranking, could devote themselves full-time to sport with the state's backing.

Now the veil is being drawn aside. As the leading Soviet male swimmer, Vladimir Salnikov, revealed in the popular weekly *Argumenty i fakty* early in 1989,

We have rid ourselves of hypocritical declarations about so-called amateurism and sporting achievements. Professionalism has been recognised and athletes no longer have to compromise themselves.[8]

A year previously, the youth monthly *Yunost* admitted that,

We got used to living a double life because many of our idols did the same. We condemned professional sport in the West and were proud that our champions were amateurs. We took it for granted that they trained for six or seven hours each day after work or study. Yet everyone knew that most athletes never went to work or college, and they met their workmates or fellow students only on pay day.[9]

It is now officially admitted that top soccer players, for example, received twice or three times the salary of the average working woman or man for playing soccer alone, and spent as many as 250 days annually in training.[10]

3. *Sport and the paramilitary*

A salient feature of the turbulent revolutions during 1989 in Eastern Europe and the continuing unrest in the Soviet Union has been the welling-up of hostility and revenge directed against the paramilitary forces that had shored up the old corrupt order. It is therefore understandable that their sponsored sports clubs should suffer by association. Soviet elite sport has always been linked to the paramilitary. In fact, since the end of World War II, the East European (and world Communist) sports system has been dominated by clubs of the security forces and armed forces (see Table 3.3). Most sports heroes, therefore, were officially soldiers or police officers, guardians of public order and role models for a disciplined, obedient and patriotic citizenry. Future sports heroes are likely to be civilians, not warriors.

Table 3.3: Sports clubs of the security and armed forces in Eastern Europe and the USSR

Country	Security Forces Club	Armed Forces Club
USSR	Dinamo (Moscow, Kiev, Minsk, Tbilisi, etc.)	TsSKA (Central Sport Club of the Army)
Bulgaria	Levski Sofia	TsSKA
GDR	Dinamo (Berlin, Dresden)	Vorwärts
Yugoslavia	Dinamo (Zagreb)	Red Star
Romania	Dinamo (Bucharest)	Steaua
Hungary	–	Honved
Poland	Dosze	Legia
Czechoslovakia	Dinamo (Prague)	Dukla Liberec
Albania	Dinamo Tirana	–

4. *Russian diktat*

For non-Russians, who made up half the 293 million population of the USSR, as well as the old East European Communist states, there existed the irritation of having to put up with a system tailored by Stalin to Russian conditions and imposed from without in contradiction of their own traditions. Sokol gymnastics were banned in Czechoslovakia and Poland after 1948. Youth organisations involved in recreation, like the YMCA (very strong, for example, in the Baltic states prior to 1939), the Scouts and Jewish Maccabi, were similarly proscribed. Pre-1939 Olympic committees were disbanded on orders from Moscow, and their members often persecuted (for example Estonia's two prewar IOC members, Friedrich Akel and Joakim Puhk, 'were put to death by the NKVD (Soviet precursor of the KGB) for their public activity').[11]

All this happened in spite of the long traditions and often superior standards existing in the non-Russian states, both within and outside the Soviet Union. For example, Lithuania won the European basketball championships in 1937 and 1939; Estonia had competed independently in the Olympics between 1920 and 1936, winning six gold, seven silver and nine bronze medals. Germany had not only pioneered sports medicine since the last century, but had competed successfully in the Olympics and staged the Games in 1936. It had also provided one of the strongest worker sports movements in the world. It is an irony that the social-democratic worker (arch-rival of the Communist worker sports movement) sport base in Leipzig was to be taken over and turned into the famous Deutsche Hochschule für Körperkultur in the postwar German Democratic Republic.

Being tied to the USSR meant following Soviet foreign policy, including that on Olympic boycotts. The Soviet Communist Party decision to boycott the 1984 Summer Olympics in Los Angeles was simply passed down to other members of the Warsaw Pact – no sports or national Olympic committees, not to mention athletes, were consulted. Romania demurred, though hardly for democratic reasons.

It was the Soviet state-controlled sports system that was adopted by, or imposed (along with other political, social and economic institutions) upon the Baltic states and those countries of Eastern Europe liberated by the Red Army in the period 1945–9. They were forced to adopt the Soviet system of state control of sport, sports science and medicine, the national fitness programme 'Prepared for Work and Defence', the sports rankings pyramid for each Olympic sport, the trade union sports societies, state 'shamateurism', a government-run Olympic committee and overall control by the security and armed forces.

Such was the extent of the Soviet blueprint being copied that very often the Soviet name was retained, however insensitive that may have been to national pride and traditions – as in the case of the KGB's Dinamo clubs, the State Committee on Physical Culture and Sport: *Gosudarstvenny komitet po fizicheskoi kulture i sportu* in the USSR; *Staatssekretariat für Körperkultur und Sport* in East Germany; and the monthly theoretical journal *Theory and Practice of Physical Culture*: *Teoriya i praktika fizicheskoi kultury* in the USSR; *Theorie und Praxis der Körperkulture* in East Germany, *Teorie a Praxe Telesné Vychovy* in Czechoslovakia, and so on. Even the very concept, Soviet-born, of 'physical culture' rather than 'sport' had to be followed slavishly.

And whenever the Soviet sports structure altered as a result of a new political line, that in the rest of Eastern Europe had to follow suit. It is hardly surprising, then, that such contempt for national traditions should finally provoke mass ire and hatred expressed so violently in the popular uprisings of late 1989 in Eastern Europe, and subsequently in the Baltic states and the various republics of the Soviet Union.

5. Drugs and child exploitation

A major reason for the strong anti-elite (i.e. Olympic) sport sentiments may be found in the current revelations in the media of the long-term *state* production, testing, monitoring and administering of performance-enhancing drugs in regard to athletes as young as 7 or 8. It is this mendacity by members of the old regime – loudly condemning drug abuse in the West as a typical excess of capitalism, while concealing its own involvement in a far more extensive programme of state manufacture and distribution of drugs – from growth stimulants to growth retardants, anabolic steriods to blood doping – that has brought Olympic sport into question.

When a number of émigré athletes, coaches and sports doctors had previously talked of widespread use of drugs in sport, their testimony bore a suspicion of 'selling out'. Even when in 1989, the one-time East German ski-jump champion and later sports doctor Hans-Georg Aschenbach sold his story alleging that GDR athletes were drugged from childhood, he was widely attacked in East and West for sensationalism. Yet the substance of what he said was never refuted. In fact, in late 1991 four one-time leading GDR swimming coaches issued a statement confessing to widespread use of anabolic steroids among GDR swimmers in the 1970s and 1980s. And a long stream of evidence has been emerging, particularly from the Soviet Union and the ex-GDR, of the state-controlled administering of drugs.[12]

Back in 1986, Yuri Vlasov, then Chairman of the USSR Weight-lifting Federation (and one-time world champion and now campaigning MP), declared that immense damage had been done to Soviet sport in general, and weightlifting in particular, by the 'coach-pharmacologist' who worked alongside the sports coach. Not only did Vlasov accuse athletes of using anabolic steroids from '1968–1970',[13] but he named names – specifically that of senior coach and USSR Sports Committee functionary Arkady Vorobyov, 'who was one of the first to distribute anabolic steroids to members of our national team'.[14] A TV report in late 1989 revealed a document, signed in 1982 by two deputy sports ministers, prescribing anabolic steroids as part of the preparation for Soviet cross-country skiers. The document set out a programme to test the effects of steroids and for research into ways of avoiding detection.[15]

It has long been known by those familiar with Communist sport that drug-taking was organised at the top and that no athlete was allowed overseas unless he or she had a clearance test before departing. At the Olympics of Montreal and Seoul, it has now been revealed, the Soviet squad had a 'hospitality' boat used as a medical centre to ensure that Soviet competitors were at least 'clean' at the last moment.[16] The Soviet coach Sergei Vaichekovsky, who was in charge of Soviet swimming from 1973 to 1982, had admitted that the use of drugs was widespread: 'From 1974 all Soviet swimmers were using banned substances. I've personally administered the drugs and advised swimmers individually on how to avoid getting caught.' He indicated that while the East German method was to give drugs during periods of intensive training, which for swimmers usually comes at the start of the year, Soviet competitors took them to within a month of major meetings.[17]

Following the Seoul Olympics of 1988 and the Ben Johnson drug scandal, Soviet senior track and field coach Igor Ter-Ovanesyan launched a well-publicised campaign against drug-taking in Soviet sport. Admitting that 'many of our athletes' take drugs, he conceded that even several school athletes had been caught taking steroids; and he advised that 'society needs proper legislation to combat this evil, seriously punishing both athletes and doctors, coaches and drug-suppliers'.[18] Many reports in the press now reveal cases of schoolchildren being given drugs to enhance their performance. Among those named was the coach V. Yatsyn, who 'fattened up his fifteen-year-old athletes with anabolic steroids'; the exposure of several positively tested schoolchildren dates back to the 1984 Schoolchildren's Spartakiad.[19]

The sport in which Soviet athletes won many Olympic medals is that of weightlifting; and here too the revelations mount. A journalist recently wrote that the world champion super-heavyweight, Vasily Alexeyev, 'took anabolic steroids. With their help he beat world records, won two Olympic and European and world championships.'[20] Other sources have uncovered drug-taking and other forms of 'doping' in cycling, rowing, body-building, gymnastics and track and field.

6. Distorted priorities

To many the worst aspect of the old system is the misplaced priorities, the gap between living standards and ordinary sports and recreation facilities, on the one hand, and the money lavished on elite sport and stars, on the other. As a Soviet sports commentator recently put it, the country won Olympic medals while being 'a land of clapped-out motor cars, evergreen tomatoes and totalitarian mendacity.'[21] Valuable resources were used to buy foreign sports equipment and pay dollar bonuses to athletes who won Olympic medals. For a gold medal at the Seoul Olympics, for example, Soviet recipients gained 12,000 rubles (6,000 for silver and 4,000 for bronze medals); since the Soviet team won 55 gold medals and 132 medals overall, it cost the Sports Committee about a million rubles (almost half paid in dollars) in bonuses alone.[22] (The official value of the ruble was approximately one ruble to one pound sterling at the time.) At the Seattle Goodwill Games in 1990, some 2.6 million rubles were set aside for bonuses (with $750 going to each gold medallist, $450 to each silver medallist and $225 to each bronze medallist).[23]

Some journalists have suggested that alongside Olympic medal tables Soviet newspapers ought to publish sports amenity comparisons: the 2,500 Soviet swimming pools by contrast with the US million plus,[24] the 102 Soviet indoor skating rinks by contrast with Canada's 10,000.[25] To give another example, before 1988 the USSR had never held sports competitions for any category of handicapped person; it sent a team of invalid athletes (thirteen blind men) to the Paralympics for the first time in Seoul. Unlike their able-bodied compatriots in the Olympic Games, who won 132 medals, the disabled athletes won no medals at all. But at least a start was made.

Even more seriously, it is now being pointed out that the country supported an elite sports system on an extremely weak and ramshackle base. It is now admitted that the nation is fifty-third in the world in per capita GNP, that as many as 100 million people, over a third of the population, live below the official poverty line, that while scarce foreign currency was being spent on expensive foreign sports equipment and paying dollar bonuses, children were dying for want of medicines, food and disposable instruments (more Soviet children than adults have died of AIDS, because of unhygienic conditions and the backward state of the health service). To one sports commentator, the sporting achievements diverted attention from the realities of Soviet life and helped to 'reinforce the most anti-human and anti-sport system in the world.'[26]

Bearing these six factors in mind, it should really come as no surprise to find that the leaders in the post-*perestroika* period are radically changing their scale of priorities. They no longer see the need to demonstrate the advantages of socialism, in so far as they are trying to distance themselves from the command economy that has failed so badly and the totalitarian system that accompanied the imposition of Communism from above.

Such a radical shift of policy is bound to cause a twinge of sadness to those who have admired aspects of Soviet (and East European) sport down the years – and not only because it provided good competition with American sport. The old system, it merits saying, was generally open to the talents in all sports, probably more so than in the West. It provided opportunities for women to play and succeed, if not on equal terms with men, at least on a higher plane than western women. It gave an opportunity to the many ethnic minorities and relatively small states within the USSR and Eastern Europe to do well internationally and help promote that pride and dignity that sports success in the glare of world publicity can bring. Nowhere in the world has there been, since the early 1950s, such reverence for Olympism, for Coubertin, for Olympic ritual and decorum. One practical embodiment of this was the contribution to Olympic solidarity with developing nations: to the training of Third World athletes, coaches, sports officials, medical officers and scholars at colleges and training camps, as well as in African, Asian and Latin American countries themselves. Much of this aid was free. None of it was disinterested, most of it going to those states whose governments generally looked to socialism rather than capitalism for their future. Further, no nation outside the Third World did more than the USSR to oppose apartheid in sport and have South Africa banned from world sports forums and arenas.

Today, in Eastern Europe and the rapidly evolving erstwhile Soviet Union, the international challenge is diluted through lack of state support; the free trade union sports societies, as well as the ubiquitous Dinamo and armed forces clubs, have given way to private sports, health and recreation clubs; women's wrestling and boxing attract more profit than women's chess and volleyball; the various nationalities prefer their own independent teams to combined effort and success. And right across the central and eastern European plain, as far as the Ural Mountains, sports and every other aid is at an end, the Third World students (in medicine and engineering as well as in sport) have all gone home as their support grants have run out. The ex-Communist states are now competitors with other poor nations for development aid from the West.

The failed Soviet coup of 19–21 August 1991 accelerated the shift from state control of and support for sport towards private, commercial sport, and a 'brain' and 'muscle' drain of top athletes, coaches, sports medics and scientists to the richest overseas 'buyer'. It further weakened Soviet interest in the Olympic movement, led to the removal of the sinecures of an army commission and 'eternal' studenthood for all top athletes, and to the dismantling of the forty Olympic sport boarding schools.[27]

Gone now are the Soviet flag and anthem: the 'CCCP' logo has gone the way of the East German state symbols, replaced by the colours and emblems of a dozen or more 'national' teams and Olympic committees, representing Russia, the Ukraine, Belorussia, Georgia, Armenia, Azerbaidzhan, Moldova, Kazakhstan, Uzbekistan, Tadzhikistan, Kirgizstan, Turkmenia with, perhaps, further fragmentation to come. The three Baltic states already have their Olympic Committees and independent teams. The result will not enhance Olympism nor necessarily merit universal applause. But there is no alternative.

Some conclusions

The rapidity of change in all areas, sport included, in Eastern Europe and the former Soviet Union would seem to indicate that the elite sport system and its attainments, far from inspiring a national pride and patriotism, tended to provoke apathy and resentment. This appears to be more apparent in those states – Poland, East Germany, Hungary, Romania, Bulgaria – which had 'revolution' and an alien sports system and values thrust upon them without reference to their indigenous traditions. A similar mood is evident, too, in Islamic areas of the old USSR. Sports stars were seen to belong to a private, elite fiefdom within the overall domain of the regime; they were not part of a shared national achievement, let alone heritage. That is not to say that in societies of hardship and totalitarian constraint, and in the face of western arrogance and attitudes that were sometimes tantamount to racial prejudice, the ordinary citizen obtained no vicarious pleasure in her/his champion's performance. But, overall, the dominant attitude was one not entirely different from Western class attitudes to sports and heroes which are not 'theirs' (e.g. the ambivalent British attitude by many workers to Olympic show jumpers, yachtsmen and fencers).

On the other hand, in countries like Czechoslovakia and Yugoslavia, as well as the Slav regions of the old Soviet Union – the Ukraine, Belorussia and Russia – the patriotic pride in sporting success and heroes would appear to have been genuine. Hence the identification by many Ukrainians with the fortunes of 'their' Dinamo Kiev soccer team, 'their' Olympic sprinting champion, Valery Borzov, 'their' gyumnast, Ludmilla Turishcheva. One reason for this may be that the socialist revolution of 1917 in the old Russian empire, and of 1946 and 1948 in the cases of Yugoslavia and Czechoslovakia, came out of their own experience and had some popular support – rather than at the end of a bayonet or gun.

That is not to say that it was Communist ideology that motivated athletes (very few would admit to that) or that Marxism–Leninism was responsible for Olympic success. A more compelling reason was that the sports system grew up with and was integral to the building of a strong national state which generated its own motivational forces and patriotic spirit. The same central control and planned application of resources, allied to State priorities and direction of labour, which initially achieved such remarkable success in constructing the infrastructure of socialist society (enabling, for example, the Soviet system to be so effective in defeating the might of the German armies) provided conditions that were more conducive to discovering, organising and developing talent in specific sports than those of the more disparate western systems. It should be added that East European sport was oriented on *Olympic* success, and its less privileged athletes fared less well in the fully professionalised and commercial sports of the West: soccer, basketball, boxing, rugby, motor racing, tennis and baseball.

Today, the inheritors of the sports system that evolved during the Communist years are faced with a choice of how sharply they should break with the past and adopt a pattern of sport based on market relations. 'Westernisers' in Eastern Europe, with public support nourished on a reaction to the Communist past, aided and prodded by those westerners eager to see the old Communist states join the 'civilised' world, abandon socialism, central planning and social provision, seem bent on rejecting the past *in toto* and embracing its antithesis.

It is possible that sport in such states will become a hybrid of the worst of both worlds, retaining the bureaucracy of the old and adding only the exploitation and corruption of some forms of western sport. The final product may well not inspire admiration. Much the same could be said of the larger reform processes under way.

No doubt, in time, a new sports nationalism will emerge and international rivalries will resume. For the moment, however, it is time to concentrate on more important things. Bread is now more vital than circuses.

Notes

1 John Hoberman, 'The transformation of East German sport', paper presented at the annual meeting of the American Association for the Advancement of Slavic Studies, Chicago, 4 November 1989, p. 1.

2 *Kultura i zhizn*, 1 November 1949, 5.

3 *Sport in der Deutschen Demokratischen Republik*, Minesterium für Wirtschaffliche Zusammenarbeit (Bonn), 1975, pp. 12–13.

4 Garri Kasparov, 'Too outspoken for a closed society?', *Moscow News*, 1, 1991, 3.
5 Vladimir Maslachenko, 'Ya po-prezhnemu v igre', *Sobesednik*, 46, 1990, 15.
6 Nikolai Rusak, 'Medali ili zdorovye?', *Argumenty i fakty*, 28 April–4 May 1990, 7.
7 'Funding challenge', *Soviet Weekly*, 11 July 1991, 16.
8 Vladimir Salnikov, 'Vremya nadyozhd', *Argumenty i fakty*, 1, 1989, 3.
9 A. Novikov, 'Pismo redaktsii', *Yunost*, 6, 1988, 9.
10 'Skolko poluchaet futbolist?', *Moskovskie novosti*, 10, 1988, 15.
11 Gounnar Paal, 'Increasing Olympic enthusiasm in Estonia', paper given at the International Symposium 'Sport ... Le Troisième Millenaire, 20–25 May 1990, Quebec, Canada, p. 2.
12 See Alois Mader, 'Verwissenschaftlichung des Sports in der DDR – sport-medizinische Erkenntnisse and ihre Anwendung', unpublished manuscript (Cologne, 1977); A. Mader and W. Hollmann, 'Sportmedizin in der DDR', *Sportwissenschaft*, 2, June 1983, 152–62; Peter Kühnst, *Des missbrauchte Sport: Die politische Instrumentalisierung des Sports in der SBZ und DDR, 1945–1957* (Verlag Wissenschaft und Politik, 1982); Renate Heinrich-Vogel, 'Mein Lebensweg vom sportbegeisterten Kind zur Hochleistungssportlerin der DDR', in Dieter Ehrich, Renate Heinrich-Vogel and Gerhard Winkler, *Die DDR Breiten-und Spitzensport* (Kopernikus Verlag, 1981), pp. 49–59; Brigitte Berendonk, *Doping-Dokumente: Von der Forschung zum Betrug* (Springer-Verlag, 1991).
13 Yuri Vlasov, 'Ya pravdu rasskazhu tebe takuyu ...', *Sovetsky sport*, 31 October 1991, 4.
14 Yuri Vlasov, 'Drugs and cruelty', *Moscow News*, 37, 1988, 15; see also A. Klaz, 'Rekordy po retseptu?' *Smena*, 4 May 1988, 3.
15 *Sovetsky sport*, 10 October 1989, 1.
16 Vasily Gromyko, 'Nash styd', *Leninskoye znamya*, 28 March 1989, 2.
17 Reported in *Corriere Dello Sport*. See Alan Page, 'Sacked Soviet official admits widescale use of drugs', *Guardian*, 2 December 1989, 20.
18 Igor Ter-Ovanesyan, 'I declare war on anabolics', *Moscow News*, 50, 1988, 15.
19 Ludmilla Chub, Alexander Pogonchenkov, 'Impotent, po ... sobstvennomu zhelaniyu', *SPID-info*, 11, November 1991, 24.
20 Sergei Dadygin, 'Damoklov mech', *Sobesednik*, 14, April 1991, 15.
21 Maslachenko.
22 D. Rennick, 'Soviet Olympians compete for pre-set quota of medals', *The Korea Herald*, 27 September 1988, 9. The author (JR) heard the Sports Minister's words at a news conference in Seoul just prior to the opening of the 1988 Summer Olympics.
23 D. Grantsev, 'Otvet na vopros', *Argumenty i fakty*, 31, 4–10 August 1990, 8.
24 Salnikov. Another author makes the point that the USSR had one swimming pool per 115,000 people, while Germany and Japan had one pool per 3,000–4,000 people, and Hungary and Czechoslovakia one per 10,000–15,000 people – see Alexander Churkin, 'Melko plavayem', *moskovskie novosti*, 3, 15 January 1989, 15.

25 A. Druzenko, 'Olimpiyskaya slava', *Koskovskie novosti*, November 1988, 15.
26 Maslachenko.
27 The sports boarding schools, which began to be established in the early 1970s, following the example of those in the GDR (which had twenty-seven in 1990), catered exclusively for Olympic sports, with the single exception of chess (at one school).

4

Sport, nationalism and cultural identity

GRANT JARVIE

The message of Murrayfield this weekend was bigger than scrummaging techniques and line-out skills. It seemed etched in emotion on the faces of the players as they sang Flower of Scotland. It boiled constantly around the arena. Sometimes events happening send a clearer signal than a thousand pieces of newspaper. Murrayfield was a message of Scottish identity and nationhood.[1]

The above remarks are the observations of one correspondent as he tried to encapsulate the complex tension and emotions that were percolating around Murrayfield prior to the Scotland versus England semi-final clash in the 1991 World Rugby Cup. The climate was structured by a multitude of factors such as Anglo-Scottish political, historical and sporting relations, the prize of a place in the 1991 World Rugby Cup final, a rising tide of nationalist patriotic fervour within Scotland as a whole and a contest between two teams whose contrasting styles of play whetted the appetite of many a rugby connoisseur. Some political commentators at the time were suggesting that the result of the game itself would be an important factor in the then-pending Kincardine–Deeside by-election. The adoption by such a conservative Scottish institution as the Scottish Rugby Union of the populist national anthem 'Flower of Scotland' at one level might be seen as insignificant and yet at another level it was a profound gesture of sentimentality which in part encapsulated the mood of the Scottish people at a particular point in time. When the song was first written it was far less popular because it was associated with the Scottish National Party.

Aspects of Scottish sport are strongly nationalist. There is a separate Scottish Football Association and Scottish Football League; football loyalties centre around Scottish teams, and football internationals, particularly against England, arouse a fierce partisanship. Other sports are also organised on a Scottish rather than a British basis while the important place of sport within Scottish popular culture is also reflected in the effect that it has on other aspects of Scottish culture such as the composition of newspapers and the time devoted to sport on Scottish television. Indeed the novelist William McIlvanney still holds to the ingenious view that if Scotland had faired better during the 1978 Football World Cup in Argentina, then the result of the 1979 referendum on Scottish devolution might have been different. In both cases, the goalposts were seemingly moved; at least the Scottish goalkeeper was not standing in them when an ageing Peruvian called Cubillas found the net with regularity in the Scottish 3–1 defeat to Peru in the opening match of Scotland's 1978 World Cup campaign, while the 1979 referendum on devolution was governed by the infamous 40 per cent rule. The rule was introduced by an expatriate Scot representing an English constituency and ironically accepted on 25 January 1979 (Burns Night) against the wishes of 80 per cent of the Scottish MPs.[2]

During the early 1990s, it was not football nor Hampden Park, the national football stadium, which seemed to reflect the feelings of the Scottish electorate but Rugby Union and in particular the events during and leading up to the clash between Scotland and England at Murrayfield, the national Rugby Union stadium. It goes without saying that sport does not provide the healthiest foundation upon which to mobilise a campaign for national or regional separatism and yet just for a second Murrayfield seemed to encapsulate not just the tension of a Rugby World Cup semi-final clash but the real tension of a Union of opposites and the potential constitutional crisis currently facing the 'divided' United Kingdom. Murrayfield itself was packed with a capacity crowd of 59,000 whose loyalties had been emotionally charged by a complex number of factors: the prospect of a Scottish victory over the 'auld enemy', memory of England's grand slam victory in 1991, the Scottish flanker John Jeffries leading out the Scottish team in his last home international before retirement, the contrast of styles between England's dour pack and Scotland's fleet-footed running backs, and the strains of the respective national anthems, the Scottish 'Flower of Scotland' and the English 'God Save the Queen'.

Yet at another level, the events at Murrayfield were also mediated by the apparently widening fissure within the fabric of the original 1707 Act of Union of the Parliaments, the anger against the poll tax which had been introduced in Scotland one year before it was introduced to the rest of the United Kingdom, and the sentiments which endorsed 'A Claim of Right for Scotland'. The Claim of Right for Scotland gave birth to the Scottish Convention, a cross-party body charged with the task of presenting detailed proposals for a Scottish Assembly which would enjoy wide support. The future governing of Scotland, after a decade of confrontation which has stretched the very fabric of the Union of the Parliaments thinner than ever before, is uncertain. Indeed, it would be unhealthy for any of the existing British political parties to dismiss the symbolism of the events at Murrayfield, even the defeat by the English, as being peripheral, meaningless, or, in part, not reflecting the political pulse of the Scottish electorate during the early 1990s.

Despite the occasional idealist claims that sport itself often transcends the conflicts and problems of modernity, the changing world conditions and relations apply to everyone. Numerous arguments might be put forward in the early 1990s for considering the relationship between sport, nationality and cultural identity in all of their meaningful or distorted forms. Firstly, the year 1992 has achieved a significance paralleled only by the year 1984 (thanks to George Orwell's classic novel – written on Jura in 1948).[3] The implementation of the Single European Act represents both a threat and a promise to traditional, national and local sporting boundaries. Secondly, global sporting productions, such as those accompanying the 1991 Rugby World Cup, have often led to images and statements about cultural homogeneity and integration. Thirdly, with South African sportsmen and sportswomen being welcomed back into the congregation, and Europe itself being shaken by the tremors of democratic upheavals and resurgent nationalism, it is almost impossible to forecast the national composition of future world sporting events.[4] Finally, rather than increasing unity and integration, some cultural critics and political theorists have argued that the natural reaction to modern internationalism and globalisation is that local, regional and national communities will hold on even tighter to those symbols, myths, memories, traditions and nostalgia which have helped to define various cultural identities, some of which are closely associated with the making of many nations.

As any critic will readily discern, this specific contribution, while it touches upon many of those central concepts which are often closely associated with nationalism, namely nationhood, national-consciousness, racism, and national sovereignty, its central concern is not so much with the complex relationship between sport and nationalism, but the way in which sport, in all its different forms and contexts, often contributes to quests for identity. Many of these identities are often reflected in representations of nationality.[5] The concept of identity is not used here to define a common denominator of patterns of life and activity, but rather the subjective feelings and valuations of any population which possesses common experiences and *many* shared cultural characteristics.[6] Sport itself, in all its different forms, both contributes to and is constitutive of, for example, Irish, English, Scottish and Welsh culture and yet within each of these amorphous identities and expressions of nationhood, it is almost impossible to distinguish exactly what identity is being reflected and what expressions of national consciousness are being symbolised or lived out. Histories come and go, people come and go, sporting examples come and go and indeed identities take on changing forms, and yet when everything has been critiqued and counter-critiqued, there is still something down there, something deep rooted which helps individuals, classes, genders, ethnie(s) and nations make sense of themselves. The forms and contexts change, but what I have called here the quest for identity is as much a question about the present as it is about the past.

In order to address these themes, I have essentially divided this chapter into two parts. The first part briefly considers an historically specific example of the complex relationship between sport, nationalism and identity. In particular this section addresses the question, why did no organisation develop in Scotland similar to the Gaelic Athletic Association in Ireland given that a close association existed between the two countries during the last two decades of the nineteenth century and the first two decades of the twentieth century? The second part of the chapter is more general in that it considers some current issues and debates concerning sport, nationalism and cultural identity.

Sport, Gaelic nationalism and Celtic culture: Michael Davitt, John Murdoch and the kilt versus knickerbocker debate 1879–1924

Scotland and Ireland have much in common: they are geographically close, have intimate ties of ethnicity, history and culture and a complex identity which, in part, has been structured by their respective relationships with the British state in general and the English in particular. The Irish experience might contain a lot of lessons for the Scots, but in general, there has been little cross-fertilisation between the two nationalist movements within the respective social formations. There are good reasons for this, the least of which are the barriers of Ireland's Catholicism and Scotland's Calvinism and the fact that when nationalism in Ireland was at its peak, nationalism in Scotland, at least Scottish nationalism as such, was at best embryonic if not non-existent.[7] The roots of the Irish problem lay in the Act of Union of 1800 which, like the Scottish Union of 1707, was meant to be incorporative and consequently submerge the respective identities of the two nation-states within a new United Kingdom.[8] For Scotland, the Westminster Parliament worked imperfectly but adequately up until the early 1920s while the 1800 Act of Union continually and systematically failed Ireland up until 1921. In many ways, Scotland's discontents were different from those of the Irish and consequently it is difficult if not impossible to compare the two nationalist movements.

If one considers in a comparative sense the cross-fertilisation between the Highlands and Ireland during the latter decades of the nineteenth century and the early two decades of the twentieth century, one is afforded insights not only into the Gaelic connection, but also the relationship between sport, politics and nationalism in two different yet similar contexts.[9] Some of the key individuals and organisations involved in the respective struggles included Michael Davitt, John Murdoch, John Mackay, the Gaelic Athletic Association, the Irish Land League, the Highland Land League, John Stuart Blackie and the Camanachd Association. Yet the crucial question that needs to be addressed, at least within the context of this discussion, is why in Scotland did no organisation emerge similar to the Gaelic Athletic Association in Ireland?

Born in 1818, John Murdoch spent most of his childhood on the Island of Islay, the closest of the Hebrides to Ireland. To Murdoch, the plight of the Irish peasantry, which he saw as analogous to the problems of the crofting community in the Highlands, was the greatest condemnation of the Anglo-Irish Union.[10] The formation of the Highland Land Law Reform Association in 1883 was in no small part due to the tireless campaigning of John Murdoch through the medium of *The Highlander*, the paper which Murdoch launched in Inverness in 1873.[11] Although the paper had become defunct by 1882, the columns of *The Highlander* reported regularly on developments within Irish nationalist politics and anti-landlord agitation in the Highlands, and in general provided a forum for debate and co-operation between Gaelic speakers and political and cultural nationalists in Scotland and Ireland. The paper also contained regular reports and views on the subject of shinty and in the kilt versus knickerbocker debate of 1878 it reproduced one of the great sporting controversies of the late nineteenth century.[12]

On 21 April, Mr A. G. Cameron not only protested against the early shinty clubs using the word Camanachd, but also suggested that the Highland Camanachd Club of London should insist on its players wearing kilts at shinty games. Alastair MacLennan, secretary of the club, sought to close the debate by responding 'a wearer of the kilt, when put *hors de combat* is anything but graceful, nay he is bare-ly decent'.[13] The Glasgow Ossian shinty club entered the fray arguing that it was ridiculous to think of a caman getting entangled in a kilt. By then it had been suggested by the Highland Camanachd Club of London that £10 wager should be placed on three knickerbockered shinty teams beating any three kilted shinty teams. Donald McPherson, secretary of Glasgow Fingal, one of the kilted clubs, suggested that there should be one game between a knickerbockered select and kilted select. The call to arms apparently never took place, with the last word seemingly being left to Ronald Walker of Glasgow Camanachd who asserted 'playing matches to doomsday won't decide which is the most suitable dress . . . a Highlander is a Highlander though he should play shinty in pantaloons'.[14]

The Highlander also reported the triple alliance of 1879 between Charles Stewart Parnell, Michael Davitt and John Devoy and the resultant rapid rise of Davitt's Irish Land League. Murdoch not only shared Davitt's views on internationalism, demands for land reform and Irish home rule, but his paper actively supported them from the beginning. It is perhaps somewhat ironic that although Highland Land League MPs had the support of Parnellities in parliament, Parnell's own opinion of the Scots is enshrined in his remark that Scotland had long since ceased to be a nation.[15] It was different with Davitt whose Highland speeches in the late 1880s openly attacked not only the landlord system, but the systematic development of the Highlands as a leisure playground for the southern aristocracy. Indeed popular forms of protest against such developments continued intermittently from the late 1880s right on into the 1920s. Davitt not only showed an interest in Scottish questions and Scottish home rule, but actively agitated for the development of a Scottish Home Rule Association which itself was founded in 1886. Murdoch by this time was in his seventies, and with the demise of *The Highlander* he spent more and more time on the advancement of the labour movement and yet he had ensured that the Irish influence on Scottish nationalist politics and Highland political struggles was not an insignificant one.

Like Murdoch, John Stuart Blackie from the Chair of Greek at Edinburgh University supported Highland land reform, Gaelic revivalism, Irish home rule and Scottish devolution. Blackie prompted the campaign for the establishment of the Chair in Celtic Studies at Edinburgh, became Vice-President of the Highland Land Law Reform Association, was regularly quoted and supported by Charles Stewart Parnell and became first Chairman of the Scottish Home Rule Association.[16] Blackie's interest in Gaelic politics and culture also included sport in the sense that he became the first president of the Edinburgh University Shinty Club, formed in 1891. Shinty, from the Chair, was not only the embodiment of Scottish Gaelic culture and identity, but also a link with the past. Similar views on shinty were shared by John Mackay, editor of the *Celtic Monthly*, ferverent supporter of Glasgow Cowal Shinty Club and the man who brought photo-feature jouralism to shinty in the last decade of the nineteenth century.[17] The first issue of the *Celtic Monthly*, printed in October 1892, listed twenty-six organised shinty clubs, with the Camanachd Association being inaugurated exactly two years later in October 1894.

Undoubtedly there were many lessons and interconnecting strands between Irish and Highland political and cultural movements during the last quarter of the nineteenth century. Like the Irish problem, the plight of the Highlands was portrayed as a classic example of the English neglect of Scottish questions. The lesson for organisations such as the Highland Land League, the Irish Land League, the Scottish Home Rule Association and the Irish Nationalist Movement seemed to be that Irish and Highland questions loomed high on Westminster's political agenda only when the respective social formations began to organise and mobilise outwith the British political framework. As I have tried to indicate here, many nationalists on both sides saw a common plight in the struggle of the Irish peasantry and the Highland crofters and yet there is a danger in putting too great an emphasis on this Gaelic bonding and pan-Celticism. It may have been a contributory factor to the political atmosphere of Scottish politics during this period and it may have provided a common framework in which questions of landownership and questions of nationalist and socialist strategies might have been raised but there is more than an ounce of truth in Lord Derby's declaration in the late 1880s that apart from a handful of Celtic enthusiasts Scotland did not want a separate parliament or even home rule.[18] Even the founder of the Scottish National Party, Dr John MacCormick, criticised those nationalists who looked at Scotland through green spectacles and the lack of historical parallel between the specific struggles between Scotland and Ireland. Such differences are just as important as the similarities but perhaps go further in explaining why no organisation equivalent to the Gaelic Athletic Association in Ireland developed in Scotland.

Although the Irish–Ireland ideal did not come to full fruition until after 1900, some of the underlying emotions behind it can be discerned in a letter written in 1884 by Archbishop Croke to Michael Cusack, founder of the Gaelic Athletic Association. The Archbishop regretted that,

> we are daily importing from England, not only her manufactured goods ... but, together with her fashions, her accents, her vicious literature, her music, her dances, and her mannerisms, her games also and her pastimes, to the detriment of our own grand national sports ... as though we are ashamed of them.[19]

The Gaelic Athletic Association was formed in Dublin in 1884 as an avowedly, unabashed nationalist organisation.[20] It was dedicated above all to the fostering and preserving of the sports of Old Ireland. While the game of hurling embodied the spirit of Irish identity on the playing fields, such sports as hockey and association football were seen to be indicative of the process of cultural British (really English) imperialism. The GAA wished both to protect Irish athletes from defeat at the hands and feet of the vastly more experienced English but also halt the process of Anglicisation. Consequently, the patriotic, political implications of the game of hurling became symbolic for both reasserting Irish cultural identity and acting as a bulwark against imported colonial sports. Three years after Gladstone came out in favour of home rule, two pro-independence members of the Liberal Party arrived in Dublin and were met at the railway station by a thousand young members of the GAA bearing hurling caman. In 1891 the funeral cortège of Charles Stewart Parnell was led through the streets of Dublin by thousands of GAA members carrying hurleys draped in black. As a symbol of defiance against English rule in Ireland it was given added potency in 1917 when the English banned the hurling caman from being carried in public. Indeed in 1971 a party of Republican women were arrested while demonstrating outside Belfast law courts but, as Hutchinson indicates, they were charged not with any public order offence, but with being in the possession of offensive weapons – hurling caman.[21]

Although Highland Games and shinty may arguably represent various visions of Gaelic culture, visions and identities which are often drawn upon to fuel the oxygen tanks of Scottish nationalism, no organisation similar to the GAA emerged in Scotland. Perhaps the only other sporting body in Britain whose welfare and difficulties have been discussed at governmental level is the Marylebone Cricket Club. Certainly the Camanachd Association had little contact with the GAA in either the late 1890s or early 1920s. A match between Glasgow Cowal and Dublin Celtic did take place in 1879, with Michael Cusack presiding, and the Camanachd Association were invited to the Tailtean Games in August 1924. An international match had been planned for 1934, until discreet approaches were made to the Camanachd Association which resulted in the announcement from Inverness that since the GAA had an 'anti-British political flavour' the Camanachd Association would have nothing to do with the proposed international hurling/shinty match.[22]

Despite the Gaelic connection being severed in this instance Irish politicians had long since recognised the advantages of being associated with Glasgow Celtic Football Club. Paradoxically Michael Davitt, founding member of the Irish Land League, strong supporter of the GAA, was also a staunch supporter of Glasgow Celtic Football Club. As patron of the club, Davitt laid the first patch of soil, specially transported from Donegal, at Celtic Park in 1892. The paradox of course is that Davitt was both an enthusiastic patron of Glasgow Celtic Football Club and a staunch political supporter of the GAA which had condemned association with the game of football. Perhaps as Murray suggests, this might be explained by the fact that Davitt allegedly reported that if he saw too many games at Celtic Park, he would forswear politics for football.[23] More realistically, it was perhaps an indication that the Irish in Scotland were about to go their own way, were about to commit themselves to a different union and were about to weaken the original ties with Ireland. By this, I do not mean that Irish–Scots did not identify with Irish causes, but that they became more involved with socialist concerns and the labour movement in Scotland which, while recognising the important cultural and political links with Ireland, in the last instance was pro-unionist in its orientation.[24]

The relationship between revolutionary socialism and extreme nationalism during the early decades of the twentieth century lies outside the scope of this chapter. In all events, in both Ireland and Scotland in the years leading up to the Easter Rising of 1916 and the years immediately following it, both movements probably came closer together than at any other time. Both James Connolly and John Maclean were born of Gaelic-speaking parents. It was the Easter Rising of 1916 and its aftermath that attracted the attention of John Maclean to Ireland, and led eventually to him acknowledging that there were lessons that Scotland could learn from the Irish predicament. For instance, Maclean made immediate connections in the Highlands with Connolly's notion that Irish society had been founded on the communal ownership of land. An increasing Irish influence was prominent in the views not only of Maclean, but also Erskine of Mar and Tom Johnston. The links between Erskine and Maclean on the one side and the Land League and the Labour Party on the other side were typical of many postwar alliances between Gaelic nationalists and various sections of the Scottish left but in the end, the attempt by Erskine, Maclean and others to draw parallels with Ireland was based on essentially a false premise. While there are many valid reasons for comparing the Highland context with Ireland, there was never any real chance of Erskine and Maclean, and the ideas associated with them, gripping the Scots' imagination in the same way as Connolly and Pearse had mobilised Irish nationalist sentiment. The Gaelic connection was strongest between the Highlands and Ireland but to extend the similar circumstances and contexts to those of Scotland and Ireland was to embrace the false premise that Scotland and Ireland were the same. Scotland at this time in its political history did not want to break out of the Act of Union, and in this fact alone lies one of the key reasons in explaining why an organisation similar to the Gaelic Athletic Association did not develop in Scotland.

Furthermore it has to be said that while periods of Scottish history have witnessed attempts to establish separate kingdoms and local fiefdoms, such as the Lordship of the Isles during the fifteenth century, in general nationalists, whether they be Gaelic, Irish or Scottish, have tended to support moves for home rule in Scotland and Ireland but not home rule for the Highlands or the Gaidhealtachd. In a simple sense while the Gaelic Athletic Association could readily identify with a form of Irish nationality in modern times, no nation other than Scotland existed for Gaelic culture in the Highlands to identify with. Indeed many modern Celtic historians have suggested that the divisions within the Gaidhealtachd are as great as the integrating factors and while one might talk of a Scottish consciousness it is perhaps spurious to talk of a unified Celtic consciousness in the Highlands of Scotland. There was certainly no specific modern political organisation in the Highlands that was marching for home rule in the Highlands and as such no political party for any sporting organisation to attach itself to.

One final point is that, in retrospect, Scottish identity, if not Scottish nationalism, was much more profoundly affected by an incident at Hampden Park which happened six years prior to Michael Davitt's visit to Celtic Park. On 30 October 1886, during a third-round Football Association cup match between Preston North End and Queen's Park, Jimmy Ross, a Scots player with Preston North End, fouled Harrower, the Queen's Park centre-forward before a crowd of 15,000.[25] The pitch was invaded by Queen's Park supporters and Ross had to be smuggled out of the ground. The incident brought to a head the differences between the Football Association and Scottish Football Association (SFA), as a result of which the SFA announced on 10 May 1887 that clubs belonging to the Association should not be members of any other national association and, consequently, ordered the Scottish teams to withdraw from the FA cup competition.[26] The crystallisation of Scottish and English football structures along national and not British lines has been used by a number of politicians and political scientists to illustrate the fact that football in Scotland, along with other institutions such as the Church of Scotland, the Royal Burghs and distinctly different educational and legal systems, has a strongly national character. Such structures often help to sharpen up national identities and reinforce a certain national consciousness.[27] Yet such concerns have not been the main focus of attention here.

Analysis of the period 1879–1924 has commanded attention for at least three important reasons: (1) it provides an illustrative example of the complex relationship between sport, politics and nationalism; (2) in a comparative sense, it affords a discussion of some of the similarities and differences between political and cultural forms of nationalism in Scotland and Ireland; and (3) it reminds us that the specificities of general theories and explanations concerning problems of politics, identity and nationality can really only be borne out with concrete historical expositions. While the next part of this chapter still draws upon Scottish and Irish examples, amongst others, it moves to the level of generality in the sense that it briefly considers some current debates concerning sport, nationalism and cultural identity.

Sport, nationalism and cultural identity: Global culture, integration and a world in union

The idea that sport itself transcends and integrates local, regional, national and European communities is an argument that has appeared in many disguises and forms. The notion that sport has some inherent property that rises above and displaces whatever major or minor social divisions there may be has often been perceived as one of the major rationales behind staging global sporting productions such as the Olympic Games, and World Rugby, Football and Athletic Championships. In the late 1970s Nigeria's Minister of Sport, Sylvanus Williams, suggested that sporting achievements not only help to integrate the people but are also a measure of the nation's greatness.[28] Similar sentiments have been echoed by a number of liberal historians who have argued that international sport and the success of the international athlete has been one of the greatest symbols of integration for many emerging African nations. The victorious athletes not only tended to legitimate the nation within the international arena but also incarnated a positive image of the nation. The underlying assumption behind this argument has been that cultural heroes/heroines along with political leaders such as Julius Nyerere of Tanzania helped to bridge the gap between national and global recognition. African citizens, argued Wallerstein, could feel an affection for the athlete and the nation, a feeling which might not have existed in the first instance.[29] Needless to say, such a process depends upon the athletes not only accepting the respective politics of the nation, but also working in tandem with the respective party structures.

The whole understanding of African social development, for Wallerstein, was firmly rooted within his perception of world systems theory, an intervention which, in part, has contributed to an understanding of global culture and the politics of the world economy.[30] The question which Wallerstein initially posited was to what extent do the core areas of the world economy expand and develop at the expense of those semi-peripheral or peripheral regions whose expansion can only be seen as a reflection of the development of the core? Although Wallerstein avoided the concept of underdevelopment, the crucial theoretical innovation in his work was not just the relational ideal between cores and peripheries but that the world system itself could be thought of as a world economy, global entity and global culture which often transcended national boundaries. Whatever the predictive power of Wallerstein's analysis, one of the crucial elements which emerges from the world systems view is that geography tends to replace history as the fundamental index of human relationships. Societies are for Wallerstein geopolitically related and, as such, do not exist at different points in a historical trajectory. The particular logic of world systems theory often breaks down when historical concrete questions are asked of it. While accepting the explanatory power of any particular framework which draws upon such notions as core, periphery, dependency and nationality, the central difficulty in any project which attempts to construct a global entity or global culture is that much of the identity, imagery and tradition which is drawn upon to construct such a collective identity is in fact historically specific and rooted in particular histories, memories and senses of continuity between generations of peoples.[31] This in itself cuts across global culture and at least for the time being means that the idea of a world in union is perhaps premature.

Yet it was precisely this message of a world in union which Kiri Te Kanewa wanted us to internalise during the World Rugby Cup of 1991. Such a premise did not rest upon the political economy of any world system – the African nations were not even represented at this global sporting production – but upon the power of communication networks to package the imagery and symbolism associated with a world in union. The term global culture in this sense is generally taken to mean the international diversification of production and consumption, a general process which is often closely linked to notions of cultural homogeneity and integration. Certainly the images, messages and symbolism of a world in union were beamed into many more homes in comparison to the 1987 World Rugby Cup in New Zealand and Australia. While only fifteen countries received pictures from the 1987 production, seventy countries watched live pictures of what one commentator referred to as Rugby's global warming.[32] In Europe *Screensport*, which broadcasts to twenty-two million homes, in twenty countries, in English, French, German and Dutch, simultaneously showed thirty of the thirty-one games live. Within Scotland, England, Ireland and Wales, Independent Television paid over £10 million to show seventy-five hours of rugby coverage. Yet I think it is fair to say that while particular television programmes, sport spectacles and advertisements may rapidly travel the globe or even the European circuit it is doubtful if the response of those viewing and listening within a variety of cultural contexts will be anything like uniform or global.[33]

The possible emergence of a European football league within the European Community and the relative free migration of sports workers throughout Europe has also prompted the notion of European integration.[34] The idea is that since the status of national boundaries will be downgraded any previous connections that were made between modern sporting practices and previous sporting nations might have to be re-evaluated. A central facet of this argument has been that modern communities tend to be more geographically than historically linked. It is further argued that this provider will be a greater potential for embracing entire populations whether it be in terms of European or global integration. Certainly those European politicians keen to highlight the efficiency of the free market and the image of a true community may look up to sport as a vehicle for building Euro-consciousness and Euro-identity. Football teams undoubtedly benefit from the migration of European talent such as the likes of Kuznetsov and Mikhailichenko at Glasgow Rangers and Kanchelskis at Manchester United. The flow of goods, people, information, knowledge and capital may indeed make it possible at one level to think of increased integration and yet at another level should a European league take shape traditional loyalties may simply be reset along alternative lines. Furthermore, it goes without saying that existing rules concerning the limits on foreign football players permissible in European competitions is not only out of step with other EEC regulations but actually contributes to the reproduction of local, regional and national identities rather than European integration.

In many respects the original nation-state has been undermined by a number of fundamental shifts since the mid twentieth century. The expansion of transnational organisations and a more complex international division of labour have certainly circumscribed the capacity of many nation-states to control their own economy. The globalisation of culture and the media has undoubtedly meant that the relationship between culture and the nation-state has become much more complex; multi-culturalism is embedded in virtually all states and any claims that people have to a single culture or a single identity becomes almost impossible to maintain.[35] At the same time centre nationalisms, be they English, French, Castilian – Spanish, have unwittingly helped to reinforce Peripheral Nationalism in at least two senses. In the first sense, changing world conditions apply to everyone and one of the consequences of recent changes is that simply re-asserting centre nationalism does not have the same force that it once had, particularly in the periphery; and in the second sense centre nationalisms have helped to reinforce peripheral nationalisms simply by asserting what peripheral nationalism are not. On the one hand, it would appear that the nation-state has entered into a phase of long-term decline and yet it is clear also that in Benedict Anderson's words the end of the era of nationalism so long prophesised is not remotely in sight.[36]

Invented traditions, imagined communities and the quest for identity

It may be that changing world conditions are about to shake many historical skeletons and unhappy national complexes that have often furnished the wardrobe of national and cultural identity. Whatever the nation in question, the quest for identity inevitably involves questions of representation, nostalgia, mythology and tradition. As several critics have pointed out, many nations themselves are fabrications or constructions, many states are not nations and indeed many nations (like Scotland at the time of writing) are not states. Above all, many modern states have had to manufacture a sense of national identity where the population is culturally and linguistically diverse. Modern states, it has been argued, have often required an explicit sense of loyalty and identification which has at times been mobilised through the identification with certain symbols, icons, hymns and prayers.[37] Hobsbawm himself suggests that mass and middle-class sport during the period 1870–1914 combined the invention of political and social traditions by providing a medium for national identification and factitious community.[38] Sport along with other mass-producing traditions became a social force of cohesion for the newly emerging Victorian middle class.

Yet even if one accepts this thesis, it is important to point out that although public entertainments is one sense became open to all during the late nineteenth century, in another sense barriers were erected to ensure that only the socially acceptable upper classes became the consumers of certain activities. That is to say activities that were formerly public – open to all – became private and as such only those of recognised social standing were admitted. In this way firm controls over participation could be asserted. Both Davidoff and Scott have implicated sport in what they refer to as the privitisation of sociability.[39] The invention of tradition in this sense revolved around, for example, the London season which got into full swing in May and lasted until the end of July: the main sports – horse riding, rowing, tennis, polo and cricket – each involved a number of key events in which all had to be seen.[40] The season ended with a mass migration to Cowes for yachting, before returning to the country homes for the autumn round of shooting, hunting and country activities. The point that is being made is simply that sporting traditions themselves, whether they are invented or not, can be both integrative and divisive, conservative and oppositional.[41] They also provide an amorphous identity in different ways for different groups of people.

Of course some contributions to the invention of tradition thesis are more acceptable than others. As a distinct aspect of national identity Scotland has often been portrayed through a Gaelic vision of Scottish culture.[42] Tartanry as a distinct aspect of this identity has, according to Hugh Trevor-Roper, been one of those traditions that was hastily contrived towards the end of Queen Victoria's reign. Tartan symbolism has certainly been reproduced through a number of Scottish sporting forms such as kilted athletes at Highland Gatherings, tartan armies which have travelled the globe in search of the holy World Cup grail and more recently, the official dress of the Scottish Rugby World Cup squad. Yet I would argue that the Highland tradition, tartanry, and indeed Scottish cultural identity is not so much an invention of tradition but a selection of tradition. Trevor-Roper's analysis is just plain wrong – tartans, clans and certain ways of life did exist prior to about 1745; they were not invented. Various social factions, such as the Highland Landlords, by virtue of their power, selected, interpreted and attributed different meanings to such cultural artefacts as tartanry, clans and what Nairn refers to as the kitsch symbols of Scottish cultural identity.[43] It is important not to divorce such romantic symbols from historically lived experience. At the level of popular culture, not even on Highland Games day do you see the bulk of the Highland people walking around in kilts, scarfs and other tartan fabrics.[44]

Whether the quest for identity draws upon romanticism, mythology, invented tradition or real objective cultural artefacts, all forms of identity are selective, particular, timebound and expressive. All nations, argues Benedict Anderson, at some stage have to indulge in some imagining.[45] The nation, it is suggested, is imagined or constructed on at least three levels, as limited in the sense that it has boundaries, as free in the sense that it is under a sovereign state and as a community which expresses itself through forms of symbolic action and comradeship. Nation-ness as well as nationalism, Anderson asserts, are built upon cultural artefacts of a particular kind. Sport itself often provides a uniquely effective medium for inculcating national feelings; it provides a form of symbolic action which states the case for the nation itself. The popular identification between athlete X, team Y and nation or community Z has led to the suggestion that sporting struggles, and international triumphs and losses, are primary expressions of imagined communities.[46] It is as if the imagined community or nation becomes more real on the terraces or the athletics track. Yet the life and death of sporting success is essentially linked in many cases to the life and death of the nation. This is not imagined but real, and an acute sense of history and specific historical circumstances invariably helps to form the expression of identity, invented or otherwise.

Certainly the relationship between sport, identity and tradition has figured in the works of a number of literary critics, many of whom have been associated with nationalist movements and nationalist struggles. One such writer was Neil Gunn whose periodical writings and novels in the 1930s and 1940s continually probed the relationship between symbolism, tradition, nationalism and culture.[47] Born in the small coastal town of Dunbeath in 1891, Gunn continually asserted that nationalism could only be interpreted out of an awareness of tradition, which for him was rooted in Highland culture. Tradition for Gunn was the essence of nationalism, which in turn lead to an outward appreciation of internationalism. While I do not wish to endorse Gunn's politics of nationalism, his writings during the 1930s are particularly insightful with regard to the discussion at hand in the sense that in one vivid example, Gunn illustrates the clear relationship between history, tradition, identity and sport.

The importance of sport within a changing way of life did not escape the attention of Gunn who, during the 1930s, continually questioned the commercialisation of the Scottish Highland Games and the spectacle of the professional athlete travelling from village to village collecting any money that local labour and patronage could gather.[48] Commenting upon one particular incident, Gunn recalls an occasion when the dancers were called together and the prize piper, who had carried off all the money that day, appeared not in the traditional Highland dress but in a blue suit and bowler hat. The judge, obviously astonished, called the piper over and asked him to explain what the rig-out meant. Not recognising the importance of the blue ribbon tradition of the best piper having the honour of playing for the dancers at the last event, the piper explained that he had wanted to catch an early train and therefore he had jettisoned his borrowed kilt so that he could beat it at the earliest moment.[49] At one level, the humorous dismissal of the incident may seem insignificant and yet at another level, the writer's point is intrinsically a serious one since what Gunn was in fact commenting upon was the decline of a Highland way of life in the 1930s and the in-roads being made by a more urban, commercialised culture which took little cognisance of tradition, local people and local customs. What seems clear about Gunn's writings about tradition and nationalism is the view that they were both inextricably linked and that the life and death of one was the life and death of the other.[50]

As E. P. Thompson has recently argued, it is not necessary to accept the comformist notion of tradition and custom since such traditions can be just as oppositional as they are conformist.[51] Rather than increasing unity and integration on a global scale, it is quite possible that the rational reaction to modern internationalism and the demise of the nation-state, in its original form, will be that local, regional and national communities will hold on even tighter to those symbols and traditions, including sporting traditions, which once gave various nations and peoples a sense of identity. The concept of identity may refer to those subjective feelings and valuations of any group of people who possess common experiences and one or more shared cultural characteristics. At least three components of those shared experiences can be mentioned: (1) a sense of continuity between the experiences of succeeding generations of groups of people; (2) shared memories of specific events and personages which have been turning points for a collective or national history; and (3) a sense of common destiny on the part of those groups sharing those experiences. This does not mean that identity is some perpetual anguishing over the past, or a lost nation, but that the concept of identity is as much about a response to the present. The central problem with any global culture, or even European culture, is that it is difficult to construct a strong form of collective identity and it is invariably threatened by many forms of national culture and indeed nationalism which can draw upon strong memories, a strong collective identity and a strong sense of history and continuity.[52]

Europe and the new Russian Federation of Independent States are themselves a patchwork of tensions which indicates that the end of the era of nationalism or imagined communities is not remotely in sight. These tensions might be crudely divided into two categories. Firstly, those tensions which directly relate to problems of nationality.[53] These may be about nations seeking to regain lost sovereignty – Lithuania, Georgia, Scotland, Estonia – or looking to achieve independence for the first time in modern history – Wales – or attempts to extend existing degrees of autonomy – Catalonia, the Ukraine – or concerns over the civil rights of minority groups such as the Germans in the South Tyrol, the Slovenes in Austria, the Hungarians in Transylvania and Slovakia. Secondly, those tensions which directly relate to existing frontiers or demarcation lines and generally includes disputes between governments. While the Helsinki agreements (Helsinki Final Act of 1975) bind all European states not to attempt to change existing borders, except by mutual agreement, the potential for conflict is forever present. In the West, such conflicts might include those over Northern Ireland; in eastern and southern Europe there is the reluctance of the United Germany to recognise Poland's western frontier, the Oder – Neisse Line. The Macedonia question forms a deeply buried Doomsday machine under what was formerly Yugoslavia, Bulgaria and Greece, while in the Caucasus the tensions between Armenia and Azerbaijan are about frontiers, minorities, nationality and religion all at once.

It would be foolish to suggest that the content and basis of nationalism in the late twentieth century is the same as the content and basis of nationalism in the late nineteenth or early twentieth century. It has been suggested that fundamentally the basis of nationalism in many cases has shifted from primordial issues of ethnicity and indeed racism to issues of territoriality.[54] Certainly new state formations might emerge and certain state boundaries will undoubtedly become malleable and changeable. There is certainly a quest for new forms of self-determination, of limited autonomy in self-managing communities, based on the rights of people to govern themselves. Although Raymond Williams never addressed the notion of nationality or nationalism, perhaps he set a possible agenda for post-nationalist movements when he argued that it is clear that if people are to defend and promote their real interests on the basis of lived and worked and placeable social identities, then 'a large part of the now alienated and centralised powers and resources must be actively regained by new actual societies which, in their own terms and nobody else's, define themselves'.[55] The lesson is perhaps that nationalist movements which take a narrow primordial route are doomed to failure, while those that mobilise new sentiments of resistance and cultural development based on fresh challenges are more likely to have some relative success.

Concluding remarks

While there is a great danger in overemphasising the role of sport in the making of nations, at a general level, the relationship between sport and nationalism has rested upon a number of common arguments: (1) that sport itself is inherently conservative and that it helps to consolidate official or centre nationalism, patriotism and racism; (2) that sport itself has some inherent property that makes it a possible instrument of national unity and integration, for example, in peripheral or emerging nations; (3) that sport itself provides a safety value or outlet of emotional energy for frustrated peoples or nations; (4) that sport itself helps to reinforce national consciousness and cultural nationalism; (5) that sport itself at times has contributed to unique political struggles some of which have been closely connected to nationalist politics and popular nationalist struggles; (6) that sport itself is often involved in the process of nationalism as a national reaction to dependency and uneven development; and (7) that sport itself, whether it be through nostalgia, mythology, invented or selected traditions, contributes to a quest for identity, albeit local, regional, cultural or global. In some cases it is easier to accept the idea that sporting forms and sporting relations help to reproduce, transform or construct the image of a community without accepting the notion of it being imagined.

However one might want to explain nationality, and the quest for identity, it is clear that questions of ethnicity, questions of language, questions of common culture, questions of dual nationality, questions of integration and disintegration and questions of territory are likely to remain connected to the complex tensions which are unfolding within Europe in the early 1990s. Some observers have suggested that while centre nationalisms and traditional nationalisms might continue to decay, peripheral nationalisms might find it easier to survive as the centre erodes. Still others have suggested that more fundamentally the basis of nationalism in the late twentieth century is changing away from a racist emphasis on primordial or ethnic/racial or sectarian ties to a definition of a nation or community based on territoriality. Yet there are problems here too, especially for those communities whose sense of nationhood and self-determination is not closely tied to clear territorial demarcation lines being established. Scotland, for example, is perhaps fortunate in having one of the clearest and least disputed borders in the world. The Scots or English cannot claim any moral or strategic superiority for this, but they should be aware of the problems which disputes about territory or the border create for other communities or groups of people. For Irish nationalists, the border is something which lies across their territory, dissecting and mutilating it. For Ulster Loyalists, it is a physical dyke against the threat of Catholic domination. But in Scotland, the line itself, as Purdie points out, is not disputed, only the political structures which straddle it.[56]

Perhaps identity is what nation-states have always had and what many dependent, peripheral or frustrated nations have continually been struggling for. Whether it be spectating at Cardiff Arms Park, Twickenham, Landsdowne Road or Hampden Park, to be involved in Scottish, Welsh, Irish or English sport is to experience a sense of history and culture. Sport itself in Scotland, England and Wales (this is not the case in Ireland) has not generally been centrally concerned with self-determinism or political devolution but rather an assertion of Scottishness, Englishness and Welshness on the part of a diverse group of interests and individuals whose identity is caught up with that of England, Scotland or Wales. Sport itself in all its different forms both contributes to and is constitutive of Irish, Scottish, English and Welsh culture and yet within each of these amorphous identities and expressions of nationhood, it is almost impossible to distinguish exactly what identity is being reflected and what expression of national consciousness is being symbolised, transformed, reproduced or even imagined. Yet there is still something down there, something deep rooted which helps individuals, groups and nations make sense of themselves. Such quests for belongingness and identity often express themselves in the quest for national recognition, new forms of self-determination and a limited autonomy for self-managing communities.

Notes

1 'Flowers sprouting over the border', The Guardian, 28 October 1991, 24.
2 Tom Gallagher, 'National identity and the working-class in Scotland', Cencrastus, 33, 1989, 15–20. For a critical account of Scottish football since the 1920s, see Stuart Cosgrove, Hampden Babylon, Canongate Press, Edinburgh, 1991.

3 George Orwell, *Nineteen Eighty-Four*, Secker and Warburg, 1949.

4 'Traditional Olympics in danger', *The Glasgow Herald*, 1 October 1991, 42.

5 For a discussion on Englishness and cricket, see R. Colls and P. Dodds, eds, *Englishness, Politics and Culture 1880–1920*, Croom Helm, 1987.

6 Anthony Smith, 'Towards a global culture?', *Theory, Culture and Society*, 7 (2), 1991, 171–92. An extended discussion of this thesis is presented in Anthony Smith, *The Ethnic Origins of Nations*, Basil Blackwell, 1989.

7 A recent discussion of the relationship between Irish and Scottish nationalism is to be found in Bob Purdie, 'The lessons of Ireland for the SNP', in Tom Gallagher, ed, *Nationalism in the Nineties*, Polygon, 1991, pp. 66–83.

8 The Irish Act of Union of 1800 was flawed from the start not least because Pitt had meant to include Catholic Emancipation but the king blocked the proposed concession. While there is more than an ounce of realism in the immortal words of Robert Burns – that the 1707 Act of Union was bought and sold for English gold by a parcel of rogues who were themselves members of the Scottish nation – the general consensus is that up until the 1920s Scotland and England existed within an equal partnership.

9 James Hunter, 'The Gaelic connection: the Highlands, Ireland and Nationalism, 1873–1922', *Scottish Historical Review*, 54, 1975, 178–205. See also James Hunter, 'The politics of Highland land reform, 1873–1895', *Scottish Historical Review*, 53, 1974, 45–68, and also David Howell, *A Lost Left*, Manchester University Press, 1986.

10 James Hunter, 'The Gaelic connection', p. 179.

11 Grant Jarvie, *Highland Games: The Making of the Myth*, Edinburgh University Press, 1991.

12 Roger Hutchinson, *Camanachd: The Story of Shinty*, Mainstream Publishing, 1989, pp. 130–6.

13 *The Highlander*, 262, 18 May 1878, 6.

14 Mr Walker also added that his preference for knickerbockers was purely practical in the sense that they were light and held their place when the player was upside down.

15 Quoted in *Scots Magazine*, viii, 1891, 37. It should also be noted that on 10 January 1880, Parnell, Dillon and John Murdoch all shared the same platform in Philadelphia promoting Celtic Radicalism.

16 When Parnell made his famous speech to the American House of representatives on 2 February 1880, he quoted with evident approval Blackie's opinion that in the pretence of governing Ireland, the English had confiscated land which by real law belonged to the people and divided it amongst 'cliques of greedy and grasping oligarchs who had done nothing for the country'. It is perhaps ironic that in a typical about-turn Blackie towards the end of his life became convinced that Ireland itself was not fit for self-government. See F. S. Lyons, *Parnell*, Fontana, 1991.

17 Roger Hutchinson, *Camanachd*, p. 136.

18 James Hunter, 'The Gaelic Connection'.

19 Quoted in F. Martin and F. J. Byrne, eds, *The Scholar Revolutionary:*

Eoin MacNeill, 1867–1945 and the Making of the New Ireland, Shannon, 1973, p. 77.

20 W. Mandle, *The Gaelic Athletic Association and Irish Nationalist Politics 1884–1924*, Christopher Helm, 1987. In general, John Sugden and Alan Bairner have done much to illustrate and explain the complex relationship between sport, politics and popular struggle in Northern Ireland. For example, see J. Sugden and A. Bairner, 'The politics of sport in Northern Ireland', *Studies*, 318, summer 1991, 133–41.

21 Roger Hutchinson, *Camanachd*, p. 32.

22 *Ibid.*, p. 186.

23 Bill Murray, *The Old Firm: Sport, Sectarianism and Society in Scotland*, John Donald, 1984, p. 73. It should also be noted that Michael Davitt, the Catholic founder of the Irish Land League, was even invited to stand as parliamentary candidate for Skye in 1887.

24 Tom Campbell and Pat Woods, *The Glory and the Dream*, Grafton Books, 1987, pp. 10–20. For a useful discussion on Michael Davitt's relationship with Glasgow Celtic Football Club, see Gerry Finn, 'Racism, religion and social prejudice: Irish Catholic clubs, soccer and Scottish society', *International Journal of the History of Sport*, 8, May 1991, 72–95.

25 Christopher Harvie, *Scotland and Nationalism: Scottish Society and Politics 1707–1977*, George Allen and Unwin, 1977, p. 37.

26 For a broader discussion on the relationship between Scottish football, nationalism and nationhood, see both James Kellas, *The Scottish Political System*, Cambridge University Press, 1973, and James Kellas, *The Politics of Nationalism and Ethnicity*, Macmillan, 1991.

27 It is often argued that it is invalid to bring Scotland into such comparisons with nation-states since it is at present a stateless nation and yet it is nevertheless a political system. There are features of statehood within that system such as separate aspects of laws, administration, church, education and sport. Such a system allocates certain values which maintain an amorphous identity.

28 The *New York Times*, 20 July 1978.

29 See William Baker and James Mangan, *Sport in Africa: Essays in Social History*, African Publishing Co, 1987, pp. 278–80.

30 Immanuel Wallerstein, *The Politics of the World Economy*, Cambridge University Press, 1984. For a useful summary and critique of this analysis, see Cairns Craig, 'Nation and history', *Cencrastus*, 19, 1984, 13–18.

31 Anthony Smith, 'Towards global culture?', *Theory, Culture and Society*, 7 (2), 1991, 171–92. In the same issue, see the debate between Boyne and Wallerstein.

32 'The games opportunity for global warming', *The Independent*, 3 October 1991, 34.

33 'Let smaller nations share in the £20m profit', *Glasgow Herald*, 30 October 1991, 31. See also 'ITV was a turn on', *The Guardian*, 6 November 1991, p. 26.

34 A number of researchers have recently highlighted the new role of football within the European Economic Community. Vic Duke, 'The sociology of football: a research agenda for the 1990s', *Sociological Review*, 3 (3), August 1991, 627–45. The National Identity Research Unit based at Glasgow

Polytechnic has published several reports on sport and the issues of European and national identity.

35 David McCrone, 'Post nationalism and the decline of the nation state', *Radical Scotland*, 49, 1991, 6–10.

36 Benedict Anderson, *Imagined Communities – Reflections on the Origin and Spread of Nationalism*, Verso, 1983.

37 Eric Hobsbawm and Terence Ranger, ed., *The Invention of Tradition*, Cambridge University Press, 1983.

38 Eric Hobsbawm, 'Mass producing traditions: Europe, 1870–1914', in Eric Hobsbawn and Terence Ranger, ed., *The Invention of Tradition*, pp. 263–307. See also Hobsbawm's discussion on sport in Eric Hobsbawm, *Nations and Nationalism since 1780*, Cambridge University Press, 1990.

39 For a discussion on this point, see John Scott, *Who Rules Britain?*, Polity Press, 1991, pp. 97–117.

40 John Scott, *Who Rules Britain?*, p. 100.

41 E. P. Thompson, *Customs in Common*, The Merlin Press, 1991.

42 Malcolm Chapman, *The Gaelic Vision in Scottish Culture*, Croom Helm, 1978.

43 Tom Nairn, *The Break Up of Britain*, Verso, 1981, p. 162.

44 Grant Jarvie, *Highland Games*.

45 Benedict Anderson, *Imagined Communities*.

46 Eric Hobsbawm has on several occasions argued with regard to football that the imagined community of millions often seems more real as a team of eleven players or more. The individual, even the one who cheers, becomes a symbol of the nation itself. Eric Hobsbawm, *Nations and Nationalism since 1780*, p. 142. See also Alan Tomlinson's use of Benedict Anderson's notion in Alan Tomlinson, 'Going global: the FIFA story', in Alan Tomlinson and Gary Whannel, *Off the Ball*, Pluto Press, 1986, p. 98.

47 For a general introduction to the work of Neil Gunn, see Diarmid Gunn and Isobel Murray, *Neil Gunn's Country: Essays in Celebration of Neil Gunn*, Chambers, 1991. See also Margery McCulloch, 'Neil Gunn: tradition and the essence of nationalism', *Centrastus*, 26, 1981, 29–34.

48 Neil Gunn, 'Highland Games', *Scots Magazine*, XV (6), 1931, 412–16.

49 *Ibid.*, 413.

50 Neil Gunn, 'Nationalism and internationalism', *Scots Magazine*, XV (3), 1931, 185–8.

51 Indeed E. P. Thompson's thesis is that customs and tradition were involved in the process of disassociation between patrician and plebian cultures in the eighteenth and early nineteenth centuries. E. P. Thompson, *Customs in Common*.

52 Although questions of culture and identity were of secondary importance to Alasdair MacIntyre, *After Virtue* rested in part upon the thesis that a sense of identity was dependent upon having an adequate sense of the traditions to which one both belongs and confronts. Alasdair MacIntyre, *After Virtue*, Duckworth, 1981.

53 Neal Ascherson, 'Old conflicts in the new Europe', *The Independent*, 18 February 1990, 3–5.

54 Much of this debate has drawn heavily on the work of David McCrone, 'Post-nationalism and the decline of the nation-state', *Radical Scotland*, 49, 1991, 6–10.
55 Raymond Williams, *Towards 2000*, Penguin, 1983, p. 183.
56 Bob Purdie, 'The lessons of Ireland for the SNP', in Tom Gallagher, ed., *Nationalism in the Nineties*, Polygon, 1991, pp. 66–83.

5

The politics of the Olympic movement

CHRISTOPHER R. HILL

The Olympic movement has always protested that politics should not be mixed with sport, yet it has always, since its re-foundation in 1896, been permeated with politics. Similarly, the movement's leaders have until recently set their faces against the taint of money and insisted that athletes should be amateurs, but now the International Olympic Committee has all but abandoned any concern about professionalism, and has successfully devoted itself to commercialising the Games up to the hilt. At present these profound changes may not pose problems for the future of the Games, because they are still 'the greatest show on earth'. But in the longer term the logic of entrepreneurial expansion could destroy them.[1]

The ancient Games' revival

It used conventionally to be held that the ancient Greek Games, held at Olympia from 776 BC until 261 AD, or perhaps as late as 393 AD, were free from politics, thanks to the 'sacred truce' entered into by warring parties for the period of the Games. However, the extent of the truce has been much exaggerated: what it meant was that competitors were allowed free passage to the Games, not that peace suddenly broke out. Nor, as used to be alleged, were the ancient Games free from professionalism. It is true that at the major contests on the Games circuit no prizes were given, but successful athletes were richly rewarded when they returned to their home cities, and those who had failed were in disgrace. There was no suggestion that the point was to take part, rather than to win.[2] However, in the nineteenth century it seems generally to have been believed that the 'Olympic ideal' involved achieving the maximum of which the human body and spirit were capable, for the love of sport and fair play, and with no overtones of material gain. This was the view propagated by Baron Pierre de Coubertin (1863–1937), the founder of the modern Games, though he seems to have been ambivalent about amateurism, even referring to it as 'this admirable mummy'.[3]

De Coubertin had forerunners, notably Dr William Penny Brookes (1809–94) who in 1850 founded the 'Olympian Games' at Much Wenlock, Shropshire. Although they sound not unlike a village fete, Brookes used them as a vehicle to disseminate his passionate belief that the curriculum of state schools should contain compulsory physical exercise. Coubertin, who of course was much younger than Brookes, shared this belief, which was strengthened when he first visited England in 1883 at the age of 20, and became deeply impressed by the educational legacy of the great Thomas Arnold, who had been headmaster of Rugby School from 1828 to 1842.[4] Later he corresponded with Brookes until shortly before the latter's death, and in 1890 special 'Olympian Games' were held in his honour when he visited Much Wenlock.

There had also been early attempts to hold Olympic Games in Greece in 1859, 1870, 1875, and 1889. They seem to have amounted to little, save those of 1870 (and to a lesser extent 1859), but the fact that they had been held at all led some Greeks to complain quite viciously that by arranging for the modern Games to be held in a different city every four years Coubertin was stealing part of the Greek heritage.[5] There may be some truth in this, but it must be remembered that Coubertin had had to use all his skills to persuade the Greeks to hold the Games of 1896, and was understandably piqued when, once they were seen to be a success, the Greeks paid no attention to him, and simply assumed that all future Games would be held at Athens. This insulting disregard of the efforts he had made strengthened his determination to find a different home for the Games every four years.[6]

Without Coubertin's political skills the Games would not have been revived in 1896, and might never have been revived at all. He used as his vehicle the Union des Sociétés Françaises des Sports Athlétiques (USFSA), and arranged that it should hold a Congress in 1894 at which the decision would be taken to press ahead with the project to revive the Games. It appears that Coubertin had been less than straightforward when he issued invitations to sports organisations throughout Europe, as well as in the United States and Australia, to send delegates to the Congress. Initially its main purpose had been represented as a discussion of amateurism, and it was only in a later version of the programme, which delegates may not have seen before they arrived, that the Olympic project was spelt out.[7]

It was his passionate wish to improve the health of the French nation, rather than a love of the Games themselves, which led him to revive the Games, although as his life went on and he became entrenched in the movement, they probably changed from being a means to an end to being an end in themselves.[8] From the start the modern Games were suffused with politics. In 1896 the Germans showed a marked hostility to them, because they were seen as a riposte by the French for their defeat in the Franco-German war. Once the first Games had been held the Greek demand to provide their permanent home was deflected only by Coubertin's devising 'intermediate' Games, which were held only once, at Athens in 1906. As he had forecast, they were not popular, because other countries wanted to hold the Games, and no one favoured a rival set of games going on in parallel with the Olympics.

Coubertin had intended that the Games should be contests between individuals, but from the start that aim was lost in nationalistic fervour. If any new attempt were now to be made to revive the original notion of the Games as contests between gifted individuals, neither National Olympic Committees nor international federations (the governing bodies of sport) would allow it.

Although virtually all Games since 1896 have been marred by unfortunate incidents of international enmity it is still claimed that the modern Games, by bringing together the youth of the world in peace and amity, show the athletes, and through them mankind at large, that there are higher things than nationalism, enmity and war. Faced with such claims one can only comment that there is little evidence that playing games together makes people like one another[9] and that if the intention is to promote understanding between members of the international sporting elite it would be infinitely cheaper and perhaps more effective to set up scholarships on the model of those founded at Oxford by Cecil Rhodes. Another claim made by the Olympic movement is more readily testable. This is its claim (like that of the Catholic Church) to universalism. One measure of success, therefore, is the extent to which the peoples of the world actually do take part. A movement which includes the (former) USSR and mainland China is, by this reckoning, more successful than one that does not.

Power in the Olympic movement

'Politics', of course, is a concept with many shades of meaning. In this chapter I use it to refer both to internal power arrangements within the Olympic movement and to the movement's reactions to, and influence upon, political events at national and international levels. Sometimes, as will be clear from the context, the two overlap. Before going any further it will be as well briefly to describe the distribution of power within the movement.

The central institution is the International Olympic Committee (IOC), set up on Coubertin's initiative to organise the Games of 1896. At first it was intended that the presidency of the committee should revolve with the Games and the first president was the chairman of the organising committee in Athens, Demetrius Vikelas. After the 1896 Games it was decided to separate the offices, and Coubertin became President until he resigned in 1925. Since then there have been only five presidents, of whom the most recent have been the American Avery Brundage (1952–72), Lord Killanin, an Irishman, though he has an English peerage (1972–80), and the current incumbent, Juan Antonio Samaranch, a native of Barcelona, who succeeded Lord Killanin after the Moscow Games of 1980. He was created a Marquis by King Juan Carlos of Spain at the end of 1991.

Samaranch has already served two terms of four years and it has been expected that he would resign after the Games of 1992, which are to be held in Barcelona. However, there have been rumours that he may wish to continue until after the next Congress of the Olympic Movement, which is to be held in Paris in 1994. In that case it would be impossible to unseat him. However, when he does go it would not be surprising if the IOC were to follow the example of the United Nations and decide that the claims of universalism would best be served by electing a successor from one of the less highly developed parts of the world.

The IOC is akin to a multinational corporation in which a great deal of work is left to the various national companies, but in

D

which ultimate power rests with the centre. (Its head office is at the Château de Vidy, Lausanne, with minor offices scattered about the city, employing in total somewhat over a hundred staff.) It is however the kind of power which has to be exercised politically rather than with brute force, if the subsidiary bodies are not to be offended, or at the very worst break away from the centre.

These subsidiaries are the National Olympic Committees (NOCs) and, less directly, the international federations (IFs). NOCs, which are nominally independent of their governments, may exist only if they are recognised by the IOC, and without an NOC a territory may not send a team to the Olympic Games. At the end of 1991 there were 170 NOCs (including those of Estonia, Latvia and Lithuania, which were recognised in 1991). They are said to represent 'countries', although some NOCs belong to colonies, like Hong Kong, or to territories of intermediate status, like Puerto Rico. It is possible that the number of NOCs may grow to an embarrassing degree, the NOCs of Croatia and Slovenia having achieved provisional recognition early in 1992, as did those of the twelve constituent Republics of the Confederation of Independent States. The twelve's recognition was conditional on their fielding joint teams at the Winter and Summer Games of 1992 at Albertville and Barcelona, but such cohesion seems unlikely to persist after 1992.

The IOC controls the NOCs partly because it confers recognition and may withdraw it. It also makes significant subventions to the NOCs, partly through the development fund known as Olympic Solidarity (which derives from a portion of the IOC's share of the sale of television rights) and partly from the profits of the IOC's marketing programme. On the other hand, the IOC cannot simply ignore the NOCs: indeed, it has had to tolerate the growth of the Association of National Olympic Committees, (ANOC), which in turn has spawned five regional associations. All these have become power blocs in their own right, providing avenues to power for such tycoons of the Olympic movement as Mario Vázquez-Raña, the President of ANOC, and for lesser lights in the regional associations, where offices are also hotly contested. It may well be that NOCs will soon be granted direct representation on the IOC itself, if not as full members, then at least for the purpose of deciding between the various cities which aspire to act as hosts to the Summer and Winter Games.

The international federations are not directly akin to subsidiary companies in the intimate sense in which this may said of the NOCs. The IFs run their own championships and, in the popular sports, earn their own considerable television rights. However, they do depend upon the IOC for admission to the Olympic programme and for subventions from the television rights earned by the Games. Like the NOCs the IFs have created several associations, whose principal business is financial, though they also provide power bases for the movement's grandees.

Though the IOC has the power to withdraw recognition from NOCs and IFs, it is inconceivable that it would do so, except in the cases of small and unimportant bodies which had few allies. But (to take an extreme example) it would be unthinkable, in practical terms, for the IOC to withdraw recognition from the United States Olympic Committee (USOC) as a means of resolving the long-running dispute between the two bodies over the share of television revenue to be allocated to USOC. To do so would risk splitting the movement and might (though this is speculative) lose the support of some of the worldwide companies (many of which are American) which are central to its marketing programme. Similarly, the IOC could never expel from the Olympic programme the International Amateur Athletic Federation, (IAAF) which, under the vigorous leadership of the often controversial Dr Primo Nebiolo, is the most powerful and richest of the federations, and in its own eyes (though perhaps not in those of the footballers) represents the most popular sport. The boot is on the other foot, for if the worst came to the worst the IAAF, and some of the other established federations, could show their strength by withdrawing from the Olympic movement altogether.

Naturally, matters would not come to this extreme conclusion, but Dr Nebiolo has already flexed his muscles by persuading the IAAF to agree to hold its own championships every two years instead of every four, despite the disapproval of many athletes. In so doing he has signalled that he is in a position to treat the Olympics as just another major event in the sporting calendar, rather than as a unique festival. Thereby, at least potentially, he devalues the Olympics in the popular mind, and thence in the estimation of advertisers.

Thus, there exists a creative tension between the three permanent legs of the Olympic milking stool (often collectively known as the

'Olympic Family'). To these must be added two temporary legs, the organising committees of the cities holding the Summer and Winter Games of a particular Olympiad (the four-year period which ends at the end of a Games). These committees' interests differ from those of the movement as a whole, because a city, having once hosted the Games, will not expect to be awarded them again for many years. It will therefore wish to maximise the ephemeral benefits, notably the sale of television rights to the United States, whereas the IOC will be anxious not to kill the goose that lays the golden egg by insisting on ridiculously high sums being paid.

Given the complexity of the movement's internal politics, a wise president will have his ears open to the ambitions of men (and some women) in every far-flung corner of the world. One individual may hope for membership of his National Olympic Committee, another for its presidency, another for the presidency of a regional association, and similar ambitions are to be found at all levels in national and international governing bodies. The president of the IOC cannot, of course, simply give such offices away, but he can influence the careers within the Olympic movement of people whom he considers deserving, and in the process make alliances.

The powers of the president are very great. Like those of any high office holder, they flourish with use, and they have flourished particularly under Samaranch. In the apparatus of the IOC itself the president disposes of much patronage. He can create committees (known as commissions), decide their membership and when they will meet, and dissolve them when they have served their purpose. His nominations to the IOC, membership of which is the highest aspiration of many sportsmen and women, are accepted virtually without question (the contested election of Mario Vázquez-Raña in 1991, when it was reported that many members had abstained from voting, was an embarrassing exception)[10] and he can have a strong influence on the composition of the Executive Board (the equivalent of a board of directors). In many countries he is received with at least as much consequence as is the Secretary-General of the United Nations. Indeed, he may believe that the Olympic movement is in the same league as the United Nations, and in a sense its rival.

Committee work, as in any other bureaucracy, is essential and, as in any organisation whose members are unpaid, it has not been easy to find men, and now women, who are rich enough and have the mental equipment to undertake the work. The average age of IOC members is high, though slowly being reduced. For those not involved with the various commissions the duties amount to no more than attending the IOC's Sessions (meetings of the full membership, held at least once a year, after fierce competition as to where they are to be held) and by far the most important duty is to choose the host cities for the Summer and Winter Games. This choice puts immense power in the hands of the membership, since the gift of the Games may revive a whole region, or put it on the map in a way which could not be achieved by years of conventional image-making.

The ninety-four IOC members are not merely bureaucrats: many of them have had distinguished careers in sport before taking to its administration; many are powerful in other fields and most are men and women of the world. Nominally they are the representatives of the Olympic movement in their countries, which is why a member is correctly referred to as the IOC member in e.g. Luxembourg, rather than as a national representatives on the IOC. However, the latter specification is closer to the truth: for example, the senior member in the United States, Robert Helmick, resigned in December 1991 and it would be virtually impossible not to fill the vacant place with another American.

Bidding for the Games

The process of bidding for the Games, on which a city may spend as much as $10 million, has become absurdly expensive and the extravagance involved is causing great anxiety to the IOC. The conscientious member will accept an invitation to visit every candidate city (or none at all, as in the case of Britain's Princess Royal, a member of the IOC since 1988). In each he or she will be received with the highest marks of esteem, so that the process of visiting the candidates, though exhausting, can be distinctly good for the ego. There are also great opportunities for corruption, but it appears that very few members take advantage of them. Allegations are made from time to time – some of the ugliest have been made by Athens since it lost the Summer Games of 1996 to Atlanta, and Robert Helmick had to resign from the IOC and USOC after allegations of conflict of interest. Efforts are being made to simplify the process of selecting the host city, so that in future it may not be necessary for every candidate city to try to persuade every IOC member to visit it.

As with other unelected bodies which have acquired great power, the IOC's most priceless asset is its integrity. In modern times it is difficult enough for such bodies to preserve their other great asset, independence. Once corruption, or even incompetence, is suspected, hitherto quiet suggestions that they ought to be formally accountable to some broader constituency may turn from suggestions into demands and prove difficult to resist.[11]

The momentous choice of city to host the Games is fraught with politics. Some decisions have seemed mistaken to the point of perversity, notably the insistence by the IOC (which of course had chosen Berlin before Hitler's takeover of power) on sticking to its choice despite all arguments to the contrary.[12] The award of the 1988 Games to Seoul, whose effects will be discussed later, seemed almost bizarre even at the time. Like that of Berlin the choice was justified in terms of its politically beneficent effects, despite the Olympic movement's claims to be above or outside politics.

As has been noted, the men and women who compose the IOC are not unworldly, and it would be foolish to expect them to ignore political perceptions when making their choice of host city. Indeed, some criterion beyond those associated with the technical suitability of a bid (that is, the adequacy of the facilities offered) is essential in modern times, when any serious contender can be relied upon to produce a bid which is technically at least adequate. Thus the choice of Tokyo for the 1964 Games symbolised the view that it was time to admit Japan back into the comity of civilised nations after the war of 1939–45; the decision to award those of 1980 to Moscow celebrated, as the IOC is proud to say, the USSR's full incorporation into the Olympic fold; if the Games of 2000 were to be awarded to Beijing the full incorporation of China into world sport would be similarly celebrated. Nor would it be altogether surprising if the awkward fact that they have never gone to Africa were laid to rest by the Games of, say, the year 2004 being held in Johannesburg.

The Games since 1972

The most hair-raising example of the Games being used for political demonstration occurred in 1972 at Munich, when Palestinian terrorists murdered Israeli athletes. There was naturally considerable feeling that the remaining events should be cancelled, but the outgoing president, Avery Brundage, decided that 'the Games must go on'.[13] Since then security has become a major preoccupation of every Games' organising committee, so much so that observers at recent Games have said that the Olympic village felt like an armed camp, although the athletes themselves, with their whole attention concentrated on winning, may not particularly notice the precautions taken on their behalf. The necessary, but incongruous, preoccupation with security can only intensify as terrorist groups recognise, just as more conventional advertisers have done, the superb possibilities for worldwide exposure offered by the Games.

In 1976 numerous Third World teams stayed away from the Montreal Games in protest against the Government of New Zealand having allowed a rugby team to tour South Africa. Since the New Zealand government was not in a position to forbid its citizens to travel and rugby is not even an Olympic sport, there was nothing the IOC could do. Indeed, it seems to have spent more time on the refusal to admit the Taiwanese team, unless the team dropped the word 'China' from its title, since the Canadian Government had by then moved to a 'one China' policy.[14]

The choices of hosts for the Games of 1980 to 1996 inclusive offer insights into the the wide range of political and financial factors underlying what at first sight might seem a relatively simple decision. In 1980 the award to Moscow symbolised, as we have seen, the full acceptance of the USSR into the Olympic movement. In 1984 Los Angeles was chosen for lack of any other contestant, bringing home forcibly to the IOC the undesirability of having only one candidate, which could then dictate its own terms. The award to Seoul of the 1988 Games caused political turmoil, to which we shall return, and the Games were saved for South Korea largely by the extraordinary efforts of Samaranch.

Boycott and counter-boycott

Samaranch's success in persuading the IOC and the world that the Games should not be removed from Korea owed something to the facts that the USA had boycotted the Moscow Games of 1980 and that the USSR had taken its revenge by boycotting those of 1984 in Los Angeles – though both sides avoided the word 'boycott' and referred to 'non-participation'.

President Carter's boycott of the Moscow Games was occasioned by the Soviet invasion of Afghanistan at the end of 1979. The President seems to have decided that a boycott would be a cheap way of showing disapproval of the Soviet action. He and his advisers seem also to have taken little trouble to brief themselves on international sport, and to have been surprised when their suggestions, made only a few months before the Olympics, that they should be moved elsewhere or that alternative Games should be held, met with short shrift. There were, of course, good arguments on both sides. On the one hand many sportspeople resented American interference in sport, and thought it wrong to deprive athletes of the supreme competitive moments for which they had trained for so long; on the other, the United States government thought it improper to back any sporting association with a country capable of so dastardly an act as invading Afghanistan, and believed that athletes should not shrink from bearing their part of the burden.[15]

Like so many basically unimportant incidents in international affairs, the boycott of the Moscow Games acquired a symbolic importance which made both sides expend enormous amounts of energy and influence upon it. In the United States extreme pressure was put on USOC to withdraw from the Games, and USOC's House of Delegates endorsed withdrawal by a handsome majority, not only because of the great pressure, but also because many Americans tend to see foreign affairs as the President's business and to believe that 'politics stops at the water's edge'. In Britain, on the other hand, where the issue caused great public debate and where the arguments received a full airing in the House of Commons, the British Olympic Association (the equivalent of an NOC) decided to defy the government and send its team to Moscow. This was a demonstration of independence which may have reassured liberals that freedom was still alive in Britain, even if they disapproved of the particular decision.[16]

It is impossible to adjudicate on the moral arguments. Many sportspeople thought it not merely inappropriate, but wrong, that President Carter should have used sport for political ends; yet the sportspeople's argument seems a little weak that if sport were shared only between teams whose governments approved of each other's actions there would be precious little international sport. The political arguments are easier to weigh up. It is clear that the President was desperate to make a firm gesture which would restore his reputation in foreign affairs, and that Mrs Thatcher would not have wasted political credit on endorsing his policy with enthusiasm had she been a more experienced Prime Minister. Naturally, there were many countries which were tied to one side or the other and had to obey their master's voice, for Moscow was as reluctant to lose the prestige conferred by the Games as was Washington to confirm it. But there was no need for Britain to play such a subservient part in what turned into a classic Cold War exercise. It could just as well have followed the line of several other major Olympic countries and not sought to persuade the Olympic authorities one way or the other.

The Soviet boycott of the Los Angeles Games, which did not come as a surprise when it was eventually announced on 8 May 1984, came at the end of a long series of complaints by Soviet officials. They were concerned about the dangers of intimidation, enticement and kidnap which might face their athletes if they ventured to the United States, the State Department's procrastination over answering Soviet requests to anchor a liner at Los Angeles and for permission for Aeroflot flights to service the Soviet teams, the refusal of a visa to the Soviet Olympic attaché (who was understood to be a KGB officer) and various other grievances. The situation was evidently made worse by the conviction of Peter Ueberroth, who was directing the Games, that his organising committee should conduct its own foreign policy, independent of that of the State Department. Such an exaggerated idea of his own importance cannot have endeared him to the professional diplomats in Washington (who did not think the Olympics of supreme significance in the scheme of things) and at the same time made it easy for Soviet officials to drive wedges between Ueberroth and the State Department.[17]

It would be a mistake simply to discount the Soviet complaints and to see them as excuses for a nakedly political decision to boycott the Olympics. Equally, the Games were not by themselves important enough in Soviet eyes to be worth a major incident in international politics. The simple explanation is probably the right one, namely that the Soviets were exacting an eye for an eye, by taking revenge for the United States' boycott, which had deeply upset the then President, Leonid Brezhnev. On the other hand, they would not

have done so had not relations between the two countries been
already strained.

The Seoul Games, 1988

Seoul and Nagoya, Japan, were the only contestants to hold the
Games of 1988 (Melbourne and Athens having dropped out) and
there was a good deal of surprise when Seoul won. To some extent
its victory can be explained by the activities of Japanese citizens who
were opposed on environmental grounds to the idea of the Games
being held at Nagoya; commercial interests may have played a part;
some members of the IOC may have seen the Games as a reward
to South Korea for many years' faithful alliance with the United
States and others may have thought it desirable to honour a newly
developing country. There is no single satisfactory explanation,
beyond the obvious one of lack of choice, and once the choice
was made Samaranch threw himself into overcoming the political
obstacles to the Games being held at Seoul.

The obstacles were enormous. The Korean peninsula had been
divided since 1945, the epitome of the Cold War, with the South
unrecognised by the Soviet bloc, and firmly tied to the West, and
the North correspondingly close to the Soviet bloc and estranged
from the West. The absence of relations between South Korea
and the Soviet bloc gave rise to the fear that the USSR and its
allies might boycott the Games if, indeed, the IOC persisted in
its intention to hold them at Seoul. The North naturally made
what capital it could from the situation by demanding that the
Games be shared between North and South, and the fears of a
Soviet boycott were compounded by the realisation that, even if
it did not wish to boycott, the USSR might be obliged to do so in
order to demonstrate loyalty to its ally and so to reassure its other
Third World adherents.

Samaranch handled these difficult circumstances with outstanding diplomatic skill and pertinacity. By negotiating with the utmost
seriousness with North Korea he showed the USSR that the Olympic
movement had done all it could to satisfy its ally's demands, and
so allowed the USSR to participate in the Games without loss of
face. This was what the Soviet leaders almost certainly wished
to do in any case, for by boycotting the Los Angeles Games
of 1984 the USSR had already strained some of its Eastern

European friendships; to boycott again might have strained them dangerously, and even dismayed some Third World allies, quite apart from the damage which would have been done to Soviet sporting achievement and to the country's international image.

The IOC had also to turn a blind eye to the authoritarian aspects of the South Korean regime, which sometimes led to excess, though it must be added that the government was influenced by the fact that extreme excess might cost it the Games. The Olympics were probably one of the factors leading to improved relations with the Soviet Union and Eastern Europe generally, and may even have played some part, as Samaranch believes, in democratising South Korea itself.[18]

Financing the Games

During Avery Brundage's period as president the IOC was not a rich organisation; indeed it was run on a shoestring. Brundage served without salary or expenses but, rich as he was, he had to recognise that the IOC must live within its means.[19] The way forward lay with television, and the first North American rights were sold in 1960 for what would nowadays seem the paltry sum of $440,000. In recent years organising committees have vied with each other to sell rights for record sums. The Seoul Games' television rights fetched $408 million worldwide, and those for Barcelona and Albertville had by the end of 1991 raised $635m and $295m respectively.

Since the first 'private enterprise Games' of 1984 at Los Angeles it has become a point of honour with organising committees to make a larger profit than their predecessors, although the trend is frowned upon by the IOC, which hopes to discourage it by requiring organising committees to turn over a proportion of the profit to the IOC. Even this sanction can be overcome, however. After the 1988 Games Seoul declared a record profit but successfully argued that a much smaller figure should be used for calculating the amount due to the IOC![20] The trend may be broken by Barcelona, where doubts have been expressed about the organising committee's ability to make a profit.

Not only does the IOC deprecate the determination to seek ever higher fees, but it thinks the concentration on income from television imprudent. It has taken action in respect of both worries. Firstly, it has declared its intention to take charge itself of the sale of television rights after 1992, instead of selling them in partnership with the host city's organising committee. This may seem a dramatic change: on the other hand, the IOC has always insisted that it owns the Games, so that a change in the way the sale of television rights is handed may be seen as a change in detail rather than of principle.

Secondly, the IOC decided that the reliance on income from television was unwise and set up a Commission to investigate possible alternative sources of income. At the IOC'S Session at Delhi in 1983 a plan was presented by the then very small firm ISL, which was 51 per cent owned by the sportsgear firm Adidas (the other 49 per cent belonged to the Japanese advertising agency Dentsu) and had as its chairman Horst Dassler, the chairman of Adidas. The presentation led to the acceptance by the IOC of a marketing programme which came to be known as TOP, for 'The Olympic Programme'. Although there may have been doubts about the wisdom of so close, albeit indirect, an association with Adidas, Dassler was perhaps the only man who could have carried the programme through. He had already acquired extraordinary influence in sports bodies of all kinds, and had been able to secure new markets by making friends with promising administrators and helping to promote their careers.

TOP was a plan whereby categories of product (such as soft drinks or credit cards) were identified, and multinational companies invited to buy worldwide rights to use the Olympic 'marks' (emblems) on their products and in their advertising.

The plan was not totally original, since Peter Ueberroth had been obliged to rely very largely on companies' sponsorship to fund the Games of 1984. The necessity had arisen because the Games' unpopularity in the State of California meant that neither State nor Federal Government money could be committed to them, although there was some Federal expenditure on security, and of course a great deal of civil service time was spent, however uselessly, on dealing with the Soviet boycott.

The difference between Ueberroth's approach and the new programme lay in the universality of the rights to be granted. Although Ueberroth had sold rights to firms to use the Olympic marks, he had sometimes, according to the IOC, failed to realise that NOCs owned the rights to the sale of their marks in their own territories. By contrast, if a company was to be offered worldwide rights in a product category in the new scheme, the individual NOCs had first to be persuaded to give up their rights to do their own deals in that category. For example, before Visa could be recruited to TOP it was necessary to persuade the British Olympic Association (BOA) to give up its established contract with American Express, an act of renunciation which is said to have been extremely lucrative for the BOA.[21]

Thus the key word is 'exclusivity'. Once a firm pays its subscription to TOP it knows that, in the category or categories of product in which it has bought rights, no competitor company will be able to use the Olympic marks on its products or in its advertising anywhere in the world. The Olympic Games are perhaps the only event which can offer advertisers this degree of exclusivity combined with in-built mass appeal. The Olympics also offer advertisers superb opportunities to invite clients to a unique event and to provide corporate hospitality of the highest order. The IOC does not, however, allow advertising boards within the Olympic arenas. The possibility has been examined, but it is thought that to relax the current ban would excite public disapproval, and so reduce the unique appeal of Olympic advertising.

From the commercial point of view, therefore, the Olympics may be seen as the supreme vehicle for worldwide advertising, coupled with the opportunity to entertain clients to an event which has the magic of the Epsom Derby, but on a vastly magnified scale. The IOC's programme does not, of course, prevent NOCs from running their own sales campaigns, for outside the product categories reserved to TOP they may continue to sell their marks, as may the organising committees of the Summer and Winter Games. However, danger may lie ahead if the IOC develops its plans to move into licensing goods on its own account, apparently without the prior authorisation of NOCs. The dangers are precisely of the kind encountered by Peter Ueberroth, namely that if the sale of rights centrally by the IOC is not co-ordinated with local sales by NOCs, a confused market may be created. This is exactly what TOP is designed to avoid, and it would be ironic if the IOC were to cause in the field of licensing the confusion which it has so skilfully avoided in TOP.

To the advertiser the choice of city to hold the Games is relatively unimportant, because they are primarily a television spectacular. What does matter is that disasters and embarrassments should be avoided. (At Munich in 1972 the terrorists' activities greatly extended the audience appeal of the Olympics in the United States, but that was in the days when the Games were relatively new to the American audience).[22] Nowadays, quite apart from humanitarian considerations, such disasters would be unwelcome to advertisers, as indeed, would non-lethal embarrassments, such as Catalonian separatists jumping into the Olympic swimming pool at Barcelona and spoiling the heats.

The Olympics, to sum up this section, are big money. We have seen that television is expected to yield at least $930m from the Summer and Winter Games of 1992. In addition, estimates for the yield from TOP range up to $180 million and the total generated locally by NOCs in those countries which are commercially active is unknown, but must be considerable. There is ample room for disagreement about how the proceeds are to be divided, which, as has been noted, provides the bulk of the business of many of the associations within the Olympic movement.

Dividing the proceeds

Now that the IOC is rich it has become accustomed to riches, and has learned to protect them. It seems reasonable to suppose that the IOC's minimum aim is to build up sufficient reserves for it to survive even if a Games were cancelled and none of the expected income were recoverable from insurance. It cannot be said with certainty that the IOC is in this position, since its accounts are private, and it would be impossible to build up an accurate picture of its financial position without access to a four-year cycle of its accounts. Nevertheless, it seems likely that it has reached at least this minimum position.

Its main sources of income are television rights and the marketing of the Olympic emblems under TOP. Other sources include special coins, the licensing of products, and local sponsorship programmes arranged by the two host cities' organising committees.

The precise division of the proceeds from the sale of television rights changes frequently, but in in 1992 it will be as follows. First 10 per cent of United States rights (Barcelona $400m and Albertville $243m), or approximately $64m, will be deducted from the total of about $930m. From the remaining $866m a top slice of 20 per cent, or $173m, will be applied to the organising committees' technical costs; of the remainder ($693m) two-thirds will be divided between the organising committees and the remaining third will go to the IOC. The IOC's share will be divided equally between the IOC itself, the IFs and the NOCs (payments to the NOCs being made through the IOC's development fund, Olympic Solidarity). Thus, each of the three constituents of the Olympic Family will receive one-ninth of 80 per cent of the total television rights (after USOC's share has been deducted), giving an IOC share of $77m.

After 1992 the Winter and Summer Games will for the first time be held in different years, with the next Winter Games being held at Lillehammer (Norway) in 1994 and the Summer Games at Atlanta in 1996. From 1994 onwards the 20 per cent for technical expenses will not be taken out before the division is made, but will be paid by the organising committee from its enhanced share of 60 per cent of the total. The Olympic Family's share will also rise – to 40 per cent – but it will become responsible for the 10 per cent of United States rights paid to the USOC.

The division of TOP is different, with half being paid (in 1992) to the organising committees (two-thirds to Barcelona and one-third to Albertville, though this proportion could change in future Olympiads); 6–8 per cent to the IOC and up to 42 per cent to the USOC and other NOCs. (It is known that the USOC's share takes the form of a top slice of 20 per cent.) TOP payments are made directly to NOCs, rather than through Olympic Solidarity for specific programmes, because they are essentially made as compensation to NOCs for rights forgone in their own territories. The NOCs' share takes the form of a flat fee ($10,000 in 1988); a standard payment of $400 per athlete in 1992 ($300 in 1988) and in about thirty major economies a negotiated fee, whose amount is a commercial secret.

Thus the IOC's income from the 1992 Games, leaving aside such additional sources as licensing and ignoring the sums which it administers for the other members of the Olympic Family, may be $77m from television rights and 6–8 per cent of TOP proceeds, which could yield the IOC a further $14 million (assuming TOP proceeds of $180 million). No account is taken here of legal or agents' fees. The latter are considerable, although ISL charges much less than the industry average for its considerable contribution to the marketing operation. Not only does the company sell the Games and service the clients, but it also has to make contracts on the IOC's behalf with each NOC, except the three which do not take part in TOP.[23]

Nor is account taken of the profits made by the Games: in the Olympic context the figures are virtually meaningless, because it is so difficult to make any rule as to which items of expenditure should be taken into the accounts and, as we have seen in the case of Seoul, creative accounting is in vogue. (The official division of profit is 10 per cent IOC, 10 per cent host NOC and 80 per cent for the benefit of sport in the host country.) Finally, no account is taken of sums earned by NOCs, nor of local sponsorship programmes arranged by the host cities. The IOC signs all such agreements, and takes 3 per cent of the value of the contracts, which will rise to 5 per cent in 1996.

The overall picture is incomplete, but enough has been said to show that the IOC is by no means poor: indeed, it may be said to have progressed from rags to riches in the space of only thirty years.

The future

The Olympic movement is faced with many problems, some of which, like drugs, are not peculiar to the Olympics, although doping could be peculiarly damaging to the Games because it so harshly contradicts the ideals of their modern founder, Baron de Coubertin. It will also eventually have to tackle the question of 'gigantism' – the tendency for the number of athletes and their entourages to grow unmanageably. But the problems which most concern readers of this book are those of commercialism and of the movement's political relationships.

Internally the movement is beset with politics, as is any large organisation, and the most pressing internal political problem is that of how cohesion is to be maintained, given the many centripetal forces that are present. As World Championships held outside the Olympics by the major sports increase in importance, so the Games risk being down graded to the status of just another professional event, and not always a top-class event at that. The extraordinary public appeal of the Olympics rests partly upon the conviction that they are still the best, and in part on their claim to be unique, because rooted in a non-commercial ideal, which still holds a kind of magic. It is hard to believe that the Games can indefinitely retain their unique appeal when, on the one hand, they have abandoned amateurism and are therefore fully competitive with other professional events, but on the other may not be able (for example, in athletics, football or tennis) to attract the best players. There are of course some sportspeople who believe that commercialism has gone too far – there may even be some who regret the passing of the days of amateurism – but their voices are subdued.

Internal politics and commercialism go together, because none of the constituent parts of the movement is prepared to forgo the advantages brought by the whole-hearted pursuit of revenue. Thus, even if the IOC were to wish to scale down its business effort (and it shows no signs of doing so) it would be unable to proceed for fear of losing the loyalty of its richer constituents.

Externally, the movement cannot escape the ambiguity of its political position. It aspires to be above or outside politics, so that it may operate independently when taking such decisions as whether or not to go to Moscow or Los Angeles. At the same time its worldwide scope, financial power and popular following have made it difficult for the movement to maintain its claim to operate according to rules different from those binding other major international organisations. So long as commercial success raises the Olympic profile yet further the movement can expect calls to grow for its independence to be curbed, perhaps even for formal accountability to some outside body.

No one suggests that the Olympics, or any other major sporting activity, can simply be immune from politics. Sophisticated sports people, like the IOC's president, Juan Antonio Samaranch, know that sport cannot be kept out of politics. What they demand is that politicians should not use sport, as they are accustomed to use other bodies, as a card in the international game. It is this demand which has been frequently ignored in the past, and which may become less sustainable as the Olympic movement increasingly takes on the character of a multinational corporation.

Notes

1 This chapter draws extensively on my *Olympic Politics*, Manchester University Press, 1992. I have not referred to it in detail.

I must also acknowledge my debt to Trevor Taylor's admirable 'Politics and the Olympic spirit', in Lincoln Allison, ed., *Sport and Politics*, the present volume's predecessor.

2 For the Ancient Games see: David C. Young, *The Olympic Myth of Greek Amateur Athletics*, Ares Publishers Inc., 1984; M. I. Finley and H. W. Pleket, *The Olympic Games: the First Thousand Years*, Chatto and Windus, 1986.

3 Pierre de Coubertin, *Mémoires Olympiques*, Bureau Internationale de Pédagogie Sportive (Lausanne), n.d., but 1931, p. 12.

4 Pierre de Coubertin, *L'Education en Angleterre, Collèges et Universités*, Librairie Hachette, 1888. His chapter on Rugby is reprinted in Norbert Mueller, ed., *Pierre de Coubertin: Textes Choisies*, Weidmann, 1986, vol. I, pp. 39–56.

5 Young, pp. 28 and 71–2.

6 Pierre de Coubertin, 'Une compagne de vingt-et-un Ans (1887–1908)', 1909, *Textes Choisies*, vol. II, pp. 131–47.

7 Young, pp. 179–81 and *Mémoires Olympiques*.

8 Carl Diem, 'Pierre de Coubertin', speech at the fiftieth anniversary celebration of the IOC, held at Lausanne, 17 and 18 June 1944, p. 6.

9 Roger C. Rees, 'The Olympic dilemma: applying the contact theory and beyond', *Quest*, 37, 1985.

10 *The Times*, 17 June 1991.

11 For Robert Helmick's resignation see *The Times*, 5 December 1991, 36, David Miller, Lausanne.

12 For the Berlin Games: R. Mandell, *The Nazi Olympics*, Souvenir Press, 1972; Duff Hart-Davis, *Hitler's Olympics: the 1936 Games*, Coronet Books, 1988 (first published by Century Hutchinson, 1986).

13 Allen Guttman, *The Games Must Go On: Avery Brundage and the Olympic Movement*, Columbia University Press, 1984.

14 Lord Killanin, *My Olympic Years*, Secker and Warburg, 1983, chapter XI, *passim*; R. Espy, *The Politics of the Olympic Games*, University of California Press, 1979, pp. 152–5; Geoffrey Miller, *Behind the Olympic Rings*, H. O. Zimman, Inc., 1979, chapter 12.

15 Killanin, chapters XVII, XVIII, XIX, *passim* and Denis Howell, *Made in Birmingham: the Memoirs of Denis Howell*, Macdonald, Queen Anne Press, 1990, pp. 292–306.

16 The House of Commons debate took place on 17 March 1980. For a racy account of it see Howell, pp. 298–302.

17 For Peter Ueberroth's account of the Los Angeles Games see his *Made in America*, (with Richard and Amy Quinn), Kingswood Press, 1986.

18 Kim Un-yong, *The Greatest Olympics: from Baden-Baden to Seoul*, Seoul Si-sa-yong-o-sa, 1990, introduction by Juan Antonio Samaranch, p. 14.

19 Fiftieth Session of the IOC, Paris, 13–18 June 1955, *Minutes*.

20 Kim, pp. 286–8.

21 Neil Wilson, *The Sports Business: the Men and the Money*, Mandarin, 1990 (first published 1988), pp. 25–6.

22 David A. Klatell and Norman Marcus, *Sports for Sale: Television, Money and the Fans*, Oxford University Press, 1988, p. 165.

23 This passage was written before the provisional recognition, early in 1992, of NOCs from Croatia, Slovenia and the twelve Republics of the Confederation of Independent States.

6

Developments in sporting law

KEN FOSTER

In the Football League, Brentford's Gary Blissett is charged with causing grievous bodily harm to Torquay's John Uzzell, who had his cheekbone fractured in a match between the teams.[1] Police are to report Alan McLeary, the Millwall defender, to the Football Association for alleged foul and abusive language to the crowd in a game against Bristol Rovers.[2] Intensive investigations by the Thames Valley Police and the British Ice Hockey Association continued into an ill-tempered match between Bracknell Bees and Murrayfield Racers in which Lee Odelein of Bracknell sustained a broken jaw and concussion after being knocked unconscious in an off-the-puck incident.[3] Gary Rees, the England and Nottingham rugby player, is charged with grievous bodily harm after an assault on a London Irish player during a friendly game.[4] All these events were reported on the sports pages of one national newspaper during one week in February 1992. And it was not an untypical week by any means. This increasing proliferation of cases of police involvement in violent play on the field is not untypical. It is just one of many examples which illustrate an accelerating trend towards increased legal intervention in sport and a decline in the myth of sport as an autonomous and separate sphere where the law has no place.

This myth of sporting autonomy has been used as an argument against legal intervention in sport; a view expressed as recently as 1986 by a judge declaring that 'sport would be better served if there was not running litigation at repeated intervals by people seeking to challenge the decisions of the ruling bodies'.[5] But this concept of sporting autonomy is a mix of different ideas. At a cultural level, it is that sport has values which are divorced from those which law is normally seen as regulating. Sport and games are seen as mere amusements, ways of passing the time for pleasure. As a private use of time, it is clearly within civil society and outside the concerns of the state. Team games as well can be seen as supporting communal and co-operative values, celebrating and rewarding co-operation and allowing harmless competition and conflict by not giving rise to the disputes of social and economic interests which the legal process is best suited to resolving and adjudicating.

But 'sporting autonomy' can also be used as a concept to describe the view that sport and the law are separate realms, where the kind of social relations involved are not amenable to being reconstructed into legal relations. Legal norms are fixed rules which prescribe rights and duties; relationships within the social world of sport are not seen in this way. The two discourses have no common language and no links between them; there is no mechanism for communication between the different norms. The result is that law is seen as an inappropriate form of controlling the social norms of sport.

Another meaning of 'sporting autonomy' refers to the debate as to the extent of state and legal intervention into sporting affairs. The principal tensions centre on viewing sport as an economic activity, as big business, against seeing sport as a leisure pastime where citizens have their free time to use as they wish. Governing bodies in sport need to be regulated and accountable, it is argued, because they control large economic resources. Whether that regulation is best achieved by voluntary self-regulation or external legal regulation becomes the focus of debate. On the whole, there has to date been a preference for voluntary regulation but in some sports legislative frameworks have been created for the sport's administration where self-regulation is considered inappropriate, horse racing being the most obvious example.

Against legal intervention, there is the view that sport is a pursuit for pleasure, not profit. In this area of private activity, legal intervention is inappropriate and unnecessary. As a private use of time, it is pre-eminently within civil society and outside the concerns of the state. At worst, any necessary regulation can be left to voluntary consensual organisations who are private clubs with no need for legal control nor accountability. A second argument is that sport creates its own 'internal law' which negates the need for external regulation and intervention. Sports have their own constitutional arrangements and organisation codes, which govern and supervise the general administration of the sport. They usually have their own supreme legislature which makes the playing rules, supervises and licenses competition, and has its own disciplinary codes for enforcing and punishing breaches of the rules. All this structure suggests that sport is a microcosm of law, with a parallel structure which shadows legal rules, and so is an adequate form of regulation without the need for further interference. Linked to this argument is the view that internal administrators and officials know the needs of their own sport best. They are better equipped to judge the best interests of sports overall, to understand the context in which it operates and to adjudicate on conflicts of interest. Outsiders, especially judges, threaten these values by opening up the possibility that remote and inappropriate decisions will be made by regulators or judges who are insufficiently tuned into the environment of the sport.

This decline in sporting autonomy has been indexed in a number of different ways in the area of sports law. There has been a marked increase in statutory intervention and control. Sport is increasingly seen as involving public interests which the state needs to regulate. In the past six years, issues such as the safety of spectators, the location of sports stadia, questions of public order at football games, the abuse of drugs in sports have all created major public concern and have given rise to statutory intervention. This form of regulation is obviously instrumental with the achieving of policy objectives as its goal.

There has also been an increase in litigation which has opened up the possibilities of judicial review. There have been a number of cases where players have challenged the decisions of governing bodies. The judges appear to be deciding such cases on a mixture of principles. On the one hand, the principle that private organisations can control their own affairs leads to a non-interventionist approach, at least as far as the substantive merits of the decision are concerned. On the other hand, there is a concern that procedural justice is observed when regulating bodies are making decisions, especially where economic interests are involved. The idea of protecting the economically weaker party from the monopoly control and exercise of power by regulating bodies is a strong theme within the English common law and it has been applied in the area of sports law.

A further theoretical framework which can be used to chart the decline of sporting autonomy is that of legal pluralism. This is the view that there are a plurality of legal orders within any social context, which are semi-autonomous in regulating their own social field. The central state is seen as only one amongst many legal orders, even if formally hierarchical. Such a viewpoint would emphasise the 'internal law' of sport, the way in which it creates its own legislation and rules, its own administrative regulation and its own procedures or processes for judgement. This 'internal law' is only influenced by external state law in a weak sense. The emphasis is on the ability of internal law to be self-regulating and create the power to control its own system. External law is limited to providing a facilitative framework which allows voluntary autonomy within fixed boundaries, which are often procedural. Any greater degree of intervention which interferes with the internal law may be subject to a process of readjustment or even denial of the external imposed norms which allows the internal law to re-assert its own relative autonomy. This process is also described by legal theorists as juridification, which refers to the process whereby social norms are transformed into legal norms. At a simple level, it merely reproduces the traditional idea of private and public realms, with private areas increasingly being subject to public or judicial control, a move from voluntarism to legalism. But it offers also a more complex version which stresses the interaction as legal norms are used to reorder the power relations within the social arena.

The developments in the law of sport in recent years have highlighted all these themes. Increased litigation, or the threat of it, has given the courts the opportunity to address the question of how far they will interfere with or overturn the decisions of governing bodies, especially where there is some economic prejudice suffered by the persons suing. The law assumes that governing bodies are private organisations and thus normally immune from judicial control. Many sporting clubs are technically unincorporated associations; they therefore have no independent legal personality. The law ignores the collective reality of their existence and treats them simply as a group of separate individuals. In principle, such groups cannot sue nor be sued; they cannot make contracts nor hold property. All legal relations are assumed to be made by, or between, the individual members but not with the group as such. The law of unincorporated associations expresses the concept of 'privacy of association'. The law is not interested in trespassing within the four walls of a private club. As contractual associations, they are difficult to supervise when the 'club' has no legal personality nor capacity. In addition, many governing bodies are merely federations of other associations, local, regional or national, and this can present an insurmountable hurdle to a legal challenge by a player, who is not in contractual membership of the relevant governing body. Adrienne Cowley, the swimmer, was declared ineligible to compete in the Commonwealth Games in 1986 by the Commonwealth Games Federation, despite her nomination by the Games Council of England, because of her South African domicile. Her legal case failed partly on the grounds that the Federation had no direct contractual relationship with her but only with the national Councils who constituted the Federation.

The main routes by which a player can challenge a governing body are 'natural justice' or by an application for judicial review. 'Natural justice' refers the procedural requirements of fairness which must be followed by any body which makes decisions over players. It includes the right to an unbiased hearing and minimum requirements of fairness, such as the need to give reasons for decisions and for proceedings to be conducted within the rules and regulations of the associations. Governing bodies of any kind are vulnerable to challenge if they fail to meet these requirements. There have, however, been suggestions that amateur players may not be able to challenge governing bodies unless their earning capacity is prejudiced. This at least was the reasoning of the Court of Appeal in 1988 when it refused to review the decision of a county tennis association not to select, for disciplinary reasons, a player for the county team.[6] An alternative reason offered in the same case was that decisions about team selection were not the kind of decision to which the rules of natural justice in any case applied.

The substance of an administrative decision by a governing bodies may also be contested on the grounds of arbitrariness or unreasonableness. This is technically 'judicial review'. The analogy is statutory or administrative bodies who exercise statutory powers. It is well established that such bodies are subject to a general principle of reasonableness, as is well illustrated in the sporting context by the decision of the House of Lords in Wheeler v.

Leicester City Council.[7] In this case, the City Council withdrew its permission for Leicester Rugby Club to use a recreation ground for training as a protest against members of the Club being selected for an England touring team to South Africa. The House of Lords held that this was a misuse of the council's statutory powers by taking into account irrelevant factors in its decisions. It was thus unreasonable and a breach of the council's duty to act fairly.

Whether this general duty to act fairly is applicable to sporting authorities, especially where they exercise a monopoly control over the industry or where they exercise statutory powers as in the case of the Jockey Club, is a question which has come up several times in recent cases. The trend in these cases has been to draw a line which normally prevents sporting decisions being reviewable on the grounds of substantive unreasonableness. In refusing an application of the chairman of the stewards at Doncaster Races to review the Jockey Club's decision to remove him as chairman, the Divisional Court in 1990 decided that the Jockey Club's powers and functions were not sufficiently in the public domain to be reviewable.[8] If the Jockey Club, whose powers are partly conferred by Royal Charter, are immune from judicial review, then it is difficult to see how any governing bodies could be controlled. However, the Court's decision in this case rested heavily on the fact that it felt bound by the higher precedent set in the Court of Appeal when it refused to review the decision of the stewards of the National Greyhound Racing Club to suspend a trainer's licence, where it was successfully argued that the presence of contractual relationship excluded the possibility of judicial review.[9] However, if the governing body's authority is derived from non-contractual powers, the situation could be different.

In another case later in 1990, the Divisional Court again refused to review the Jockey Club.[10] Here, a company had built a new racecourse in Telford on the expectation that the Jockey Club would allocate it fifteen fixtures during 1991. When the Jockey Club refused to do so, to the obvious economic prejudice of the company, the Courts again refused to intervene albeit with some disquiet. Mr Justice Simon Brown argued for a distinction between areas of decision-making where private law concepts of agreement and contract were adequate, which 'affected only those voluntarily and willingly subscribing to its rules and procedures', and those areas where there was a wide enough public interest to justify judicial review in cases when governing bodies are exercising a 'quasi-licensing power'. Thus, if it had been necessary, he might have held the Jockey Club reviewable in this case, although on the facts he held that a legitimate expectation of being given the fixtures had not been created.

Although the dividing line as expressed by these cases may appear to be a purely legal distinction between when private law remedies based on contract and when public law remedies based on unreasonableness are available, nevertheless the distinction has important social consequences. To define an area of decision-making as private or contractual means the rules and constitution of the sporting association have priority and the decision-making process can only be challenged when the rules are not followed and then only by a contracting party. If the rules themselves are unfair or biased against those without the social or economic powers to change them, even if they have a formal contractual power in law, then the potential for arbitrary government is increased. On the other hand, to define an area of decision-making as public means that it can be opened up to independent external scrutiny and more importantly perhaps recognise the rights of the paying public to be considered. The keen race-goer in Telford is effectively denied any interest when the judges are prepared to treat the licensing of a new racecourse and the allocation of fixtures to it as a purely private matter for the Jockey Club.

Another major development in recent years has been the increasing trend for governing bodies to operate in the shadow of the law and in fear of legal intervention. The process at work here is a complex interaction between the law of the land, the 'internal law' of the sport and the respective authorities for enforcing both. It can best be illustrated by the changing attitude of the police and the football authorities towards violence by players on the field. At one time, the view was clearly taken that whatever happened on the field of play was essentially a matter for football authorities and the referee. Players hitting each other were in the first instance punishable by the referee within the rules of the game. If it resulted in a caution or a sending-off, then the football authorities had clear powers to discipline the offenders usually by banning them from playing in a specified number of future games. In addition, the player's club could also exercise its power to fine players, common in professional players' contracts. The system was self-regulating and apparently outside the concern of the law of the land.

Yet, such assaults are clearly criminal offences and there is no defence available because you are playing a game. As activities outside the laws of the game, and the reasonable expectation of what might happen even outside then, then in principle they are no different from any other kind of punch-up. At some point around 1987, some local police forces began to take this view. The most notorious example was when four players were successfully prosecuted for their conduct during a Rangers v. Celtic game in 1987.[11] This led to a mild panic on the part of the football authorities that such occurrences would become commonplace, almost to the point of police officers entering the field of play to arrest players. That this was not entirely fanciful was illustrated when a police officer entered a dressing room at half-time to caution a player for the use of foul language against a linesman.

The consequence was a marked change in the attitude of the English FA towards violence on the field. When Paul Davis, of Arsenal, broke the jaw of an opponent in 1988, the FA suspended Davis for nine matches and fined him £3,000, an unusually harsh if not unprecedented punishment. A general mêlée between Arsenal and Norwich towards the end of a game in 1989 caused the FA to fine both clubs heavily, £30,000 and £50,000 respectively. This prompted an outburst by Alan Eastwood, the chairman of the Police Federation, who was quoted as saying, 'This is a joke. These offences demanded a reduction in league points. Any sort of fine would have been a joke, but these amounts are totally meaningless.'[12] As Norwich City reported a pre-tax profit of £71,000 in that season, a £50,000 fine may appear a stiff one to their supporters. These statements were reinforced by the then Sports Minister, Colin Moynihan, who was also quoted as saying 'Now my greatest desire is to see the Football League urgently introduce the deduction of points as an additional penalty in future'.[13] The predictable consequence was the unprecedented deduction of league points from Arsenal and Manchester United in 1990, after a similar occurrence. Here seems to a clear example of the 'internal law' being much more strictly enforced in order to try and prevent the external criminal law invading the sport.

This is not an isolated example, although it may be the most obvious. In December 1991, it was reported that the RSPCA was unhappy with the Jockey Club's failure to take appropriate action against a jockey for the excessive use of his whip on a horse.[14] The threat of a private prosecution was issued by the RSPCA, no doubt with a similar aim of trying to get the Jockey Club to alter either its own internal rules or to enforce its existing rules in a different manner.

A more sophisticated example of this interaction between the internal law and the external law is the way in which legal concepts themselves can get imported in the regulations and the practice of governing bodies. Disciplinary proceedings have in general become formalised and legalistic, and several governing bodies have amended their disciplinary orders in the light of legal challenges by players.

A different issue is raised by the questions which surround the legal regulation of economic interests within sport. The large amount of money generated by professional sport has led increasingly to problems when the allocation and control of these resources is within the direct or indirect control of the governing bodies. The administrative structure of these bodies does not always contribute to the most efficient use and maximisation of the money within the game. Legal challenges are likely when players are deprived or hindered in the opportunity to maximise their earnings, when clubs are not allowed a similar freedom to maximise their profits and when governing bodies restrict or control participation in competition in order to make competitions more attractive or competitive.

The legal principle at work here is the restraint of trade doctrine, which requires restrictions on players' freedom to choose where and for whom they play to be justified by the criteria of whether the restraints are reasonable and in the public interest. This doctrine can surface in a variety of ways in sport, but most have a common thread in the monopolistic control that governing bodies have in their sport, especially in its professional aspects. The potential for conflicts which this causes between the interest of the governing bodies in the overall economic health of the sport as a whole and the particular interest of the players or clubs is not always capable of resolution within the sport itself. The governing body is often both judge and jury on specific issues. In a recent High Court case, Michael Watson, a professional boxer, successfully challenged his contract with Mickey Duff, the promoter and his manager, on the grounds that it was unfair.[15] Because Duff acted both as a promoter of bouts and as Watson's manager, there was a conflict of interest. As a promoter, Duff could have wished to include Watson in one of his promotions to make a more attractive bill when as manager he may have objectively advised his fighter that the particular match or opponent was unsuitable. In light of this potential conflict of interest, a contract which did not give the boxer a right to negotiate his fights on his own behalf was unenforceable. The British Boxing Board of Control were encouraged by the judge to find ways of separating the roles of manager and promoter, so that they were effectively independent of each other.

A similar argument about the economic ability to control sport arose in the litigation between the Football League and the Football Association over the formation of a Premier League. The legal issue was the FA's right to form a Premier League by taking the present First Division clubs out of the jurisdiction of the Football League. Its argument was that as football's supreme governing body in England it had the power within its own constitution to form a league, even if that power was not directly specified in that constitution. The Football League's counter-argument was partly based on the monopoly that would be created by a Premier League. Although the ultimate outcome was favourable to the FA, it was on the narrow legal grounds as to the validity of the notice of six months to be given by the clubs who wished to leave. What was left open, possibility for further legal contest, was the extent to which the Football League could challenge the FA's manoeuvres as an anti-competitive tendency.

Also at stake in this litigation was the question of the administrative structure of football, and the desirability of two competing associations. The FA represents the national game, both amateur and professional, as the sport's governing body, whilst the Football League has the immediate economic interests of all its clubs to consider. The clear dissatisfaction of the elite clubs within the Football League with an administrative structure which they feel gives too much power, especially financial control, to clubs outside the First Division has been one of the root causes behind the problems of football. The question that is raised is how far sport should be allowed to regulate its own administrative structures, or how far does a wide public interest require statutory or legal regulation of these structures.

This has been recently posed by the Home Affairs Select Committee in relation to the governance of horse racing. The sport has always attracted more government interest than most sports, principally because of the state's fiscal interest in the revenue generated by gambling. Traditionally, the sport has been run by the Jockey Club who are responsible for the organisation and administration of horse racing. However, much of the financial assistance to racing is provided by the Horse race Betting Levy Board. This body has the statutory power to raise a levy on bookmakers, which is then distributed to racing in accordance with what the Board views as the best interests of racing. The money is used to improve the facilities at racecourses, to support prize-money to ensure a widespread fixture list and a number of related purposes. In addition, there is a Horse racing Advisory Council.

The Select Committee's report was severely critical of the Jockey Club's management. It was described as 'hardly a democratic organisation, and is perhaps the antithesis of all that the phrase "classless society" represents'. It was criticised for being ineffective, and not representative of different interests within the sport. The Committee's recommendations include a suggestion for a single ruling body, a British Horse racing Authority, which would combine the financial powers of the Levy Board and the administrative powers of the Jockey Club and the Horse racing Advisory Council.

Despite these recommendations, the Select Committee's Report is very much imbued with the philosophy of deregulation, and concludes that the government should not be directly involved. Although the health of the betting market has clear implications for the state, as it takes tax directly from the bets made by punters, nevertheless the report states 'We believe that the very different spirit of the 1990s means that the involvement of government now seems very anachronistic. It is not part of government's duty to sustain a racing industry ... We believe that the involvement of the Home Office and of legislation in the financing of horse-racing but not the financing of greyhound racing or cricket, for example, is anomalous.' This argument stems from the crux of the Select Committee's analysis that racing is underfunded but that it was not therefore assumed that it is the responsibility of either the bookmakers or the government to ensure its prosperity.

Another area in which the economic regulation of sport has

loomed large recently is broadcasting and media rights. An increasing proportion of sport's revenues is gained from the sale of broadcasting rights, especially in sports such as football and boxing which are judged by broadcasters to be the most popular. Such rights are thus valuable commodities. Two linked questions have predominated in recent legal developments. One is whether the sale of exclusive rights to an event is legally defensible. Obviously, exclusive rights to a major event are a more important commodity than shared or other limited rights. The legality of contracts for exclusive rights is questionable in the light of European competition. Any arrangement which gives a monopoly right to a business over and above its competitors can in principle be challenged under Article 85 of the Treaty of Rome. But even if such a contract may survive such a challenge, the recent case of BBC v. BSB suggests that broadcasting competitors may still nevertheless use clips from their rival coverage in limited circumstances.[16] The protection of exclusive rights depends ultimately on the owner of those rights being able to defend them by suing for a breach of their copyright. But BBC v. BSB established that the statutory defence of fair dealing is available in clips from sporting events if the material used was no more than necessary for the news reporting of current events. Mr Justice Scott's decision suggests firstly, that the event be 'news' and indicates a limit of twenty-four hours (this prevents rivals using footage as background material in their other programmes); secondly, that a time limit of ninety seconds might be desirable so that the news reporting did not transform itself into a rival sports coverage, and thirdly, that the event had to be a major sporting event (the immediate context of the case was the coverage of the 1990 World Cup Finals) which was important enough to justify its inclusion in a news programme. The leeway allowed by the judgement seems to have been used by all of the terrestrial and satellite stations. What is difficult to judge is whether the ruling has lessened the attraction or lowered the price of exclusive rights deals.

There is a related problem here as to who owns the rights to sports events. In principle, the ownership belongs to the organisers of the event although who this is is not always entirely straightforward. Do, for example, the television rights to an FA cup game belong to the home club (as hosts), to both clubs jointly (as participants) or the FA (as organiser of the competition)? In practice, football solves the problem by forcing clubs, as a regulation of the cup, into giving up any individual rights so that a package can be sold to broadcasters as a more attractive proposition. In legal terms, the answer would probably be the same that the organisations of the event are the legal owners of the broadcasting rights. Yet when a governing body or a league sells exclusive rights, they may still be vulnerable legally. As a cartel or monopoly selling exclusive rights, they are doubly open to challenge under the competition laws. For this reason, individual clubs such as Sunderland and Chelsea have shown signs of being prepared to challenge the monopoly of the Football League to sell the rights of all football played under their control.

A further problem area is whether a governing body, such as the FA, can protect its domestic games by preventing the screening by broadcasters of other games at the same time, on the grounds that live coverage will cause lower gates. BSkyB's coverage of football in 1991–2 has been severely hampered by such restrictions. It has backtracked on showing live coverage of Scottish Cup football on Sundays after a complaint from the League of Ireland, where its broadcasts can be received, and also on showing live coverage of Italian League football on the grounds that its broadcasts can be illegally received in Italy.[17] The enforcement mechanisms being used by the football authorities in these examples seem open to legal challenge. In the Irish example, it was the League of Ireland invoking its rights under the constitution of UEFA, the European football federation. This amounts to a mutual pact between the national governing bodies to prevent broadcasters transmitting foreign games at the same time as their own games. It is enforced by the national associations accepting an obligation to discipline any club within their own jurisdiction which allows such a game to be broadcast or by UEFA itself taking direct powers to fine clubs. As a restrictive practice preventing clubs from selling their rights to games, these regulations will doubtless soon be challenged, probably by one of the satellite broadcasters. In the Italian example, the pressure appears to have come from RAI, the Italian state broadcaster, who have contractual rights with the Italian League to show highlights immediately after the games. They presumably feared that the availability of live coverage, even via a small number of illegal decoders, would harm their interests. The agreement that RAI has to supply BSkyB with pictures was thus used to restrict the live coverage.

A final example on broadcasting law illustrates the considerable powers possessed by the European Commission. In February 1991, they effectively closed down Eurosport, a satellite channel. Eurosport had been established as a consortium owned 50 per cent by Sky Television, now BSkyB, and 50 per cent by the European Broadcasting Union, which is a group of all the major public service broadcasters within Europe. Commercial broadcasters, both terrestrial and satellite, are excluded from the EBU. EBU had a mutual agreement, whereby if one broadcaster televised a sports event in their own country, then such coverage was offered free to all other members of the consortium. As in practice almost all major European sporting events are sold to public service broadcasters, this gave EBU an effective monopoly. The Commission ruled these arrangements illegal under Article 85 after a complaint by Screensport, a rival satellite channel.[18] The Commission judged that potential competitors, such as Sky and the BBC, were co-operating together as a joint venture and thus denying access to other broadcasters. As Eurosport was receiving preferential access, via EBU's coverage, this was also to the detriment of potential competitors. It ordered BSkyB to divest itself of its shareholding and when it was unable to do so before the Commission's deadline, Eurosport closed temporarily. The channel restarted when TF1 became a shareholder, thus technically avoiding the Commission's ruling as TF1 is a public service broadcaster. Whether EBU's effective monopoly, which it retains, will survive the attention of Brussels is open to question.

Other areas where legal regulation has also increased recently are football hooliganism and the safety of sports grounds. These issues have continued to dominate the Government's agenda for sport over the past five years. There has been a steady stream of legislation designed to combat football hooliganism, much of it specifically targeted at the perceived problems of football and creating criminal offences from otherwise normally lawful activity when done at or near a football match.

Wide-ranging controls over football games were first introduced by the Sporting Events (Control of Alcohol etc.) Act 1985. This Act created the concept of a 'designated sporting event', which includes all Football League games, and then made it an offence to carry liquor at, or near a sporting event and even to carry liquor in a motor vehicle or train travelling to or from the event. It also made it an offence to possess any article capable of causing injury at or near the venue of a sporting event. These are widely-defined and wide-ranging offences. They are backed up by police powers to stop and search transport and to search spectators on reasonable suspicion. The net effect of these provisions is to give the police almost unlimited powers to supervise and control the movement of spectators going to grounds.

Further legislation was introduced in 1986 when the government introduced a new Public Order Act. Several of the offences in this Act are of particular relevance to football hooliganism. Section 4 creates a new offence called 'fear or provocation of violence', which is committed when a person uses threatening, abusive or insulting words or behaviour with intent to cause another person to believe that immediate unlawful violence will be used or provoked against them. Although a wide offence, the essence of section 4 is still the threat of violence and it is uncertain as to how far it can deal with the minor acts of hooliganism, such as the chanting of obscene or racist abuse at football games, which are not necessarily accompanied by a real threat of immediate violence. Section 5 of the Public Order Act 1986 creates a wider offence that of using threatening, abusive or insulting words of behaviour, or disorderly behaviour which causes any person within hearing or sight to be harassed, alarmed or distressed. This is an extremely wide offence and has been criticised by many commentators for just that reason. It uses the criminal law against what appears at worst to be anti-social behaviour that causes alarm or distress. The offence also unusually carried a specific power of arrest for an offence which is punishable only by a fine. Nevertheless, the usefulness of section 5 for the policing of football games is self-evident.

Despite these new laws, the Final Report of the Taylor Inquiry into the Hillsborough disaster considered that the current framework was inadequate.[19] Taylor felt that three activities had the potential for causing disorder, namely throwing missiles, chanting obscene or racist abuse, and invading the pitch. The Popplewell Inquiry into the Bradford fire of 1985, when the main stand at Bradford had caught fire causing fifty-five deaths, had previously considered the same question.[20] It had recommended the creation of a specific offence of disorderly conduct at a sports ground. This had not been implemented, partly because the Home Office felt it wrong in principle to treat football or sports grounds as a special case, even though this principle had already clearly been breached

E

in the 1985 Act in relation to carrying and consuming alcohol. Taylor rejected this argument on the grounds that, although these activities would be anti-social nuisance anywhere, they had an extra potential for leading to serious disorder within a sports ground. In addition, Taylor considered that sections 4 and 5 of the Public Order Act 1986 were inadequate to cover these activities, in particular because it was so difficult to prove that harassment, alarm or distress had been caused rather than for example merely disgust at racial abuse. He therefore recommended the creation of a specific offence to cover throwing a missile, chanting obscene or racialist abuse, and going on the pitch without reasonable excuse.[21] These recommendations have now been implemented by a brief statute, the Football (Offences) Act 1991.

The government has also acted to give magistrates greater power to act against 'known hooligans'. The Public Order Act 1986 gave a court the power to make an exclusion order on a person convicted of an offence connected with football. Such an order prohibited the offenders from attending any football match. These powers have not however been widely used by the courts and the enforcement of them by clubs is obviously difficult. The government intended to replace them by the stronger deterrent of depriving offenders of their membership under the proposed national membership scheme which was introduced by the Football Spectators Act 1989. This hare-brained idea was firmly put in its place by the Taylor Inquiry which concluded that: 'I have grave doubts about the feasibility of the national membership scheme and serious misgivings about its likely impact on safety. I also have grave doubts about the chances of its achieving its purposes and am very anxious about its potential impact on police commitments and control of spectators.'[22] With this strong condemnation of the scheme, the government retreated and Part I of the Act, which deals with the scheme, has not been implemented. However, Part II of the Act extended the concept of exclusion orders in order to try and prevent convicted hooligans from travelling to matches abroad. These new powers are described as restriction orders and imposed a duty on offenders convicted in relation to football a duty to report at a police station when designated matches are being played abroad, principally those in which the national team are playing.

The Taylor inquiry was also directly concerned with the safety of sports grounds, another issue on which there is now a considerable legislative framework. Specific legislation had been introduced in 1975 to implement the recommendations of the Wheatly report which had inquired into the Ibrox disaster in which sixty-six spectators had died.[23] The legislation was updated by the Fire Safety and Safety of Places of Sport Act 1987. This Act similarly followed a judicial inquiry, the Popplewell report, into the Bradford fire of 1985.[24] This legislation established a framework for safety by requiring sports grounds to have a safety certificate issued by the local authority, although since 1987 the Home Secretary has had to specify the terms and conditions which a Safety Certificate should include. In practice, the major guidelines which are followed are those contained in a Home Office Guide known as the Green Guide.

The Taylor inquiry into the Hillsborough disaster concentrated the majority of its recommendations on safety and its related aspects. The root cause of the disaster in its analysis was the overcrowding into two specific areas, and the remedies lay mainly into trying to prevent such a re-occurrence. This is reflected in its main recommendations of all-seater stadia for the first two divisions by the 1993/4 season, and in the meantime progressively reducing the maximum capacity for the standing terraces. This achieves the major aim of safety because of Taylor's assumption that all-seater stadia are inherently safer.

What receives least attention in Taylor's analysis is the problem of policing. This is not unsurprising given the framework of analysis used, that of safety. But it arguably leads to a lop-sided perspective of the basic problems. The only specific proposals in relation to police planning are concerned essentially with safety, with recommendations such as that ticketless fans should not be admitted, arrest procedures should be streamlined to minimise the time that a police officer is absent, options to postpone kick-off or to suggest early or Sunday kick-offs.

None of these recommendations address themselves to the overall problems of policing football matches. The legal liability for Hillsborough was fairly quickly accepted by the police. Their role in failing to control the crowd, in allowing an overcrowding of a particular part of the ground to an extent that was obvious to the naked eye, and the apparent initial reaction that the problem was one of hooliganism have all been identified as contributory causes in the events. The liability of Sheffield Wednesday FC, as legal occupiers of the ground, in relation to inadequate signposting inside the ground, the state of crash barriers, and the arrangement of the terraces is still the subject of legal proceedings.

I concluded my chapter in our previous edition by predicting that 'the increased commercialisation . . . of sport . . . seems certain to lead to greater legal intervention'.[25] The developments in the law since then have mainly fulfilled that prophecy. The original analysis proposed a crude relation between increased commercialisation and the juridification of sport, and events since then have confirmed that conclusion. Sport is more commercial, the law more present. The argument is now not whether and why the law should intervene, but when the law does intervene, how and to what extent it should.

The juridification of sport is clear to anyone who has even only a nodding acquaintance with the back pages of the newspapers or the news headlines. There is more legislation, on safety at sports grounds in particular. More demands for legal controls on sport, such as the calling for a total ban on boxing. More criminal offences that the football spectator may commit and more police powers to enforce them. Even though the judges are continuing to show their traditional caution in interfering in the affairs of what they view as private clubs, there is also a recognition that the economic interests involved call for greater judicial scrutiny, especially of decisions which affect players' earnings and livelihood, and a halting but significant movement to opening more governing bodies, such as the Jockey Club, to judicial review. Litigation in sports seems on the increase. Writs are flying in many directions, especially but not exclusively in relation to disciplinary proceedings by governing bodies. In the last three years alone, there have been challenges to cricket authorities over the re-admission of South Africa to international competition, to the Jockey Club over the result of the 1990 Oaks, boxers freeing themselves from oppressive contracts with their manager, football clubs threatening action over poaching of managers, a major sports satellite channel closed for being anti-competitive, the FA and the Football League fighting their battle in court, players being prosecuted for assaults on the field. This explosion of litigation has been reflected in an increased interest by lawyers. Sports law is increasingly treated as a sub-division of the law. Books and articles have been written; legal practitioners specialise in it; courses are taught in universities and top legal firms have sports and leisure departments.

In an attempt to forestall much of this intervention and litigation, sport is increasingly looking to voluntary self-regulation and arbitration. There is already a private international arbitration system for the settlement of legal disputes in sport established by the International Olympic Committee, known as the CAS (Court of Arbitration for Sport). The Central Council for Physical Recreation (CCPR) has recently proposed the creation of a similar body at the national level.[26] There have been attempts by the major sports to review and to co-ordinate the internal disciplinary procedures on drug offences of different governing bodies. Whilst devices such as private arbitration tribunals may help to keep sport out of the courtroom, it will not stem the tide of juridification. Lawyers will still be used, legal concepts employed, and conflicts of interest will be defined and processed in a quasi-legal manner.

And this trend is not just a British phenomena. Internationally, there is also more intervention and litigation. To cite just one example, the Federal Trade Commission is currently investigating the US Golf tour on charges of monopoly and restraint of trade.[27] Likewise, international governing bodies face increasing difficulty as players challenge their decisions in a variety of national courts; the IAAF was unable to make effective its two-year ban on Butch Reynolds for testing positively for steroids when the American federation were threatened with a lawsuit in the American courts.[28] The Pandora's box has been opened world-wide and the consequences will remain with sport for the indefinite future.

Notes

1 *Guardian*, 24 February 1992.
2 *Ibid.*
3 *Guardian*, 25 February 1992.
4 *Guardian*, 29 February 1992.
5 Sir Nicolas Browne-Wilkinson in *Cowley* v. *Heatley*, *The Times*, 24.
6 *Currie* v. *Barton*, *The Times*, 19 September 1988.
7 [1985] 3 W.L.R. 335.
8 *R.* v. *Jockey Club, ex parte Massingberd-Mundy*, *The Times*, 3 January 1990.
9 *Pett* v. *Greyhound Racing Authority Ltd. (No. 2)* [1970] 1 Q.B. 46.
10 *R.* v. *Jockey Club, ex parte RAM Racecourses Ltd. Independent*, 14th April 1990.
11 *The Times*, 3 November 1987.
12 *The Times*, 28 November 1989.

13 *Ibid.*
14 *Guardian*, 7 December 1991.
15 *Guardian*, 27 March 1991.
16 *The Times*, 22 January 1991.
17 *Guardian*, 7 December 1991.
18 *The Times*, 21 February 1991.
19 *The Hillsborough Stadium Disaster: Inquiry by the Rt Hon Lord Justice Taylor Interim Report* (1990), Cm. 962, Chapter 9.
20 *Final Report on Crowd Safety and Control by Mr Justice Popplewell* (1986), Cmnd. 9710.
21 *Hillsborough Interim Report.*, para. 292
22 *Ibid.*, para. 419.
23 *Report of the Inquiry into Crowd Safety at Sports Grounds* (1972), Cmnd. 4952.
24 Note 22 above.
25 Lincoln Allison, ed., *The Politics of Sport*, Manchester University Press, 1986, p. 64.
26 *Guardian*, 30 November 1991.
27 *Independent*, 13 March 1991.
28 *Guardian*, 12 June 1991.

7

Politicians and sport: uses and abuses

TERRY MONNINGTON

In January 1989, after 2,923 days in office as President of the United States of America, Ronald Reagan flew out of Andrews Air Force base bound for retirement in California. From the terminal building hung a banner proclaiming that 'Air Force One Flies Once More For The Gipper'.[1] The poignancy of this farewell message lies in the name 'Gipper'.

Reagan used everyday symbolism to make a political statement. In the form of modern day parables that were pure and uncomplicated he endeavoured to give life to his principles. Throughout his political career his speeches were peppered with a common phrase, 'There's a story . . .', which prefaced yet another of his well-used anecdotes. These stories about provincial men and women thinly veiled his ideological and emotional beliefs.

The Gipper was perhaps one of Reagan's most successful film roles and was certainly a character with whom he closely identified. The role of George Gipp provided Reagan with one of his early breaks in Hollywood when Warner Brothers planned to make a film, *Knute Rockne – All American*. The subject of the film was a Norwegian who coached Notre Dame University football from 1918 until 1931. The success of this coach in the years leading up to the Depression reputedly inspired a nation. The story-line of this film provided Reagan in his subsequent political career with an ideal medium through which he could express his fundamental beliefs. The Commencement address at Notre Dame in 1981 provided Reagan with an audience well beyond the confines of the University, for this was his first foray out of the White House since he was shot in an assassination attempt. A national audience was guaranteed.

The central characters in the *Knute Rockne* film, Gipp and Rockne, provided Reagan with two archetypal American heroes, symbols of patriotism; a central tenet of Reagan's philosophy to rekindle personal faith and optimism within the American people.

In the Notre Dame speech Reagan wove a political ideology into the story portraying Rockne as much more than a football coach. Rockne became a moral educator and a father figure for the American nation; an individual to inspire the nation's populace once again. Reagan explained,

> As a coach, [Rockne] did more than teach young men to play a game. He believed truly that the noblest work of man was building the character of man. And maybe that's why he was a living legend. No man connected with football has ever achieved the stature or occupied the singular niche in the nation that he carved out for himself, not just in sport, but in our entire social structure.[2]

George Gipp, the character that Reagan played and immortalised, and in fact became so closely identified with, was a member of the Notre Dame team, but died while still a student. He was reputed to have relayed a message to his team mates from his death bed, exhorting them to 'win one for Gipper'.

Reagan's film interpretation of Gipp was as a conformist, a character trait significantly divergent from the real Gipp. But in all of his story-telling Reagan was only too willing to digress from historical fact to give credence. Eventually he was to believe the myth that he had created.

Rockne also used Gipp's immortal lines eight years after the boy's death in a period of crisis for the team when petty jealousies and friction were undermining the unity of the team. Reagan used this football story during the Notre Dame speech and on numerous subsequent occasions to convey a moral learning experience and a message to the American people. The challenges to the students of Notre Dame and the nation as a whole were beyond the confines of the football field and were for a cause greater than themselves. They were being called on to pull together for the national team. To reinforce his message, Reagan likened Rockne's footballers, who turned a potential defeat into victory after being inspired by Gipp's death-bed wish, to the Founding Fathers of the American Constitution who were galvanised into action by a vision and a cause again much greater than themselves.

Reagan had infinite faith in the lessons of history for contemporary America and the Gipper story provided an immensely strong emotional association in a society where sport has such status. Sport in the USA is a major cultural practice; being a spectator or participant is perceived to be almost a duty.

The Notre Dame speech concluded with a rallying call to the nation. Like Rockne's half-time exhortation, Reagan claimed that the economic difficulties, social ills and embattled national prestige which confronted the American people were a consequence of failures of the Democratic Party and in particular the former presidential incumbent, Jimmy Carter. Reagan presented his vision for the future as a half-time pep talk. He endeavoured to evoke the strength and vitality of youth to pull together to win the match and restore the pre-eminence of the USA. The call was 'to win one for Gipper'; win one for America and win one for Reagan who was the contemporary Gipper.

Reagan also professed to be the modern-day Rockne and as coach to the nation he believed that the moral fortitude that brought victory on the football field to the home team at Notre Dame in the 1930s was what was required to confront the problems facing America in the early 1980s. Communism and the 'Evil Soviet Empire' were the opposing team that was an ever present threat, but a threat that could be beaten by unity and strength within the American team.

This sporting analogy was to be an ever-recurring theme throughout the Reagan presidency as he endeavoured to restore national self-confidence and prestige, severely tarnished by the Vietnam war and the taking of American hostages in Tehran. Reagan regarded these tasks as paramount, more important than specific policy initiatives.

The willingness of international leaders, as well as lesser politicians, to use sport to further their own political ambitions has characterised sport throughout history and certainly since the activity began to be formerly structured in the nineteenth century. The German gymnastics movement of the middle decades of that century, known as Turnen, was a highly centralised and organised association with clear political objectives. It could be argued that none of the modern Olympic Games have ever been independent of political activity. The globalisation of television since the 1950s has not only revolutionised sport, but has provided politicians and political systems with a policy tool of immense potential.

Sport in the former Eastern bloc countries was for many years regarded as a valid means of reinforcing a particular political ideology; success in sport being equated with success by association for Communism. African leaders have been more than willing to utilise sport as they have travelled the rocky road of creating nation-states since the 1960s. Sport was seen by these leaders as a cheap and simple way to develop the sentiment of national loyalty and to gain international status for themselves and their country. A love of sport and a desire to gain success as a participant or supporter was, in the case of many citizens of Africa, the only common bond. More recently, with an African consciousness becoming increasingly apparent, sport has been seen to be a valuable means of fostering African unity.[3] In addition, spectators and participants are potential voters who can be subjected to overt and covert political indoctrination, a process that can be reinforced by the use of nationalistic symbols. Politicians universally use sporting contests as a means of communicating political messages to particular groups, drafting in international sportsmen and women to lend credence to their arguments.

The use of sport by politicians in recent years has in many instances proved to be most successful. But the use of sport in this way has often had negative consequences for both the politicians and sport itself. Its use has occasionally appeared to be counter-productive, despite high aims and impressive rhetoric. Sport has often suffered when brought into the political arena, abused and then left to lick its wounds. It is the analysis of this potential use and the inevitable scope for abuse of sport by two particular politicians, Ronald Reagan and Margaret Thatcher, that provides the focus of attention of this chapter. Their willingness to use sport as a political weapon was clearly not unique. Sport did not even feature very specifically on their action agendas. What was, however, most significant was the fact that here were perhaps two of the most influential politicians of the late twentieth century who were prepared to utilise and politicise sport in such an overt manner. Reagan proved to be the arch-exponent of sporting rhetoric to engender national enthusiasm in support of the supposed 'Reagan Revolution'. In contrast Thatcher was more concerned to use sport to implement social policy and further her foreign policy objectives.

She expressed no affinity for sport either through word or deed. Her use, or abuse, of sport to accomplish policy objectives was in fact, in many instances, to alienate the relevant sporting communities.

The close identification of Reagan with sport and sporting men and women was a classic example of a political leader endeavouring to become a sports populist to win the hearts and minds of their electorate. Sport has since the 1950s operated, in the opinion of successive American presidents, as a unifying metaphor within the USA; a means by which the American people can be encouraged to rally around a political leader and around the American flag. But the use of sport in this way does not necessarily succeed with all politicians. The sporting image and the identification with sport has to be developed and refined over a considerable period of time. A successful sporting career, real or imagined, as in the case of Ronald Reagan and Gerald Ford, provided an invaluable foundation on which to create such an image. The identification of American politicians with the frontiersman of old appears now to be out-dated, replaced apparently more appropriately with a sporting or military image that portrays success, pre-eminence and leadership qualities. It is significant that in the United Kingdom the close identification of political leaders with sport has been less in evidence. Edward Heath was a sailor of some repute, Harold Wilson an ardent soccer fan and John Major an avid follower of both football and cricket. But in the case of the latter two politicians, although their association with sport has provided a supposed opportunity to identify with the people, it has had limited impact and is a political card that is far from exploited. In the British context such an association is not deemed to provide much political mileage. Traditional attitudes suggest that in Britain sport is more compartmentalised in people's value system in contrast to that of the USA. Sport as a leisure time pursuit, whether active or passive, not least as a consequence of the continued significance of the nineteenth-century work ethic, is deemed to be an activity that should be divorced from the pressures and influences of workaday life. Hence the rearguard action to maintain the myth of apolitical sport.

The identification of British politicians with sport has consequently proved mildly amusing to the British electorate, but nothing more. The sporting activities of John Major since entering Downing Street have provided media exposure to a politician who has, as yet, failed to excite the popular press or television audiences. His desire to take a mini version of the Oval cricket ground on to the mythical desert island of BBC Radio 4, along with John Arlott's commentary of Donald Bradman's last Test cricket appearance, may well have provided an insight into the prime minister's sporting interests, but it is unlikely to have significantly improved his performance in the 1992 election. The potential of benefiting at the ballot box from developing a sports populist persona among British politicians is further diminished by the class associations of many British sports. Identifying with a specific sport might associate a politician with a particular social class; an association that would adversely affect their popularity with the electorate who identify more closely with another social class.

The appearance of John Major at the Five Nations rugby clash between England and Ireland in January 1992 in the company of two international figures, the President of Eire, Mary Robinson and President de Klerk of South Africa, was a potentially significant political statement in a sporting context, given the ongoing troubles in Northern Ireland and the rapidly changing political scene in South Africa. Yet the media reaction was condemnatory. The incident was seen as a reflection of Major's political naivety, considering the rigid policy line of the Irish government with respect to South Africa.

The absence of Margaret Thatcher from this list of recent British prime ministers is no accident. There is no real evidence to suggest that she has had any real or significant interest in sport, either as a participant or as an observer. Nevertheless, she has been an instrumentalist with respect to the political use of sport, a politician willing to utilise sport as an instrument to promulgate social policy and to provide a platform to confirm her foreign policy convictions. Sport was largely peripheral to her main agenda. If a sports issue forced its way on to that agenda, as in the case of football, then no special privileges or dispensations were perceived necessary. The football hooligan was a British export that Thatcher regarded as a political embarrassment at a critical point in her discussions on the future of Britain in Europe, an unnecessary adjunct in her export drive into the European Community. She contended that legislative action was appropriate to control this element of sport, even in the face of universal condemnation from the majority of sporting authorities. The specificity of this approach is the subject of analysis in the second half of this chapter.

To return to the American context, the pathos of *Knute Rockne* was all the more powerful because Reagan was not only a high school and college footballer during the period of Rockne's pre-eminence as a coach, but it was a period when he was formulating his career aspirations and personal ideals. He was consolidating a love of sports and sporting heroes. In his youth Reagan was not regarded as a natural footballer because of his light frame and rather reserved character. But success on the sports field was perhaps a means of gaining status among his peers. High school and subsequent college sporting honours were, however, not to lead to a professional sports career. His immediate ambition on leaving college was to be a radio sports commentator.

During a successful audition for a part-time sports announcer's job in Davenport, Iowa, Reagan recounted from memory the final quarter of a football game involving his former Eureka College team. The significance was not only his ability to tell a good story, but his willingness to embellish that story, alter historical fact to convey a message and still to retain apparent authenticity; an authenticity that he was apparently even to believe himself. This ability to merge fact with fiction was to be refined in his subsequent post as a radio announcer in Des Moines. He was required to present a match commentary utilising limited information received by telegraph wire. Such commentaries were to be maintained even when the wire went dead. This story-telling technique was to become the basis of his future political rhetoric.

His ensuing employment as a star of fifty-two movies, spanning a quarter of a century, provided further opportunities to create imaginary situations and characters that would provide, in his political career, a wealth of story-lines to convey his own beliefs and ideology.

In November 1980, Reagan achieved a landslide election victory to become President of the USA. His guiding principles revolved around a number of basic beliefs: a free market and free trade, a love of his country, distrust of government with a desire 'to get government off the back the people' and peace through strength. These principles were presented in simplistic form as a conflict between good and evil. He lacked in-depth technical knowledge relating to these issues and revealed a reluctance to reverse this situation; briefings bored him and he was regarded as being intellectually lazy. He simply did not grasp the intricacies of social and economic policy. He was not able to manage the presidency and so became increasingly dependent on cabinet government as much out of necessity as conviction. He set the broad policy agenda, but relied on his senior staff for detailed imposition. His leadership potential was further marred by his frequent lapses in memory and by his ability to fall asleep during briefings and even important meetings.

But his failure to command government coexisted with his greatest asset: his ability to lead the nation. Reagan believed in himself and was forever the optimist. He was to become 'the great communicator', able to convey his ideas and develop a real bond with the electorate. He managed to disarm his critics and convert the majority of the American people to his views, mobilising public opinion on to his side. He was a man of the people with whom they could closely identify. His simple solutions were those of 'the guy at the bar'.

His beliefs were based on lifetime experiences, newspaper stories and articles in *Newsweek* and the *Reader's Digest*. These beliefs were translated into policy statements and rallying speeches. Myth and reality were merged to provide what was a good story. Authenticity was rarely questioned. He used limited facts and figures to reinforce his arguments, but the strength of his message was often transmitted by way of anecdotes. He relied heavily on 'for instance' stories. The phrase, 'There's a story' was a common introduction that gave vitality to his principles. His skill and ability to convey a message by analogy and often intricate anecdotes was honed during his days as a radio sports commentator and as an actor. Through voice modulation and the use of local dialects he was able to embellish his stories. He was to become more concerned with his performance than with the actual content of the presentation. The content and its eventual implementation as policy was to be the responsibility of his aides.

These stories were constantly used throughout his presidency to make a political statement, willing to play fast and loose with fact in order to carry his audience. The analogies and anecdotes were drawn from his early careers and from history. Sport and the movies provided an infinite source of material. They were also subjects for which he had a wealth of knowledge, supported by a life time of experiences. The confidence with which he pontificated on the movies and sport contrasted embarrassingly with his lack of understanding of economic matters, modern technology and foreign affairs.

Knute Rockne and the Gipper were themes to which he constantly returned. He also often related a story originally set in his old school, Dixon High, which told of a young footballer who admitted to an unknowing referee a rule infringement, an admission that cost the home team the match. Reagan often repeated this story to reinforce his belief in honesty. The venue, the player, who was occasionally Reagan himself, were constantly changed, despite the implied suggestion that the story was genuine. It is, however, probable that Reagan believed the myth that he had created.

Reagan supplemented his sporting analogies and anecdotes with a wealth of one liners, again designed to proffer a simple, but critical message. They proved popular with his audiences and despite their origin they became identified with Reagan. When he was shot in March 1981 he was reported to have said to Nancy Reagan, 'Honey, I forgot to duck!'[4] The words, in fact, were those of Jack Dempsey, explaining his reason for defeat in a heavy weight title contest against Gene Tunney in 1926. In his desire to confirm his patriotism and to rekindle the patriotism of the nation he regularly misquoted the words of Joe DiMaggio, one of America's most respected baseball players, by stating that 'He was lucky to be an American'.[5] DiMaggio, in his autobiography, had actually said that 'he was lucky to be a Yankee'.

Unlike many of his presidential predecessors, particularly Richard Nixon, Reagan did not use 'locker room diplomacy' or organise his trips around the football season calendar. He did, however, regularly invite national champions and championship teams to the White House to meet the media and provide a valuable photo-call. Such actions were perceived to give credence by association to his image and to his policies. Even away from home such opportunities were rarely missed. In mid-April 1984, prior to his much publicised trip to China, he took the opportunity for a photo-call on his stop-over in Hawaii. The venue for the press was the beach where Reagan, stripped to a pair of shorts and followed by his entourage of security staff, pretended to be the star quarter-back, using a coconut as the ball. The aim was ostensibly to present the president as a fit and healthy leader. The real objective was to give him an opportunity to rest and readjust to a new time zone and so hopefully avoid falling asleep when meeting the Chinese leaders!

In 1984 the Reagan presidency was in its golden age. Policy successes were achieved at home and abroad, while his re-election prospects were near guaranteed. The Olympic Games of that year, held in Los Angeles, were an unprecedented success for the American team, made the easier by the absence of the majority of Eastern-bloc athletes. The potential of the Games as an election ally was not missed by Reagan and his aides.

The victories of the US athletes were used by the Reagan administration to reinforce the success story of Reagan's first term. He had supposedly restored American pride and revitalised the nation's prestige in the international arena. The athletes' triumphs were a consequence of the new-found national confidence and self-respect that the Reagan presidency had orchestrated. During the Games, Reagan identified the American athletes with the nation's military apparatus and the athletic contests as the frontline. The successes of the athletes were seen in this imagery as reflecting the superiority of the nation in international diplomacy, the achievements of the President and the Republican Party.

Every photo-call opportunity and speaking engagement was seized upon to associate Reagan, his party and his ideology more closely with the triumphant American athletes. These included his opening address at the Los Angeles Coliseum which gave him an international audience linked by satellite. In his address to the American athletes he urged them to seek success for themselves, their families and their country and 'do it for Gipper'. He thinly veiled the fact that he believed that he too was running for victory, to become the team number one and captain of the American team. But the task for Reagan was not perceived to be difficult. Much of his campaign for re-election was likened 'to a long victory lap in which the only task of the triumphant victor was to jog easily around the stadium, gracefully accepting the tributes of the adoring crowd'.[6]

Mondale endeavoured to use sporting analogies in his campaign, but he lacked Reagan's conviction. Reagan had made the Games and the sporting analogy his own. If individual Americans rejected Reagan's perception of history and his dreams for the future, they would, after the election, be on 'the losing team'. This judgement was applied equally to his assessment of the position of the USSR. He questioned his audience at a campaign rally in Missouri, 'Didn't you get the feeling that the Soviets must have been relieved when the closing ceremonies for the Olympics were over? But one thing they'll never see is the closing ceremonies for America'.[7] In the post-games breakfast speech he likened the athletes to international ambassadors for their country. He reflected, 'That I couldn't help but think that if the people of the world judged Americans by what they saw of you, then they'd think, "Americans? Well they're generous and full of serious effort; they're full of high spirits; they're motivated by all the best things. They're truly a nation of champions"'.[8]

Even the transference of the Olympic Torch across America by a multitude of carriers of all ages, the fit and the handicapped, was referred to by Reagan to relay an image. These individuals were regarded as equally important as the American athletes and were extolled as victors, as true Americans. He had received these heroes at the White House in May, when he declared that 'Our young people are running for their country, running for greatness, for achievement, for that moving thing in man that makes him push on to the impossible'.[9]

Each successive Reagan campaign speech utilised at least one sporting analogy or anecdote. The formula was well tried and tested and proved universally successful. Reagan's proclamations were to be interrupted constantly by the chanting of 'USA! USA! USA!', mirroring the public displays of patriotism expressed by the home crowd at the 1984 Olympics.

Reagan's nomination acceptance speech in August again referred back to the Games. He regarded the American people, like their athletes, as true champions, with their Olympic successes fostering enhanced patriotism. An eventual victory in the forthcoming elections would open a new season that offered new expectations and good fortune. The presidential contest with the Democratic candidate was portrayed as a contest between two coaches to gain the national coach's job. The choice was clear. 'And come November, the American people will tell Coach tax-hike [Mondale] to go find another team someplace else'.[10]

Reagan seemed to be a winner before he even ran, but the Republican Party complacency was exposed in a televised face-to-face debate with Mondale in October. Reagan was depicted as muddled and unable to express a cogent argument. The real truth about the health of the nation was in fact already apparent. It was evident that Reagan's massive defence spending programme, undertaken

without any significant tax increases, had resulted in an inevitable
failure to balance the national budget; a development that was alien
to the Republican tradition. During the campaign, Reagan had also
failed to proffer any new policy initiatives or ideas. His near total
dependence on his aides was evident. His critics claimed that his
single contribution to his re-election campaign was his adaptation
of Al Jolson's comment in the first talking picture entitled *The Jazz
Singer*, 'You ain't seen nothing yet!'

Despite his critics, his detachment from White House staff
operations, his disinclination to sustain the cerebral combat of
press conferences, his verbal gaffes and inattentiveness to facts he
was re-elected in November 1984. For all his shortcomings, Reagan
had restored pride in the American people and an optimism in the
future. Reagan was at his best in front of the media and a public
audience relating simple, but effective stories and anecdotes that
were designed to relay his own uncomplicated policy principles
and philosophies. The relative naivety of his politics was, however,
thinly veiled. But this did not appear to concern much of the
American electorate. He made them feel good about themselves
and about America. Mondale had by comparison focused only on
the nation's problems. In early 1985 he condensed his inauguration
ceremony, ostensibly so as not to clash with the televising of
the football Superbowl. He did, however, arrange to have an
appearance on-air during the game and so commanded the largest
national television audience for that year. The sporting context was
again exploited to make political capital.

There was a further shadow that hung over the 'Morning Again'
landslide victory of Reagan in the November 1984 elections. The
Afro-American voters were noticeable by their absence from the
Reagan ranks. He had long professed to abhor racial prejudice
and had invariably relied upon sporting anecdotes to support this
assertion. He was often to relate a story dating back to his Eureka
College days. Reagan recalled that on a football trip to his home
town of Dixon, a fellow team member, who was black, was refused
hotel accommodation, so Reagan took him to his family home.
Reagan maintained a life-long association with this team-mate until
his death in 1981.

Reagan also regularly reminisced, particularly when meeting
black groups, about his stand against racism during his radio
broadcasting days. He claimed that he had regularly cited his

opposition to the barring of Afro-American baseball players from the Major Leagues prior to 1947. This his aides referred to as 'The Jackie Robinson story'.

But Afro-Americans generally regarded Reagan as indifferent to their problems. His unwillingness to use the power of the Federal government or the legislature to offer succour in their fight for civil rights was never forgotten. Yet this failure to solicit the support of the Afro-American voters did not seriously damage his credibility or his electoral chances. A generation earlier the consequences would have potentially been very different.

The 1960s had been a period in American politics when the racial issue had been paramount. The Black Power movement was in its ascendency. Racial tension, segregation and discrimination were major political issues. The international media were constantly referring to the activities of the dominant players; men such as Dr Martin Luther King and Governor George Wallace professed their message across a political chasm. The sporting milieu provided numerous examples of both subtle and overt acts of segregation, discrimination or racism, similar to those encountered in other social institutions. These problems were apparent at every level of sporting contest involving American athletes. But it was on the international stage and in the Olympic arena in particular that racism in the USA was to command the attention of the world's media. The threat of a Black American boycott of the Mexico Olympics in 1968, orchestrated by the black American academic Harry Edwards, and the subsequent black protest by several Black American athletes including Tommie Smith and John Carlos in the Olympic stadium, contrived to expose to the world the racism that permeated American life. Tommie Smith succinctly expressed the frustrations felt by many of the black athletes: 'When we're winning, we're Americans. Otherwise, we're just negroes.'[11]

Such statements and actions were politically damaging to the incumbent US administration of President Johnson and embarrassing to the American people. Yet within a very short space of time the black issue in sport largely disappeared from the popular press and even the scientific literature. At the Munich Olympic Games in 1972 there was a much less publicised 'semi-protest' against racial unfairness involving the two Black American 400m medallists, Vince Matthews and Wayne Collett. Their protest was conceived as expressing irreverence with respect to the American flag and anthem. Their actions were seen as simply bad manners or moral cowardice and elicited a crescendo of whistles from the crowd. The lifetime ban imposed on the two athletes by the IOC the following day largely ended interest in the incident. The black power protest in sport was yesterday's news. During the Reagan administration these Olympic protests were forgotten memories for most Americans. To the young generation, held spellbound by the Los Angeles successes of the American athletes, the 1960s protesters were virtual unknowns.

Racial discrimination in the USA, in a society that prides itself on meritocratic ideals, was as much apparent in the Reagan era as it is in the 1990s. The arrangement of quotas of blacks on a sports team, as well as stacking, are still contentious issues. The potential for upward social mobility for the ethnic minorities through sport is still more myth than reality. But neither the 1980s and 1990s nor the years of the Reagan presidency have been the right time for the black protest movement to once more overcome its inertia. The black radicalism of the 1960s had been consigned to history. America in 1984 under Reagan was at ease with itself, and certainly did not want any domestic issues to undermine this feeling of satisfaction. Reagan advised the people, in his own inimitable way, that they should feel proud with respect to themselves and their country.

The apparent lack of concern expressed by Reagan for civil rights issues was not restricted to the problems of the Afro-Americans. He was also reluctant to support Federal government intervention to enforce Title IX, which was an amendment to the Constitution, outlawing sexual discrimination. A Supreme Court decision in 1984 (Grove City College v. Bell) seriously damaged the cause of the anti-sex discrimination lobby groups. Reagan proved to be indifferent to their requests for action to reverse the Court's decision. When, eventually in 1988 a Civil Rights Restoration Bill was presented to nullify the Court's 1984 ruling, Reagan vetoed it. However, the Congress in turn overruled the veto and the Bill became law.

Opposition to the Reagan administration became more apparent and openly expressed during 1986. The mid-term Senate elections of that year proved to be the arena where Reagan was to experience a major reverse. It was evident that the Republican Party was in danger of losing control of the Senate and every seat was a potential battleground.

One critical seat was in the State of Nevada where the popular Senator Laxalt was retiring. His Republican successor was a Jim Santini. In a last desperate effort to influence the voting public and save the seat for the Republicans, the Party called on their remaining trump card, Ronald Reagan. The plea was, 'When you go to the polls, win one for Jim Santini, win one for the future and for America's future, and yes, win one for the Gipper'.[12] The Republican candidate still lost!

In another contest in Orange County in California Reagan was again drafted in to support the local candidate. His rallying call once more endeavoured to identify the voters more closely with Reagan and to imply that it was almost the voters' patriotic duty to vote for Reagan's man. Reagan implored the people to 'Remind future generations that a former sports commentator, Dutch Reagan, came to town for the last campaign'. Then came the patriotic statement, 'I'm proud to be an American cause there ain't no doubt, I love this land. God bless America!'[13] The audience's response was the Olympic chant that had resounded around the Los Angeles Coliseum in the heady days of 1984, 'USA! USA! USA!' But the old Reagan magic was again found wanting as the Democrats eventually recorded another victory in their successful campaign to secure a majority in the Senate.

The loss of control of the Senate was inevitably a severe blow to Reagan, but the revelations surrounding the Iran – Contra affair significantly damaged his personal prestige and his integrity. For many months the impeachment of the President was a real possibility. When Secretary of State George Shultz distanced himself from 'the sale of arms to Iran' debacle during a CBS television broadcast, 'Face the Nation', on 16 November 1986 the die appeared to be cast. The following day there appeared in the influential *Washington Post* a leading article that referred to the TV programme as 'Gipperdammerung'; a play on the German word, Götterdämmerung, meaning the twilight of the gods.

The remaining two years in office proved very difficult for Reagan. Many now saw him as a 'Lame-Duck President'. Yet by the end of his second and final term in office, his standing as a major world leader was paramount. His policy of confronting the 'Evil Empire', the Soviet Union, from a position of strength following the massive arms build-up of the USA, had, he believed, succeeded in bringing Gorbachev to the negotiating table. When the election campaign of 1988 began, with Reagan's Vice-President now the Republican Party's front runner, Reagan's star was once more in the ascendancy. The actor-President was once more apparently in charge. The old clichés, one-liners, sporting analogies and anecdotes were once more called upon to generate support for the Bush – Quayle ticket. Almost inevitably, at the Republican Convention of 1988, Reagan called on George Bush in a highly emotional speech to 'Go out and win one more for Gipper'. In a final campaign speech the sporting analogy was central to Reagan's rallying call to the voters. 'The USA was never meant to be a second-rate nation. So, like our Olympic athletes, let's aim for the stars and go for gold . . . America's best days are yet to come.'[14]

This is not the place to judge the Reagan presidency. It is clear that he failed to gain fiscal control. His 1980 campaign promise to balance the Federal budget by getting rid of waste, fraud and abuse had proved unachievable. He never appreciated that his obsession to strengthen the military without significant tax increases was impossible. The Reagan generation was 'eating the country's seed corn'. Nevertheless, inflation was significantly reduced; so too, unemployment. Perhaps most significantly of all, Americans once more felt able to walk tall in the world community. When Reagan flew out of Andrews Air Force base in January 1989, he left office with a higher public-approval rating than any modern American president. The people still loved the Gipper.

On the international stage Reagan was something of an enigma. Foreign leaders, including Gorbachev and Thatcher, questioned how such a man could become the leader of the most powerful democracy in the world. They had invariably heard his jokes, his anecdotes and his rather simplistic ideas. But Reagan the communicator and Reagan the man both confused and entranced them. Reagan was an anglophile who loved to visit England and savour its history. Invitations to Windsor Castle and Buckingham Palace were prized, second only to those to number 10 Downing Street and an audience with Mrs Thatcher! His respect and admiration for her dated back to their first meeting in 1975 when he prophetically commented that she would 'make an magnificent prime minister'.[15] The esteem was reciprocated. In 1983 Prime Minister Thatcher expressed her feelings towards Reagan when she declared, 'I've come to know you as a personal friend who can be relied on in times of danger'.[16]

This co-operation and mutual support remained a feature of international diplomacy throughout the 1980s. Just before Reagan left office he visited London in June 1988 following his summit meeting with Gorbachev in Moscow. In Mrs Thatcher's speech, congratulating Reagan on his successful meeting, she concluded with the words 'God bless America'. The comment was greeted with ecstatic applause. The strength of her relationship with the USA and with Ronald Reagan was clearly evident. But it was not to be their only bond. They were both converts to the neo-liberal, 'New Right' political principles that emphasised the importance of moving away from a dependency to an enterprise culture. They both in their way supported the principle of minimalistic government, advocating a reduced role for the state in the economy and greater power to market forces. It was evident that Reagan only had a superficial grasp of the theoretical premises that underlay the 'New Right' principles. In contrast Margaret Thatcher's depth of understanding came from her extensive reading of monographs published by the Centre for Policy Studies and the Adam Smith Institute and the two most influential 'New Right' theoreticians, Friedrich Hayek and Milton Friedmann. She and Sir Keith Joseph were in turn to popularise a simplified form of the views of these two authors and subsequently to make their ideas the basis of her economic policy throughout the 1980s.

When Thatcher came to office in 1979 with a landslide victory over Labour, she was seen to break the mould of postwar consensus politics. Tight monetary control, public expenditure cuts, denationalisation and a reduction in personal taxation were the basis of her policy programme. Other key elements to her manifesto were a stress on vigorous enforcement of law and order and a restatement of traditional family values that emphasised self-help and individualism.

Consensus politics had been a result of wartime coalition government that had spawned a belief in egalitarianism and collectivism. An awareness of the social and economic malaise that was Britain's legacy from World War II prompted successive postwar governments to expand the apparatus of the welfare state that the wartime Beveridge report had put in motion. The acceptance of consensus politics stretched well beyond the establishment of the welfare state. In foreign affairs support for decolonisation, NATO and the nuclear deterrent were supported by successive governments of whatever political hue. On the domestic front, high public expenditure, full employment, state management of the economy and a reduced role of the market and even nationalisation of many of the basic industries received at least tacit all-party support.

The cracks in this consensus were to appear during the early 1970s, when the Callaghan government was forced by an international economic crisis to acquiesce to an International Monetary Fund loan requirement to reject Keynesian economic principles in the face of stagflation and reduce public spending, control inflation and lower public borrowing. Monetarism had begun, an economic philosophy that was a central policy principle of the early Thatcher years.

The arrival of Mrs Thatcher in Downing Street coincided with a clear need for new policy initiatives to reverse the economic decline of Britain. High inflation and rising unemployment were regarded as reaching critical levels. There was, too, a need to restore the country's prestige in the international arena. The similarities to the problems that were to confront Reagan when he arrived at the White House in 1980 are only too apparent.

Disagreement has been much in evidence whether or not Thatcher's policies constitute a coherent whole that can be regarded as 'Thatcherism'. She certainly had some fundamental beliefs that had a sound theoretical credibility. But these principles were adapted to take account of neo-liberal views and traditional Tory values. Change was also a consequence of 'events, ideas and actors'.[17] The central policy tenet of monetarism was abandoned by 1986 to be replaced by no single theoretical economic doctrine. Although the lady may have professed not to be 'for turning', her term of office was characterised by continual pragmatic and ideological compromises. Political expediency dictated that such actions were necessary.

Privatisation was successful, at least in terms of selling off many of the former nationalised industries. But the 'rolling-back of the state' to reduce the responsibility of government in the market place was continually subjected to reassessment and reversals. The objective was to reduce the tax burden on the electorate and so free capital for investment and expenditure in the market place. The provisions of the welfare state were seen to be particularly excessive. In practice, such expenditure multiplied throughout the 1980s. Rising investment in the Health Service, Education and Social Security payments was significant and in fact this growth was eventually used by the Conservative Party publicity machine to confirm the government's caring image. Thatcher was also determined to reverse the decline in the strength of Britain's defence forces. This, too, inevitably led to significant increases in public expenditure.

Given the nature of the Thatcher government's apparently new political doctrine and subsequent policy initiatives, what place did sport have in the political forums of Whitehall? Despite the obvious attempts at image-creation for Thatcher that party mandarins endeavoured to refine and the creation of a world stateswoman of undisputed stature, her approach to government was significantly different to that of Reagan. She had a detailed grasp of both economic matters and foreign affairs. Her intellect was rarely questioned. Her style of leadership was increasingly presidential, much to the detriment of cabinet government. She consequently was often at odds with her ministers. Her increasing reliance on external advisers and forceful interference in departmental activities was to alienate many and lead to serious rifts and eventually the departure of many senior ministers. Her intervention in all aspects of government stems from many factors. She had a forceful character and was a workaholic. She invariably used her advisers and think-tanks with skill and certainly had a definitive, ideological basis to her policies.

What then was the place and role of sport in the government of this ideologist? British traditions, like those of America, have made successive governments during the twentieth century reluctant to intervene directly in the field of sport. The pluralist basis of sports administration has until recently been either respected or deemed a generally no-go area for political action. British politicians have also avoided, with the possible exception of the current prime minister, John Major, any real overt association with sport. Attendance at an FA Cup Final, Wimbledon, or involvement in yachting were acceptable. But the close identifying with sportsmen and women and successful teams has not been anywhere near as popular a political stratagem undertaken in the UK by senior politicians as in the USA. Thatcher was no exception. In her speech during the Maastrict Summit debate in parliament on 20 November 1991, she indicated that her political style had 'required the occasional use of the handbag', but as the *Guardian's* report suggested, '... now it would have to be done with a cricket bat'.

Any possible interest in popular sports has been well disguised. An association with the Scottish FA Cup competition was an action out of character. A visit to the illfated Commonwealth Games in Edinburgh was a duty that proved to be a political embarrassment. A photo-call with perhaps one of this country's most controversial footballers, Paul Gascoigne, again proved to be somewhat of an embarrassment when he wrapped his arm around her. Unlike Reagan, she had no store of sporting anecdotes, analogies or one-liners which she was ready to use to win over an audience. This was not her style of politics. It is also doubtful if any British audience would accept such an approach, or be influenced by this form of rhetoric.

Nevertheless in her own way, Mrs Thatcher has significantly altered the sporting agenda in Britain and has shown a readiness both to use sport for political ends and to intervene in the sports context when she deemed it necessary. Under Thatcher, sport was used and arguably abused in a very definite, if selective manner. Sport to Thatcher appeared to be a political tool just like any other. Sport was also an arena for forceful intervention when circumstances necessitated, but rarely as an image enhancer.

The imposition of public spending cuts in the leisure sector by the Thatcher government, especially that undertaken by the embattled local authorities, as part of welfare economies, was considered inevitable; a case of 'last in ... first out'. The 1975 White Paper published by the then Labour government, had been seen as a significant watershed for sport as it revealed a government acceptance that the principle of social democratisation should be extended to sport. This area of public-sector policy was now regarded as 'a part of the general fabric of the social services'.[18] It accepted that government, through local authorities and such government agencies as the Sports Council, had a responsibility to promote and market sport to satisfy not only existing demand, but also latent demand among inactive individuals and groups. But the reversal under Thatcher of this expansive leisure policy was not as dramatic as expected. Certainly public expenditure, with respect to leisure provision, was reduced, but throughout the economic crises of the 1980s, local authorities continued to invest hundreds of millions of pounds in sport, particularly in sports and recreation facilities. The likelihood that investment, in what was traditionally a 'Cinderella' area of state involvement, would suffer seriously in a period of severe economic distress when cost-benefit analysis ruled did not occur.

Thatcher and the Conservatives saw themselves very much as the party of law and order and consequently this area of policy action received much attention. The state of the economy during the 1980s and the social, as well as economic distress associated with unemployment, were considered by Thatcher to be potential problems that could give rise to serious social disorder. The problems were compounded by growing racial tension and it was in the inner cities that the possible flash-points were considered most likely to occur. Investment cuts in the provision of recreation facilities or opportunities were thought potentially to deepen the crisis. The policy consequence of these beliefs was that leisure expenditure by local authorities, though reduced, was maintained at a significantly high level. Additional funding for leisure provision also came through various government agencies, in particular Manpower Services, the Urban Programme and the Sports Council.

Support for the creation of 'priority areas' and 'positive discrimination' in favour of specific social groups with respect to leisure expenditure in order to alleviate social tensions and reduce delinquency and vandalism had a long history through the 1970s and 1980s. The House of Lords report on 'Leisure', published in 1973, the 1975 government White Paper on 'Sport and Recreation' and the 1977 'Policy for the Inner Cities' White Paper had all justified public expenditure for this reason. During the 1980s, the Thatcher government vigorously pursued a policy of inner-city regeneration, which included recreational facilities and opportunity investment, in support of social order considerations. The arguments in favour of such investment were to be reinforced by the 'Scarman Report' on the inner-city riots of 1981.

Public investment in leisure by the Thatcher government thus continued a policy initiative begun under Labour in the 1970s. But the significant difference now was that justification swung away from provision 'as need' in support of welfare principles to provision 'as a means'; a means to maintain public order. The mark of Thatcherism on leisure-expenditure was confirmed. Her concern for the maintenance of public order became further apparent when she intervened personally in the football hooliganism debate.

The problem of football-crowd violence was not a new one, when in 1985 the tragic scenes at the Heysel Stadium in Belgium, culminating in the death of thirty-nine spectators following the outbreak of serious crowd disorder, were beamed live to a reputed worldwide TV audience of 100 million. But the horror of the occasion and the potential embarrassment for the government and the Prime Minister in particular, as Britain was once more seen to be exporting its football hooligan problem abroad, prompted direct intervention by Mrs Thatcher. The consequent embarrassment experienced by the Prime Minister following the Heysel Stadium incident was not a new experience for Mrs Thatcher. She had been visiting Italy in 1980 when crowd disorder during the European Football Championships, also in Italy, was attributed to English supporters.

The loss of life at the Heysel Stadium and the further fatalities that occurred in 1989 at the Hillsborough ground, home of Sheffield Wednesday football club, prevented the problem of crowd disorder at football matches disappearing from the political agenda. It was apparent, in the opinion of Mrs Thatcher, that the football authorities were either unwilling or incapable of finding any solution to the problem. It appeared to her that the machinery of government had to be mobilised to find a solution, or at least to contain the problem. Her eventual response was a Football Spectators Bill which was pushed through parliament despite widespread opposition. The football authorities failed to convince her that the problem was not one associated purely with football. The problem in their opinion was a manifestation of a much deeper social malaise. The public debate that surrounded the passage of this bill is well documented elsewhere.[19] So too are the implications of Mrs Thatcher's demand for all English football clubs to be withdrawn from European competitions. What is important here is the blatant way that sport was once more the battlefield on which the law and order debate was fought. The then recent social disorder associated with the miners' strike strengthened her resolve to maintain a high profile for this law and order debate.

A week after the Heysel Stadium disaster Mrs Thatcher rose in the House of Commons to outline her proposed five-point plan to contain the problem of crowd disorder. The actual passage of the Bill through parliament was handled by her Minister for Sport, Colin Moynihan, but it was evident that Thatcher was in control.

This personal identification with the Football Spectators Bill was, however, to rebound on Mrs Thatcher. The Taylor Report on the Hillsborough incident rejected the core element of the Bill, namely the proposed football club membership scheme.

The characteristic forceful intervention of Mrs Thatcher in policy implementation, which was much in evidence during the passage of the Football Spectators Bill, had been similarly apparent earlier in her administration in 1980, again in the sports arena. The major debate in international politics in 1980 was the Soviet Union's actions in Afghanistan. It was not only the intervention of that country in the domestic affairs of another sovereign state, but also the reported atrocities perpetrated there that aroused international concern. Direct action was impossible by either the British or American governments. In an endeavour to cause as much embarrassment to the Soviet government as possible the Carter administration in the USA implemented a boycott of the forthcoming Olympic Games in Moscow that summer. Mrs Thatcher intervened personally in support of the American Games boycott and called on British athletes and the British Olympic Association to boycott the Games also.

The very limited success of this British boycott is again well documented history, but its significance less so. The real diplomatic value of the American boycott in influencing the government of the USSR, according to a study by J. H. Frey,[20] was minimal. He revealed that analysis of top-level contacts between the USA and USSR governments around the time of the Moscow Games made no reference to the boycott. The use of sport in this context was more for media and public consumption.

The consequence for the British political scene was not only an early indication of Thatcher's tendency to become involved directly in a wide range of policy matters, but also her willingness to ride roughshod over the heads of her ministers. The then Minister for Sport, Hector Munroe, was not even called to speak in the House of Commons debate on the Moscow Olympics, held in March 1980.

For Mrs Thatcher her intervention into the sporting arena proved to be a political disaster. Although she was not prepared to go as far as Jimmy Carter in withdrawing the British competitors from the Games, she did consider seizing the passports of British competitors until advised as to the likely illegality of such an action. Attempts to persuade the British Olympic Association to refuse to send a team met with a frosty response.

Threats of dismissal were even made to members of the British team who were public employees if they chose to take their holidays at a time that would allow them to travel to Moscow for the Games. Several of the athletes faced with this threat resigned from their jobs rather than acquiesce to this overt pressure. In the end, with only a limited number of enforced absences, a British team attended the Games, competing under the Olympic flag. For the British government and Mrs Thatcher in particular, the entire incident was an embarrassment; an example of political naivety and a failed attempt to bring British sport in to the Cold-War political arena.

Five years later, when the Heysel Stadium incident was debated in Cabinet, it was Mrs Thatcher and her senior ministers who were involved, not Colin Moynihan. Moynihan had, as Macfarlane suggested, 'become a member of the smallest and most unimportant trade union in the House, the Trade Union of Ministers with special responsibility for Sport'.[21]

The forceful diplomatic stand that Mrs Thatcher took with respect to the Soviet intervention into Afghanistan and her support for the American boycott of the Moscow Olympics contrasts with her position on South Africa. She maintained the support of the British government for the Gleneagles Agreement signed by Callaghan in 1977, which discouraged sporting links with South Africa. But she has often been criticised as selective in her isolation policy with respect to that country by maintaining diplomatic and trade links. Sport was apparently an easy public policy weapon, without any real diplomatic or political recoil, to express the British government's opposition to another country's conduct in its domestic affairs.

Mrs Thatcher's reluctance to take such a firm stand over sporting contacts with South Africa as she had with respect to the USSR in 1980, along with her obvious eagerness to avoid bringing South Africa to its knees through the imposition of economic sanctions, alienated many of the member nations of the British Commonwealth. The policy consequence was for many of these nations was the boycott of the 1986 Commonwealth Games in Edinburgh. Mrs Thatcher was held to be personally responsible for their absence from the Games.

There are several other areas where sport has experienced the consequences of 'Thatcherism'. These have occurred when reforms such as compulsory competitive tendering, local management of schools, the 'opting-out' of schools from local authority control and actual local authority restructuring have been implemented. In addition, the current debate over the national curriculum in physical education bears the imprint of Thatcherism. But it is important to appreciate a subtle, yet important difference here. Sport is affected in these instances as a consequence of policy, rather than being used as an instrument of policy implementation.

A final consideration must be the relationship of Mrs Thatcher to the Sports Council. She came to power with a 'New Right' ideological belief that government 'Quangos' (Quasi-autonimous non-governmental organisations) should be curtailed in power and number. The reality was that after eleven years in office the importance of such bodies was not significantly reduced. In particular, the Sports Council remained in existence, with an enhanced role and much increased grant from government. However, it too did not remain isolated from the tentacles of Thatcherism. Increasingly the Council was subjected to 'clientism' as successive Ministers for Sport, closely directed by Mrs Thatcher, more rigidly interpreted the Council's Royal Charter and regarded the body as an 'executive arm of government'. In particular the Council increasingly mirrored the government's stance on the role of sport in the maintenance of public order. A coincidental policy-match or an example of the guiding hand of government? Have the most appropriate policy initiatives for sport that the Sports Council should have been pursuing, been compromised or stifled as a result of government interference?

The hand of Thatcher with respect to sport, despite her apparent indifference to the activity itself, was clearly evident during her premiership. Sport was used and perhaps abused in a very distinctive manner. The jury remains out, however, still considering its verdict on the consequences of her policies for sport.

Thus two highly visible politicians, Margaret Thatcher and Ronald Reagan, have in their own particular manner utilised sport as a valuable medium to further their own political objectives. They both left office when their finest hours were perhaps already behind them. But they have left a political legacy that is both significant in terms of policy successes as well as failures, and also in terms of style. 'The Gipper' and the 'Iron lady' have assured themselves a place in the annals of both political, as well as sporting, history.

Notes

1 Lou Cannon, *President Reagan The Role of a Lifetime*. Simon and Schuster, 1991, p. 27.
2 Paul Erikson, *Reagan Speaks*. New York University Press, 1985, p. 41.
3 See Terry Monnington, 'The politics of black African sport', in Lincoln Allison, ed., *The Politics of Sport*, Manchester University Press, 1986, pp. 149–173.
4 L. Cannon, *op. cit.*, p. 123.
5 *Ibid.*, p. 460.
6 *Ibid.*, p. 495.
7 P. Erikson, *op. cit.*, p. 109.
8 *Ibid.*, p. 106.
9 L. Cannon, *op. cit.*, p. 495.
10 P. Erikson, *op. cit.*, p. 106.
11 Alan Tomlinson and Garry Whannel, eds, *Five Ring Circus*, Pluto Press, 1984, p. 28.
12 L. Cannon, *op. cit.*, p. 673.
13 *Ibid.*, p. 674.
14 *Ibid.*, p. 515.
15 *Ibid.*, p. 464.
16 *Ibid.*, p. 464.
17 Dennis Kavanagh, *Thatcherism and British Politics*. Oxford University Press, 1987, p. 17.
18 Department of the Enviroment, *Sport and Recreation*, Cmnd. 6200, 1975, p. 1.
19 See Barrie Houlihan, *The Government and Politics of Sport*, Routledge, 1991.
20 Reported in Jay Coakley, *Sport in Society: Issuses and Controversies*, Times Mirror/Mosby Col. Publishing, 1990.
21 Neil McFarlane, *Sport and Politics*, Collins/Willow, 1986, p. 63.

8

Sport and the end of *apartheid*

ADRIAN GUELKE

Without reform, South Africa hasn't got a sporting chance. Vote yes on March 17 and keep South Africa in the game' – Advertisement of the Private Sector Initiative during the South African referendum campaign in 1992.[1]

The role played by sport in the referendum among South Africa Whites on whether to continue with the reform process started by President de Klerk owed much to the accidental coincidence in timing between the campaign and the cricket World Cup. By polling day the South African cricket team had exceeded all expectations in reaching the semi-finals. The advertisement quoted above showed a deserted and overgrown cricket field with broken wickets and contrasted that with South African cricketers celebrating their victory over Australia at the start of the competition. The message that a 'no' vote would mean an instant return to total sporting isolation was underlined by the declaration by the President of the United Cricket Board of South Africa that the South African team would have no alternative but to withdraw from the competition if de Klerk was defeated.[2] Billboards at the grounds where the South African cricket team played urged South Africa to vote yes.[3] The unexpected landslide in favour of reform in the referendum was made possible, in part, by a very high turnout among English-speaking voters, who responded to an extensive advertising campaign that aroused their fears of international isolation in the event of a 'no' majority. Sport played a prominent part in this campaign, since it was one area in which the reform process had brought the Whites benefits at little or no cost.

General White acceptance of the principle of racial integration in sport made it a wholly unproductive issue for the 'no' campaign.

Superficially, South Africa's return to international sport constitutes a reward for the country's abandonment of the policy of *apartheid* and this is simply the other side of the coin of the country's sporting isolation as a punishment for *apartheid*. From this perspective, *apartheid* politicised the country's sporting relations with the outside world and the abandonment of the policy has permitted their normalisation. In practice, this simple view of the course of South Africa's sporting relations with the rest of the world requires considerable qualification. Firstly, the country's isolation was never total. A few sporting codes were hardly affected by boycotts, particularly those of an individual rather than a team character or those, such as ocean-going yachting, where participation tended to be confined to the wealthy of the First World. Even during the political unrest in the mid 1980s sporting events in South Africa attracted foreign participants. For example, according to the annual report of the Department of National Education, 2,807 foreign sportsmen, sportswomen and coaches visited South Africa in 1985. In the same year 1,691 South African sportsmen, sportswomen and coaches travelled abroad.[4]

Secondly, the intensity of the country's isolation often bore little relationship either to the degree of *apartheid* practised in the sport in question or to the general level of social segregation in South Africa. The first decade of the policy of *apartheid* after the National Party came to power in 1948 had very little impact upon South Africa's international sporting relations. The International Table Tennis Federation was wholly exceptional in invoking sanctions against South Africa over the practice of *apartheid* in the sport in 1956. In fact, the country's sporting isolation in the 1970s and 1980s coincided with, as well as contributed towards, the beginnings of the erosion of *apartheid*, particularly in the realm of social segregation. However, the gradual – and partial – relaxation of social segregation was followed by an intensification rather than any easing of the country's sporting isolation. As recently as July 1989, sports ministers from twenty-three countries belonging to the Council of Europe meeting in Reykjavik unanimously adopted a statement condemning the continuation of sporting contacts with South Africa and criticising countries which had failed to cut all sporting ties with South Africa. In the same month, Canada strengthened still further its sports boycott of South Africa by extending its application to sporting contacts between Canadians and South Africans anywhere in the world.[5]

Thirdly, South Africa's readmission (or admission, as anti-*apartheid* groups prefer to term it) to international competition has only been weakly related to the conditions prevailing in individual sporting codes, though the organisational framework governing individual codes has played an important role in securing entry/re-entry into international competition. This point is developed further below. Fourthly, the transformation in the international position of South African sport is the result of complex political manoeuvring by the main political factions in the country and is a far cry from the depoliticisation of sport. In no sport has the transformation been so dramatic as in that of cricket and no sport provides a better illustration of the continuing salience of politics to sport and vice versa than cricket. In November 1991, South Africa played three one-day test matches against India, the first in Calcutta where the visitors were greeted by a standing ovation from a record crowd. India won the series by two matches to one. The South African cricket team's official tour of India took place at short notice following the cancellation of a planned tour by Pakistan after threats by Hindu fundamentalists to the Pakistani players. That South African cricket's emergence from isolation should take place in India was the more remarkable considering the absence of formal ties between India and South Africa, dating back to India's diplomatic breach with South Africa in 1948.

The path for South Africa's entry/re-entry into international cricket in 1991 had been cleared by the reorganisation of South African cricket into the United Cricket Board of South Africa (UCBSA) in June, the consequent admission of the UCBSA into the International Cricket Council (ICC) in July, and the lifting of the moratorium on international sporting links by the National Olympic and Sports Congress on 1 October. A final obstacle was cleared with the decision of the Commonwealth Heads of Government meeting in Harare to lift immediately people-to-people sanctions later the same month. Included under this rubric were sanctions on travel, tourism and air links, on cultural, academic and scientific exchanges, and on sport. The lifting of sporting sanctions was made subject to the condition of the consent of the approporiate sports bodies in South Africa. The decision was in line with the recommendations of the Commonwealth foreign ministers' meeting in New Delhi in September for a phased easing of sanctions, starting with people-to-people sanctions.

By the time the UCBSA received the invitation from the Board of Control for Cricket in India, South African participation in the World Cup in Australia and New Zealand in 1992 was already assured as a result of the unanimous decision of a meeting of the ICC in Sharjah in October. Further, India had agreed to a nine-week tour of South Africa starting in November 1992 and the test series with India was to be followed by a shorter four-week tour of South Africa by Pakistan. These prospects were reflected in the way that the UCBSA presented its acceptance of the invitation as a special favour to the Indians. The managing director of the UCBSA, Ali Bacher, explained that South Africa was not too well-prepared in purely cricketing terms to undertake a tour, but that the UCBSA had felt morally obliged to lend a hand.

> [The Indians] had learnt with deep disappointment that the tour by Pakistan had been cancelled and the Indian public has been starved of international cricket since about 1988. While we were [in India] we were approached by not only Modhavrao Scindia, the Board of Control for Cricket in India president, and the Minister of Civil Aviation and Tourism, but also by ANC representatives in India and the leader of the the Indian anti-apartheid movement. They all pleaded for us to tour.[6]

In 1988 the Test and County Cricket Board cancelled a tour by England of India because of the Indian Government's policy to refuse to admit players blacklisted by the United Nations over their sporting links with South Africa.

But notwithstanding Bacher's show of reluctance about the tour, the invitation to India represented a remarkable change in the position of South African cricket compared to the situation twenty months earlier when demonstrations had forced the curtailment of a tour of South Africa by a rebel England cricket team led by Mike Gatting. That tour had been a nightmare for Bacher and other representatives of the South African cricketing establishment. Plans for the rebel tour emerged publicly in July 1989 after the South African Cricket Union (SACU) had been denied a hearing by the ICC to put its case for readmission. In August, the British sports minister, Colin Moynihan, made an appeal to cricketers not to go to South Africa, arguing that the tour presented a threat to the Commonwealth Games. In September, the Anti-Apartheid Movement staged a demonstration outside Lords cricket ground to protest against the tour. The criticism of the tour in Britain was not without effect. Phillip Defreitas and Roland Butcher pulled out of the team, after they came under intense pressure from the Black community in Britain not to undermine the campaign against apartheid by their participation. In general, there was little sympathy for the rebels. The tour was seen as damaging to England's future test prospects since under the policy that the ICC had adopted in January, a player who went to South Africa as a member of an unofficial national team faced a five-year ban from test cricket. Consequently, it appeared that the rebels were putting the opportunity to make a lot of money out of the South African situation ahead of representing their country. But the reaction the rebels encountered in England was mild in comparison with the reception the tourists received when they arrived in South Africa.

The rebels arrived in South Africa on 19 January 1990. A mass protest had been arranged to greet them at their point of arrival, Jan Smuts airport outside Johannesburg. Police roadblocks succeeded in preventing several thousand demonstrators from reaching the airport, but a group of about 150 managed to evade the roadblocks and to get into the airport, where singing and chanting they were confronted by police wielding batons and using dogs. Forty demonstrators were injured in the mêlée. There were further large demonstrations outside the grounds where the rebels played. At two of the luxury hotels the rebels stayed in, there were protest strikes by staff belonging to the South African Commercial, Catering and Allied Workers Union. In an effort to defuse the situation, the managing director of SACU, Dr Ali Bacher, had talks with the police urging them to exercise restraint in their handling of demonstrations. After riots followed police action to prevent a march on De Beers Country Club in Kimberley, he even approached a magistrate to get permission for those against the tour to hold a protest outside the grounds. He did the same in Bloemfontein, where eight hundred people took part in a protest outside the city's cricket ground on 30 January. The game itself attracted a crowd of only 150 spectators.[7]

The tour coincided with a watershed in the political history of the country. On 2 February, President de Klerk announced the unbanning of the African National Congress (ANC), the Pan-Africanist Congress (PAC), and the South African Communist Party and the lifting of restrictions on thirty-three other organisations. On 11 February Nelson Mandela was released from jail. In the context of these momentous events, the confrontation over the tour seemed an unwelcome distraction from more important issues facing the country. On 14 February Bacher announced that the tour was being curtailed. In return the National Sports Congress (NSC), the organisation behind the demonstrations against the rebels, had agreed not to hold protests at the tour's remaining games. Bacher revealed that a third party had lent on both SACU and the NSC to find a solution. He accepted that the tour had been divisive and that SACU had underestimated the feeling against it. He said that SACU had decided to shorten the tour 'to show its support for the dramatic changes' announced by the President on 2 February.[8] At the same time, plans for the rebel team's second visit due to start in November 1990 were left in abeyance.

The opposition that Gatting's rebel team encountered was on a scale much greater than any previous such side in any sport had faced in South Africa. There had been six main rebel cricket tours during the 1980s. An England team, nicknamed the Dirty Dozen by the press, visited South Africa in 1982 following an official England tour of India. It was followed by a team from Sri Lanka. In January 1983, a rebel team from the West Indies arrived for a short tour. At the end of the year there was a second and longer tour by the rebels from the West Indies. This pattern was repeated two years later with an Australian side visiting South Africa in the 1985–6 season and again in 1986–7. There was considerable unrest in South Africa through the mid-1980s, reflected in the existence of a state of emergency during both Australian tours. SACU's President claimed that the tours had lifted spirits by taking people's minds off caspirs (vehicles the police used to quell unrest) and burning tyres. By contrast, at the end of the first tour the captain of the Australian rebels, Kim Hughes, was quoted in the South African press as describing South Africa as a peaceful country compared to India, Pakistan, and the West Indies (*sic*). Controversy was also generated by the very large sum of money each of the visitors received to take part in the tours. There were attempts to disrupt the second tour by a group calling itself the Commando of Angry Sportspersons. Before the arrival of the tourists, the Commando poured oil on the pitch at Newlands and daubed the ground with slogans. There were a number of other relatively minor incidents during the tour itself.[9]

Rebel tours constituted one of the principal strategies of establishment (or White-dominated) sports bodies seeking to counter the country's sporting isolation during the 1980s. While the main aim of the strategy was simply to provide South African teams with international competition they would otherwise be denied, it was also hoped that the tours would damage the credibility of the boycotts against South African sport and disrupt the consensus that existed among foreign sports bodies on links with South Africa. Through the 1980s the South African cricketing establishment, in particular, hoped for a split in world cricket on racial lines over the issue that would permit the return of South Africa to international competition, at least with the 'White' states. In 1985 Graeme Pollock, a leading figure in South African cricket whose test career as one of the world's finest batsmen had been cut short by South Africa's isolation, candidly admitted that this was one of the purposes behind the organisation of rebel tours, declaring: 'The more disruptions we can make in world cricket, the better it will be for us in the long term.'[10] There were times during the 1980s when the organisation of world cricket must have appeared to the administrators of SACU tantalisingly close to a breakdown. For example, in July 1983 an attempt by the Conservative MP John Carlisle to persuade the MCC to undertake a cricket tour of South Africa was defeated by MCC members, who supported the committee's opposition to the proposal by 6,604 votes to 4,344.[11]

An obvious disadvantage of the strategy of rebel tours was that it tended to alienate foreign sports administrators because of the disruption rebel tours caused. That made it more difficult for South African establishment sports bodies to win support for reconsideration of the boycott on the grounds of a particular sport's progress towards integrated sport since the ban on South African participation in international competition in the sport in question had been imposed. Attempts to convince the outside world that fundamental change had taken place in the organisation of South African sport was the main strategy pursued by establishment sports bodies during the 1970s. This strategy encountered three major obstacles: the limits to integration permitted by government policy and White sporting opinion; the stance of the non-racial sports movement within South Africa, which supported a moratorium on South African participation in international competition; and, finally, acceptance by much of international opinion of the argument that *apartheid* off the field of play prevented properly integrated sport in South Africa. South Africa's sporting isolation itself prompted changes in government policy, but change came step by step and too slowly to halt the trend towards isolation, let alone to reverse the trend.

In the 1970s 'multinational' sport was the rubric under which the government allowed integration to take place. Initially, it applied only to top-level competitions involving foreign participants. Then the requirement of a foreign presence was dropped in the case of sports unable to attract overseas participants to 'open internationals'. In 1976 the government extended the principle of 'multinational' competition to sport at club level. The South African Cricket Association (SACA) interpreted the new policy as permitting fully integrated sport at club level and entered into negotiations with the non-racial sports body, the South African Cricket Board of Control, to normalise cricket on this basis. Mixed leagues were established. However, the effort to unify cricket at this juncture foundered after government policy was clarified as intended to allow matches between clubs of different races, but not the establishment of multi-racial clubs. To the dismay of supporters of non-racial cricket this interpretation of the limits of the policy was not challenged by SACA. It merely sought guidance on the possibility of individual exceptions. That destroyed the prospects for unity, despite the creation of the South African Cricket Union with a formally non-racial constitution. But while the government made clear its opposition to multi-racial clubs, it did not legislate against their existence as such. Indeed, the government made much of the right of any sports club to determine its membership in its overseas propaganda outlining the new sports policy. Of course, this principle cut two ways. On the one hand, it made it possible for clubs to become multi-racial in their membership, though they still remained subject to laws limiting social integration, such as the Liquor Act. On the other hand, it also underscored the right of clubs to restrict their membership on racial grounds. The Minister of Sport and Recreation, Piet Koornhof, fended off right-wing pressure from inside the National Party to outlaw multi-racial clubs by claiming a 99.9955 per cent success rate in achieving the objective of the government's new sports policy to discourage multi-racial clubs, while allowing competition between White and Black clubs.[12]

After the confusion caused by the new sports policy and political unrest in South Africa in 1976 and 1977, there was a distinct hardening of opinion within the non-racial sports movement in South Africa. It was encapsulated in the slogan that there could be 'no normal sport in an abnormal society'.[13] Further changes in the government's sports policy, its adoption of the principle of sporting autonomy and amendments to the Group Areas Act, the Liquor Act and the Black Urban Areas Consolidation Act to prevent these acts from impinging on sporting events, failed to end the division between establishment and non-racial sports bodies in South Africa or to persuade international sports bodies to end the boycotts. Rebel tours constituted one of the responses of establishment sports bodies to the impasse. Another response, as sports administrators and the competitors themselves came to accept that an end to the country's sporting isolation depended upon more general social and political change within South Africa, was increased criticism of *apartheid* in general from those involved in sports. It was particularly marked during the 1987 election campaign for the White House of Assembly. The National Party was strongly criticised for damaging sport by prominent sports personalities, such as Tommy Bedford, a former Springbok rugby captain. At the same time, voters were urged to support the 'reform alliance', consisting of the Progressive Federal Party, the New Republic Party and a number of prominent independent candidates. The President of the South African Rugby Board (SARB), Dr Danie Craven, was the most prominent signatory of the 'Stellenbosch statement' issued shortly before polling day. It declared:

> We Stellenbosch sportsmen and women will support and encourage others to support those in party-political contests, including independent candidates, who are united in a common search for sincere and urgent initiatives to ensure a normal and peaceful life for all South Africans.[14]

But while the independent candidate in Stellenbosch did well (without winning the seat), in the country as a whole there was a sharp swing to the right among White voters.

Despite the outcome of the election, the stance that some of those involved in the organisation of sport had taken against *apartheid* during the campaign did not go unnoticed. In the mid-1980s South Africa was in the grip of a political crisis. In August 1984 'Coloured' and Indian voters had given massive support to a well-organised boycott of the first elections under a new constitution which established a 'Coloured' House of Representatives and an Indian House of Delegates alongside the existing White House of Assembly. They thereby destroyed the legitimacy of the new dispensation at a stroke. At the same time, there was unrest in the African townships leading in July 1985 to the declaration of a state of emergency in many areas. Unfavourable international reaction to the government's handling of the situation, especially after President Botha disappointed expectations that he would announce major reforms in a speech to the Natal provincial congress of the National Party, prompted a collapse in the value of the South African currency the following month. These difficulties led to calls from the more liberal sections of White opinion in the country for the government to enter into negotiations with the ANC. Although the ANC had been a banned organisation since 1960, it was widely accepted by the government's critics that the organisation enjoyed mass support among Blacks. For its part, the ANC was keen to forge alliances with Whites opposed to *apartheid*.

In September 1985, a delegation of prominent South African businessmen headed by the chairman of the Anglo-American Corporation, Gavin Relly, held talks with ANC leaders at the organisation's headquarters in Zambia. The next month the ANC leadership in exile met a delegation from the Progressive Federal Party. Delegations of clergy, students and members of trade unions followed. There were further 'safaris' to talk to the ANC in 1986 and 1987, including a meeting in Dakar, Senegal in July 1987 between an eighteen member ANC delegation and a delegation of mainly Afrikaans-speaking politicians, journalists, academics and clergy. The two delegations issued a joint communiqué supporting a negotiated settlement and calling for the unbanning of the ANC and the release of political prisoners. In 1988 sport became part of this process. In September Dr Danie Craven revealed that members of the ANC had been present at a meeting between a representative of the South African Rugby Board and African sports officials earlier in the year. In October Craven himself met with ANC officials and representatives of the non-racial South African Rugby Union in Harare. It was agreed that SARB and SARU should establish a single non-racial controlling body for the sport. The ANC for its part 'undertook to use its good offices to ensure that non-racial South African rugby takes its rightful place in world rugby'.[15] The clear implication of the ANC's position was that it was prepared to countenance South African participation in international sport well in advance of the complete dismantling of *apartheid* and the establishment of majority rule.

The Harare meeting provoked a storm of protest. It caused a split in the SARB executive committee. The Vice-President, Fritz Eloff, ironically also at the time chairman of the International Rugby Board, criticised Craven for making a joint statement with a 'terrorist organisation'.[16] (This was a common theme of Craven's critics, as in July two people had been killed and thirty-five injured in a car bomb outside Ellis Park, Johnnesburg's main rugby stadium. The attack had been widely attributed to the ANC. Without denying that the attack might have been carried out by agents it had trained, the ANC condemned the bombing as contrary to its policy on civilian targets.) The government's adoption of a policy of sporting autonomy had led to the abolition of the Department of Sports and Leisure and the inclusion of a Directorate for Sports Advancement within the Department of National Education. Consequently, the Minister of National Education (F. W. de Klerk) led the government's attack on Craven's meeting with the ANC. De Klerk described the talks as 'absolutely unacceptable' and arranged a meeting with SARB's executive committee to convey the government's opposition.[17] At the same time, the ANC ran into a measure of criticism from anti-*apartheid* groups inside and outside South Africa for creating confusion by its statements and thereby undermining the sports boycott.

In the event, the ANC's initiative on rugby ran into the sand. SARB and SARU failed to resolve their differences and the prospect of unity between the sports bodies faded with SARB's preparations for the celebration of the centenary of rugby in South Africa. Its plans included two tests between the Springboks and a World XV. As this represented a major breach of the sports boycott, it inevitably led to conflict between SARB and the anti-*apartheid* lobby, including the London-based South African Non-Racial Olympic Committee (SANROC). None the less, the games took place in September 1989, without serious incident or the dire consequences for international sport that the chairman of SANROC, Sam Ramsamy, had predicted if they went ahead. In South Africa, in spite of the use of the state of emergency to discourage protests there were several demonstrations against the World XV before and during the tour. First National Bank, which sponsored the games, was the main target of the demonstrations. The ANC's intervention in sport was not confined to rugby. It also acted as an intermediary between soccer's various governing bodies with the objective of setting in train the creation of a single, non-racial body for soccer in South Africa.

The ANC's external initiatives in the field of sport were linked to significant developments within the non-racial sports movement inside South Africa. Since it was set up in 1973, the South African Council of Sport (SACOS) had acted as an umbrella organisation for the movement. SACOS supported strict adherence to the international sports boycott of South Africa and to the principles of non-racialism within the country. It barred membership to any organisation participating in 'multinational' sport. It also banned its affiliates from using facilities requiring a permit under the Group Areas Act. Its policy of non-collaboration with *apartheid* structures even extended for a time to placing sporting facilities at Black universities out of bounds to its affiliates. There was also disagreement within the organisation before the training of coaches overseas for SACOS affiliates was accepted as permissible in terms of the international boycott of South Africa. SACOS shunned any business in receipt of government funds. The practical effect of SACOS's high-minded application of its principles was limited influence over the mass of Blacks who participated in sport in circumstances that made compliance with SACOS's rules difficult if not impossible.

During the 1970s there was little criticism of SACOS from anti-*apartheid* groups as it was seen as an important symbol of resistance to *apartheid* and because the organisation was credited with helping to secure the international isolation of South Africa's establishment sports bodies. However, the growth of trade unions based in the Black working class in the 1980s led to a much more critical view of SACOS's whole approach. Trade unions were used to bargaining within the system and saw deals with employers, local authorities or even the government itself as the way by which they advanced the interests of their members and increased their power and influence. Trade union leaders increasingly came to regard SACOS's policy of non-collaboration as an obstacle to the development of a mass-based non-racial sports movement.[18] Their concerns gave rise to an initiative in 1988 to establish a new umbrella sports organisation, the National Sports Congress (NSC). It was formally constituted at a conference at the University of Witwatersrand in July 1989. Among those present were representatives of several SACOS affiliates. The conference endorsed as objectives of the NSC the creation of a single non-racial sports movement aligned to the Mass Democratic Movement (MDM), the formation of single national bodies for each sporting code, assistance to communities to improve their sporting facilities and working with the MDM for the dismantling of *apartheid*.

In his address to the conference, the Rector of the University of the Western Cape, Jakes Gerwel, praised the contribution that SACOS had made in the past to non-racial sport, but was candid about the organisation's shortcomings in the context of the changed situation within the country. He began by referring to the meeting between President Botha and Nelson Mandela earlier in the month, placing it in the context of the crisis of the White power bloc and the success of democratic forces in establishing their legitimacy. He then went on to analyse the reasons for 'the non-existence of a vibrant non-racial, mass sports movement'.[19] One of the problems he identified was that 'while SACOS has been able to penetrate the Indian and Coloured communities, it has not really succeeded in penetrating the African townships'.[20] He also pointed out that the non-racial sports movement had failed to attract Whites into its fold, in contrast to the success of the MDM in winning the support of significant numbers of Whites. Finally, he tackled the issue of the moratorium on international tours, arguing that a rethink was necessary in line with the refinement of the objective of the cultural and academic boycott as being to isolate racist South Africa while strengthening democratic initiatives.

The creation of the NSC divided the non-racial sports movement. The main lobby for the boycott abroad, SANROC, also split into two factions, one supporting the founder of the organisation, Dennis Brutus, the majority, Sam Ramsamy. The latter was castigated by South African sports journalists as a hardline isolationist.[21] To add to the complications SACOS decided to set up its own London office. The reason was SANROC's support for the NSC. Amidst all this division, it was evident that the line being espoused by the NSC was in tune with the ANC's general strategy of seeking to maximise its support among Whites and with the ANC's sports initiatives of 1988. The NSC's alignment with the MDM, the ANC's internal ally, underscored the connection. Given the general thrust of the NSC's policies, it was somewhat ironic that its political clout should have first been demonstrated through a show of militancy: the organisation of the opposition to the Gatting tour at the beginning of 1990. The effectiveness of its protests demonstrated the value of its link with the trade union movement through the MDM. But its readiness to accept a compromise over the tour also reflected its political alignment. The third party that Dr Ali Bacher referred to as leaning on both SACU and the NSC to find a solution was not the government, but the ANC. In fact, the government's policy of sporting autonomy has tended to place it on the sidelines in the dramatic process that has brought about South Africa's entry/re-entry into international sporting competition.

The fundamental basis of the process has been the unification of establishment and non-racial bodies in a single national body for each sporting code. Once achieved, international acceptance of the new body (invariably with a new name and set of initials) has usually followed rapidly. To secure unification with their non-racial counterparts, establishment sports bodies have been required to accept the moratorium on tours in the interim. Before unification began to pay dividends in 1991, sports administrators ran into strong criticism for accepting this condition.[22] Less controversially, a programme to promote the sport in the townships has also usually been a part of the deal on unification. A further condition that the non-racial sports movement has imposed has been the abandonment of the symbols associated with the old dispensation (rightly or wrongly): the flag, the national anthem and the Springbok. The dropping of the Springbok has been a particularly emotive issue, especially as the symbol predates not merely *apartheid* but even the establishment of the Union of South Africa in 1910. The Springbok was first used as the emblem of the South African rugby team touring Britain in 1906. Supporters of keeping the Springbok symbol have argued that it is a wholly apolitical indigenous animal, but what has counted against it among Blacks was the attempts as late as the 1970s to restrict the award of Springbok colours to Whites only. The readiness of establishment sports bodies to concede the point for the sake of unity and international competition has infuriated conservative Whites. Typical of right-wing reaction has been the comment of the English-language daily, *Citizen*: 'Alas, our sports administrators have cravenly capitulated to the ANC and must now dance to its tune. Shame on them'.[23]

The sporting arena where symbols have inevitably loomed largest has been the Olympics. The story of how South Africa secured an invitation to the summer games in Barcelona in 1992 parallels cricket's success in gaining entry/re-entry into international competition. The key figure in the process was the chairman of SANROC, Sam Ramsamy. The first step in the process was a meeting in Harare of South African sports administrators. Represented in Harare were five different umbrella sports bodies from inside and outside the country: SANROC, SACOS, the National and Olympic Sports Congress (NOSC) – as NSC had been renamed – the South African National Olympic Committee (SANOC), and the Confederation of South African Sport (COSAS). A steering committee representing the five organisations was set up. At its initiative the National Olympic Committee of South Africa (NOCSA) was established in March 1991, with an interim executive headed by Sam Ramsamy, just ahead of an IOC mission to South Africa. IOC recognition of NOCSA followed with South Africa's full acceptance paving the way to an invitation to Barcelona subject to a number of conditions from compliance with the Olympic Charter to the abolition of *apartheid*. The repeal during 1991 of the laws known as the pillars of *apartheid* – the Land Acts, the Group Areas Act, and the Population Registration Act (even though its repeal does not spell the immediate end of racial classification) – was deemed sufficient to meet the latter condition. On 6 November, Ramsamy was able to announce NOCSA's acceptance of an invitation from the IOC to compete in Barcelona. He explained that representation of particular sports in the team would depend on the existence of a unified controlling body for the sport in question and its support for a programme to tackle the inequalities of provision that had resulted from *apartheid*. He also revealed that the South African team would use a specially designed flag at the Olympics and that

Beethoven's 'Ode to Joy' and not 'Die Stem' would be played for any South African gold-medal winners.

But while South Africa's admission/re-admission to international sport has happened much more quickly than even those most directly involved in the process thought possible, there have been difficulties and disagreements along the way. There was a minor storm over the participation of a South African gymnastics team in world championships in the United States in 1991 in defiance of the moratorium. In this case there was no non-racial counterpart to the establishment controlling body for the sport. At the same time, SACOS and some of its affiliates have resisted the lifting of the moratorium and raised difficulties over unification. For example, the SACOS affiliate, the Tennis Association of South Africa, refused to join the new 'unified' controlling body for tennis, Tennis South Africa, and when the Association of Tennis Professionals World Doubles Championships were held in Johannesburg in November and December 1991, staged a placard demonstration in protest. When difficulties have arisen in the negotiations among the different sporting bodies, the assistance of the ANC has frequently been sought. The key figure from the ANC on sports issues has been Steve Tshwete, a prisoner for fifteen years on Robben Island. In prison he was President of the Robben Island Amateur Athletic Association and of the Robben Island Rugby Board. He has played a crucial role in the process of unification in both cricket and in rugby, which formed a non-racial controlling body in December 1991 paving the way for a tour of South Africa by the All Blacks in 1992.

Sport has clearly been an issue through which the ANC has sought to woo White opinion and initially at least most of the competitiors benefiting from the ending of South Africa's sporting isolation will be White. For example, the cricket team that toured India in November 1991 was entirely White, while the squad for the World Cup contained a single Black player, the veteran Omar Henry. While the idea that there should be token representation in sports teams of Blacks has not won much support and runs counter to the ANC's non-racial philosophy, there has been some dissatisfaction that, for example, the cricket selectors at the provincial level have overlooked the claims of players who competed in the non-racial leagues before unification.[24] Further, the extent of Black South African participation in a particular sport has not been a factor in how quickly the moratorium has been lifted. Ironically, in a sport where Blacks are well represented among the players and which has mass support in the townships, soccer, the sports administrators were slow to reach agreement on the organisational changes needed to secure international recognition, with the consequence of South Africa's exclusion from the draw for the 1994 World Cup. By contrast, the Baltic states managed to secure their place in the preliminary round of the tournament (South Africa was later admitted to the qualifying round after a default.).

Politically, the ANC has won credit in the South African media for its role in ending the country's sporting isolation.[25] However, that has in no way moderated the criticism it has been subjected to from the White establishment for its support for the maintenance of at least some economic sanctions until the process of transition is further advanced. In addition, the ANC has had to share the credit for the sports breakthrough with President de Klerk, whose commitment to the abolition of *apartheid* many have seen as the primary factor in ending South Africa's isolation in sport.[26] Indeed, the government has presented the ending of South Africa's sporting isolation as a prime example of the general crumbling of sanctions in response to President de Klerk's reforms and the ANC's role has by implication been dismissed as the case of an organisation simply making a virtue of its support for the inevitable. A reasonable conclusion is that both the government and the ANC have derived political benefits from the process that has led to the end of South Africa's sporting isolation. The main losers have been the supporters of apartheid on the extreme right. Sport has not provided a persuasive context for the argument that making concessions to international opinion brings no rewards, as the referendum on reform showed. From an international perspective, South Africa's participation in international sport projects the image of a changed society. This is not a false image, but it does tend to obscure the difficulty of the transition that South Africa still faces and which the death of more than six thousand people in political violence since Mandela was released underlines. In areas other than sport White and Black interests are going to be far more difficult to reconcile, notwithstanding White endorsement for the reform process in the warm glow of South Africa's cricketing victories.

The case of *apartheid* in sport has provided one of the most dramatic examples of the intertwining of politics and sport. The issue made household names of Basil D'Oliveira, the Black South African cricketer whom the South African government refused to accept as part of an England touring team in 1968, and Peter Hain, who led the protests against the Springbok rugby team touring the British Isles in 1969–70. Isolation prompted moves towards integration in the sports most affected by boycotts. However, the direct impact on South African politics of the sports issue was relatively slight. The South African government's readiness to accept Black players as part of visiting touring teams, apart from the special case of D'Oliveira, prompted the formation of an extreme right-wing political party, the Herstigte Nasionale Party (HNP) but the party gained very few votes over its objections to any integration in sport. The HNP remained marginalised until 1981 when negative reaction to economic reform boosted its popularity. The National Party lost ground to the United Party among English-speaking voters in the 1970 general election in part owing to the sports boycotts, but the shift of opinion was small, only slightly reducing the government's large majority.

As one of the first areas of social life to be integrated, sport played a prominent role in the unravelling of *apartheid*. But its influence was diffuse. Further, while sport played an important role in puncturing social segregation in the early 1970s, there were other pressures on the South African government to relax the rigid enforcement of petty *apartheid*, such as the country's establishment of diplomatic relations with other African countries. The easing of social segration brought about a change in White attitudes so that by the 1980s the principle of racial integration in sport was widely accepted. At the same time there was growing recognition that it would take more than changes in the organisation of sport to end the boycotts. While this was a factor in the readiness of Whites to accept change in other areas, it was a very minor one. Economic pressures, especially after the passage of the Comprehensive Anti-Apartheid Act by the United States in 1986, loomed much larger in both the thinking of Whites and the calculations of the government. Thus, an explicit objective of the reforms embraced by President de Klerk was to meet the conditions laid down in the American legislation for the lifting of sanctions.

The role that sport has played in the reform process owes much to the desire of the ANC to use sport to convince Whites of the *bona fides* of its non-racial policy. The ANC has been criticised for reversing the boycotts too quickly, permitting South African

participation in international sport before Black voting rights have
been achieved. However, the ANC can point to the outcome of
the 1992 White referendum as a vindication of its strategy.[27]
This is not to underestimate the importance to the government
of sport as a means of promoting international acceptance of the
new South Africa. In practice, this has meant that the interests of
the government and of the ANC in ending the sports boycotts have
tended to coincide. This has a wider significance. Co-operation
between the government and the ANC over the sports issue has
provided a positive model of what might be achieved with the
establishment of a more harmonious political relationship between
the two. As such, it has served as a much needed source of hope
for a country deeply affected by recession, drought, a high level
of political violence and widespread uncertainty about what the
future holds.

Notes

1 *The Weekly Mail*, Johannesburg, 6–12 March 1992.
2 *The Irish Times*, Dublin, 18 March 1992.
3 *The Star Weekly*, Johannesburg, 4 March 1992.
4 *Department of National Education: Annual Report*, Pretoria, 1986, p. 50.
5 Carole Cooper *et al.*, *Race Relations Survey 1989/90*, South African Institute
   of Race Relations, Johannesburg, 1990, p. 18.
6 Trevor Chesterfield, 'South African cricketers lend a hand', *The Star Weekly*,
   Johannesburg, 6 November 1991.
7 Cooper *et al.* (1990), *op. cit.*, p. 24.
8 *Ibid.*, p. 25.
9 Carole Cooper *et al.*, *Race Relations Survey 1986: Part 1*, South African
   Institute of Race Relations, Johannesburg, 1987, p. 302.
10 *The Age*, Melbourne, 20 December 1985.
11 Lincoln Allison, ed., *The Politics of Sport*, Manchester University Press,
   1986, p. 139.
12 Loraine Gordon *et al.*, *A Survey of Race Relations in South Africa 1977*, South
   African Institute of Race Relations (Johannesburg), 1978, p. 559.
13 A slogan coined by Hassan Howa of the South African Cricket Board. See Basil
   D'Oliveira (with Patrick Murphy), *Time to Declare*, Dent, 1980, pp. 146–7.
14 *Sunday Times*, Johannesburg, 3 May 1987.
15 *The Times*, London, 17 October 1988.
16 *The Star Weekly*, Johannesburg, 16 November 1988.
17 *The Star*, Johannesburg, 2 November 1988.
18 See, for example, Alec Erwin, 'Sport: the turning point', in Cheryl Roberts, ed.,
   Sport and Transformation, Township Publishing Co-operative (Cape Town),
   1989, pp. 43–50.

19 Jakes Gerwel, 'Towards a disciplined, healthy sports movement in preparation for a post-apartheid South Africa' in Roberts, ed., *op. cit.*, p. 62.

20 *Ibid.*, p. 64.

21 See, for example, Alan Robinson, 'SANROC – the secret struggle', *Front File: Southern African Brief*, London, October 1989, p. 7.

22 See, for example, *Rapport*, Johannesburg, 11 November 1990.

23 Quoted in *Focus on South Africa*, Cape Town, January 1992, p. 15.

24 See, for example, Ameen Akwalwaya, 'Forward to the past?', *The Weekly Mail*, Johannesburg, 11–17 October 1991.

25 See, for example, Hector Sauer, 'On the sports front, Mandela beats FW to the punch', *The Star Weekly*, Johannesburg, 6 November 1991.

26 See, for example, Dave Beattie, 'Don't use the past to hold back the future', *The Star Weekly*, Johannesburg, 29 May 1991.

27 See, for example, Allister Sparks, 'An African miracle', *Observer*, London, 22 March 1992. Bob Cloete of the South African Embassy in London made helpful comments on an earlier draft of this chapter, for which I am most grateful.

9

National identity, community relations and the sporting life in Northern Ireland

JOHN SUGDEN AND ALAN BAIRNER

An enthusiasm for sport is shared by Irishmen and women from both sides of the border and in Northern Ireland in equal measure by Protestants and Catholics. Indeed there is a view amongst certain journalists, politicians and senior sports administrators that sport provides a forum within which members of the Province's separate communities can come together as participants and as supporters in the collective celebration of the sporting achievements of fellow Irishmen such as the boxer Barry McGuigan. However, while there is evidence that sport can fulfil an integrative function in Northern Ireland, the place of sport in Northern Irish popular culture and its role in the Province's divided political environment is far more complex than this idealistic view would suggest.

In 1986, we analysed the relationship between sport, culture and politics in Northern Ireland by examining the social network surrounding Gaelic games, Rugby Union and association football.[1] Since then, there have been many further examples of sport and politics becoming entwined in the Province. Some of these involved the three areas which we reviewed in 1986 whilst others relate to different sports and broader aspects of leisure and recreation. In this chapter we summarise the position adopted in 1986 and, where necessary, update the situation as it pertains to the Gaelic Athletic Association (GAA), Rugby Union and association football. Following this we broaden the base of our original analysis in three ways. Firstly, we increase the number of sports by looking at cricket, hockey and cycling. Secondly we analyse central and local government involvement in the provision of leisure and recreation services, particularly in Belfast. Finally and briefly, we look at government-suported community relations inititives which feature sport and related forms of recreation.

The GAA provides perhaps the clearest example of the inseparability of sport and politics in Northern Ireland. The Association's political roots are deep. It is no coincidence that the organisation was founded in the last quarter of the nineteenth century at the same time as other important vehicles for Irish political and cultural nationalism were beginning to take shape. Although a general concern for the physical health of the nation may have been in the minds of some of the Association's founding members and patrons, for people such as Archbishop Croke, the Land Leaguer Michael Davitt and C. S. Parnell, the development of an indigenous, all-Ireland sporting movement was also viewed as an opportunity for nurturing a sense of Irish national identity. Furthermore, the GAA was seen as a bulwark against the spread of English influence in the shape of 'foreign' (English) sports and pastimes.

The political character of the GAA has never been straightforward, largely because the factionalism which has been characteristic of Irish nationalist political life in general has been reproduced within its ranks. The organisation was united in its desire to see an independent Ireland, but it barely survived the decades spanning the turn of the nineteenth century because of serious internal conflict between those who sought to end British rule by military means and those who favoured using the constitutional methods. Similarly, in the early 1920s, after partition had led to civil war in the new Irish Free State, Gaelic sportsmen were to be found on both sides of the conflict. Through dealing with such internecine turmoil, the early leaders of the GAA learned that for the organisation to survive and continue to serve as a broad base for Irish nationalism, it had to distance itself from any formal association with one or other political faction. However, this did not mean that the GAA became apolitical. To this day its constitution demands an independent thirty-two-county Ireland and it is only within recent memory that the Ban, a series of articles designed to prevent Gaels participating in non-Irish games and to exclude members of the police and armed forces, was expunged from the GAA rule-book as it applies to the twenty-six counties of the Irish Republic. The two main aims of the Ban were to prohibit Gaels from playing and watching non-Irish games and to exclude members of the British security forces from Gaelic sport.

The removal in 1971 of that element of the Ban relating to participation in 'foreign' games was a clear sign that in the Republic of Ireland the GAA no longer saw such games as a threat to Irish national identity. The fact that the element of the Ban pertaining to British security forces continues to operate in the six counties of Northern Ireland, however, is evidence of the very different role which the GAA plays in terms of its relationship with the British state. In Northern Ireland, the GAA continues to perform the role which it previously played throughout Ireland during the struggle for independence from Britain. As a body, it has been careful to avoid direct and formal association with any of the various strands of Republicanism. However, individual Gaelic clubs and individual GAA members have been implicated in the Province's political turmoil through a variety of actions including vociferous support for the Republican hunger strikers in the late 1970s. In addition, the Ban, the flying of the Irish national flag at Gaelic games, the use of Gaelic as the official language for Ulster branch meetings of the Association, the brandishing of the hurley stick in demonstrations and the naming of the Provincial stadium in Belfast Casement Park, in honour of the Republican hero and British traitor Sir Roger Casement, has done little to encourage Northern Ireland's Protestant community that the GAA is anything other than a symbolic rallying point for the enemy within.

At national, regional and local levels, the British government in Northern Ireland treat the GAA in a range of sometimes contradictory ways including benevolence, suspicion and harassment. Operating from an agenda which views any form of organised sport as good for social discipline and moral enhancement, the Sports Council for Northern Ireland provides a certain amount of grant aid for Gaelic clubs within its jurisdiction. There is some logic in this strategy. While the GAA does symbolise Irish rather than British nationality, active members of Gaelic clubs tend to direct their nationalism into events on the field of play rather than becoming involved in more overtly subversive political action. In this way many thousands of young Catholics can display an affinity with the general cause of Irish nationalism whilst finding sanctuary from the violence of Republican political struggle. However, because of the Ban, the level of government funding is strictly limited and the Association continues to be regarded with suspicion by central government agencies.

The fact that GAA is funded at all by any government body in Northern Ireland causes great consternation amongst many of the Province's Unionist politicians. In one case the Unionist dominated Craigavon Borough Council refused planning permission to a local Gaelic club which wished to build new playing fields in the town. St Peter's Gaelic Athletic Club took the Council to court and won its case. The council members involved were fined heavily because, according to the presiding High Court judge, they had been guilty of discriminating against St Peters out of sectarian bias. This is an extreme example of the hostility of elected Unionist politicians towards the GAA which is present in all of the Province's twenty-six district councils.[2]

Likewise, because of the Ban and a traditional mistrust of anything celebratory of Gaelic-Irishness in the North, the security forces are suspicious of the GAA and monitor its activities very closely. Pointing to incidents such as the construction of a military barracks on Gaelic playing fields in Crossmaglen, the temporary occupation of Casement Park, the constant harassment of Gaelic players and supporters and the shooting by a British soldier of Aiden McEnespie on his way to play a Gaelic football match, many Gaels feel that this monitoring is part of a systematic tradition of oppression which can be traced back through Irish history to the first 'Bloody Sunday', 20 November 1920, when a detachment of Black and Tans scrambled over the walls of Croke Park in Dublin and shot dead thirteen spectators and players enjoying a Gaelic football match.

The mistrust of the security forces in their regard for the GAA is shared by many of Northern Ireland's Protestant civilians for whom the activities of the Association are a constant, if largely symbolic, reminder of the political threat to the Union with Britain. This was illustrated graphically in 1991 when the County Down Gaelic football team won the all-Ireland final in Dublin. While this was the cause of much rejoicing amongst Northern Ireland's Catholics, the response from many loyalists, who view with great trepidation anything described as all-Irish, was generally muted. A minority actively sought to disrupt the celebrations which took place when the coveted Sam Maguire trophy was paraded north of the border. Several trains carrying returning Down fans from Dublin to towns in Northern Ireland were stoned as they passed through loyalist neighbourhoods. Not long afterwards a GAA club house was badly damaged by an arson attack. The most extreme position was taken by the Ulster Freedom Fighters (UFF), a loyalist paramilitary organisation, who issued death threats to all active GAA members. In an attempt to explain their position, the UFF accused the GAA of acting as a front for the Provisional IRA.

With considerable justification senior officials vigorously deny the charge that the GAA is directly involved with those who use non-constitutional methods to further the nationalist cause. However, that the Association is bound up with the politics of division in Northern Ireland is beyond dispute. Its level of politicisation depends on what definition of politics is chosen. If politics is narrowly defined in terms of interactions involving formal government processes, political parties and kindred associations, then, as a body, the political profile of the Association in the Province is kept deliberately low. If, however, one operates with a broader definition, one which includes those cultural organisations through which separate collective identities are maintained and upon which more formal political positions are constructed, then the GAA must be considered as an important player in the politics of division.

At this level of cultural politics it is tempting to assume that the main foreign games to which the GAA was originally opposed, namely Rugby Union and association football, continue to be the preserve of Irish Protestants and those who feel affiliated to the British rather than the Irish way of life. However, not only do these games differ markedly from Gaelic sports in terms of their cultural and political impact, but equally significantly they diverge from each other in ways which further reflect the complex nuances of Irish political life. At first glance the main difference between Rugby Union and association football is that the former has been more successful than the latter in establishing and maintaining links between the two parts of Ireland. It is well known for example that the Irish international rugby team is drawn from the whole of Ireland, whereas Northern Ireland and the Republic of Ireland are represented separately in international soccer. In addition, all Ireland rugby leagues were established in season 1990/1, to no small degree facilitated by the good cross-border relationships which had existed at the level of club rugby for many years previously. This again is in marked contrast to the situation in association football over which separate administrative bodies based in Dublin and

Belfast have presided with, more or less, strictly segregated league and cup competitions since Partition.

Nevertheless, although it can be generally accepted that Rugby Union and association football are different features of the Irish political landscape, it would be an over simplification to conclude that the former is integrative and the latter divisive. One of the most common explanations for rugby's ability to function in an all-Ireland context is that it is an essentially middle-class game. Just as in England, in Ireland, north and south, the game is central to the physical education curriculum of elite public and grammar schools and is an important focus for university sport. There is also a widespread all-Ireland network of private rugby clubs through which contacts and values acquired in school are developed and extended. In general the Irish middle classes have been happy to maintain cross-border contacts regardless of their political affiliations. Links made through sports such as golf, cricket, hockey and show jumping emphasise the point as does the existence, in different spheres, of a whole range of all-Irish professional and business associations. The result is a veneer of civilised behaviour which may conceal deeper feelings, but which transcends these for specific purposes. These include the playing and enjoying of a good game of rugby which, after all, is only sport and thus, according to cherished middle-class values, has nothing to do with politics. However, while at the level of culture and to a limited extent only, the rugby fraternity may help to bind an all-Ireland middle class, it tends at the same time to exacerbate other social divisions by alienating working-class communities on both sides of the border. Thus, any horizontal integrative function rugby may perform must be balanced against those vertical class divisions which it helps to sustain.

In addition to class, another explanation for the harmonious nature of Irish rugby revolves around its low profile and its amateur status. Until very recently, with the exception of international fixtures, rugby has had a relatively small public following and a commensurately low level of media attention. In short, it has not been accompanied by the passionate, generalised and regionalised partisanship which so often accompanies Gaelic football and soccer. In this way the potential of the game to act as a catalyst for cross-border and cross-community conflict has been diminished. However, with the introduction of an all-Ireland senior league the stakes have been raised considerably. The abandonment of an informal arrangement of 'friendlies' in favour of a very competitive and hierarchical league system has already led to great commercial emphasis, a boost in spectator numbers and a marked increase in media coverage. This heightening of the game's profile at a local and regional level is bound to sharpen cross-border rivalries to a point where the political division of Ireland may become a factor. Indeed, there is evidence that the latter may already be an issue within the Ireland's international rugby fraternity.

In the past, questions concerning what flag should be flown, whose anthem should be aired and where internationals should be played have all led to political controversy within the Irish Rugby Football Union. At present, the hiring and firing of managers and coaches and the selection of players for the international team continue to stir emotions on each side of the border. The fact that currently all home internationals are played in Dublin, at Lansdowne Road, under the Tricolour and preceded by the national anthem of the Republic of Ireland cannot be taken as a sign that all those who play international rugby for Ireland or support the Irish team are Irish patriots. Most of the northern players consider themselves to be British first and Irish second, but they are willing to set aside temporally their first allegiance in order to play their chosen sport at the highest level available to them. It is significant that during the Rugby World Cup in 1991 the only players who sang the 'Soldier's Song', the Irish national anthem, before the start of each game were the minority of players who were indigenous to the Republic of Ireland. Players from Ulster and those whose Irish eligibility was vested in relatives either did not know the words to the national anthem or did not choose to sing them. During the five nations championships, the majority of Protestant rugby fans in the Northern Ireland support the Irish team in much the same way as the Scots and Welsh support their own national teams and they are particularly eager to seen Ireland do well against England. However, this does not easily translate into a political preference. Indeed, the example of hockey outlined below leads us to believe that if the British Lions excluded selection from the Republic of Ireland and if the Republic of Ireland played in a tournament which included the Lions, there can be little doubt that most of Northern Ireland's rugby players and supporters would throw their weight behind the British.

Thus, under closer scrutiny the claims for the integrative power of Rugby Union are weakened. This is especially the case within the boundaries of Northern Ireland where the game is not only almost exclusively middle-class, but also overwhelmingly Protestant. Rugby clubs in Northern Ireland do not make constitutional statements concerning the union with Britain and neither do they bar Catholics from membership. Thus, they claim to be non-sectarian. However, rugby clubs in the Province depend on an education system which is divided along sectarian lines and which offers an equally divided games curriculum. This informal sporting *apartheid* is reproduced in adult life through a network of rugby clubs which become focal points of a subculture which plays an important role in maintaining the social cohesion of Northern Ireland's Protestant middle class. Rugby Union in Northern Ireland remains almost exclusively Protestant so that horizontal integration between communities remains as unlikely as vertical integration among social classes.

As the most popular sport in the world, association football is often regarded as having a unique power to bring together regardless of age, gender, nationality, class, religious and ethnic affiliation and political belief. In Ireland, therefore, it might be assumed that, unlike Gaelic games and Rugby Union with their particular forms of exclusivity, soccer has the integrative potential which peace-makers so avidly seek in sport. This is particularly so as the game appears to be growing in popularity in the Republic of Ireland with a possible long-term threat to support for Gaelic games. Although it may be that the performances of the national side have created what is merely a temporary rise in interest in the 'foreign' game, there is no doubt that the Irish have enjoyed their taste of something which the Gaelic sports movement had effectively denied to them: namely, the opportunity to compete at the highest international level and, moreover, to beat the English at their own game.

In contrast, north of the border, soccer at an internatioanl level is currently going through a transitional period. Attendances at international matches dropped to lower levels than at any time since the early 1970s and in part this was a reflection of a series of poor performances. However, although Northern Ireland recruits its players from both communities in the Province, the context in which home games are played at Windsor Park in Belfast, the headquarters of the once exclusively Protestant Linfield FC, is so heavily laden with loyalist imagery that many Catholics find it increasingly difficult to identify with their 'national' side and many have changed their allegiance to the relatively more successful Irish Republic side. This issue was given added prominence at the beginning of 1992 when a local newspaper, the *Sunday Life*[3] drew attention to comments made by Linfield manager Eric Bowyer in a Linfield fanzine. Bowyer made it clear that in the prevailing circumstances he could not envisage signing a Catholic player. Despite the policy reiterated by club secretary Derek Brooks not to 'exclude from its staff anyone by reason of colour, race or religion',[4] Linfield came under attack from the Irish National Caucus in the United States who demanded that the Irish Football Association should sever its ties with Windsor Park and threatened to disrupt Northern Ireland's participation should they qualify for the 1994 World Cup finals in the United States. The secretary of the IFA, David Bowen, defended Linfield from the charge of sectarianism and pointed out that the IFA's relationship with Linfield is underpinned by a £3 million programme of ground improvements largely funded by the government. Although Mr Bowen acknowlegded that a boycott campaign would be embarrassing, he was confident that his organisation would receive full backing from FIFA.[5] However, Linfield succumbed to a variety of pressures in the summer of 1992 and signed Chris Cullen a catholic, from Cliftonville.

Sectarianism does not present a problem for the majority of those who at present constitute Northern Ireland's support. Indeed, it is precisely because the Northern Ireland football team remains as one of the strongest reminders of the Province's separate political identity that Protestant supporters have remained loyal and regard Catholic shifts in allegiance as the latest example of the perfidy of the enemy within. Ironically, therefore, whilst the rising popularity of soccer in the Republic may have a progressive impact in terms of loosening the cultural stranglehold of the GAA, in Northern Ireland its effect has been to further polarise the two communities.

Attempts to increase cross-border soccer contacts have met with considerable resistance in Northern Ireland where there are real fears that closer ties would ultimately diminish the Province's independent international status in the eyes of FIFA. Furthermore, competitions and individual matches involving teams from Northern Ireland and the Irish Republic have frequently been marred by crowd trouble which, in the eyes of many administrators, would only get worse if an all-Ireland league or cup competition were to be introduced in the present political context. Underlying these pragmatic considerations, however, is the weight of opinion of the vast majority of Protestant supporters in the North who are opposed to any form of unity as a matter of political principle. So clearly have the battle lines been drawn that for Derry City, a club based in Northern Ireland but with a predominantly Catholic following and a ground situated close to the nationalist Bogside, it proved easier to gain admission to the southern-based League of Ireland than re-entry to the northern Irish League which it had been obliged to leave in 1972 because of the security situation. The Derry City case provides insight into the way in which inter-community rivalry creates problems for the administration of soccer within Northern Ireland.

Thus, if there is a single sport which does most often emphasises the polarity of Northern Irish society it is association football. Ironically, this is precisely because, unlike either Gaelic sport or Rugby Union, soccer is popular within both communities. Thus, there are many opportunities within the game for cross-community contact which can result in sectarian confrontation and even violence. The history of football in Northern Ireland is littered with manifestations of sectarian rivalry both on and off the pitch and in recent years there have been several very serious incidents. The riot which took place during and after the Irish Cup match between Linfield and Donegal Celtic in 1989 was one of the worst in the history of professional football in Ireland and this was caused by sectarian undercurrents. However, potentially, the most damaging incident occurred during Cliftonville's fixture with Glenavon in 1991 when loyalist paramilitaries tossed a grenade on to the terraces occupied by Cliftonville supporters. Cliftonville's support is largely drawn from Catholic neighbourhoods. The grenade fell short, undoubtedly saving many from death and mutilation.

Also, at a lower level, leagues and teams within leagues tend to be organised in such a way that some degree of separation between Catholic and Protestant players is maintained. However, in other important ways soccer achieves far more than either Gaelic games or Rugby Union in terms of providing common ground for Catholics and Protestants. At a senior level, with the exception of Linfield, it is usual for Catholics and Protestants to play together in the same teams. Neither is it unknown for Catholics and Protestants to support the same senior teams. For example, although support for the Scotish Old Firm of Celtic and Rangers mirrors community division this is not the case with regard to support for English league teams. It is common for Catholics and Protestants to support the same team and to travel together to England to do so. Indeed, this also provides an opportunity for the development of cross-border soccer friendships through encounters with the large volume of travelling support from the Republic of Ireland. Finally, despite the segregated school system, soccer is the main sport of many Protestant and Catholic schools and a network of inter-school leagues and representative schoolboy teams makes it possible to provide integrated sporting experiences for many young players. Thus, while in terms of direct sectarian conflict, soccer may be the most politically volatile sport in Nothern Ireland, it may also be one of the games with the greatest potential to have a positive impact on the Province's deeply divided popular culture. To what extent that potential remains unlocked is a question for the game's administrators on both sides of the border.

The various codes of football are by no means the only popular sports in Northern Ireland. While it would be wrong to claim that all aspects of all sports in Northern Ireland are politicised, most sports, at one time or another, have to negotiate problems which are related to the wider political conflict. Major team sports, because they tend to attract larger followings, seem to be most vulnerable to political manipulation. However, this has not been the case with competitive cycling which enjoys a huge following throughout Ireland and has been unable to avoid becoming entangled in sectarian politics. The main issue for competitive cyclists in Ireland revolves around national affiliation. In the early 1980s the world governing body, the International Cycling Federation (ICF) introduced legislation whereby member countries could only be represented through a single national association. This immediately rekindled a long-standing political dispute within the sport's governing body in Northern Ireland, the Northern Irish Cycling Federation (NICF) which had strong links with both the Irish and the British cycling federations.

Ever since its foundation at the beginning of the century, elements within the NICF have been vehemently opposed to the notion of a single, all-Ireland governing body. In the first place the NICF developed within the structure of the British Cycling Federation (BCF), an arrangement which suited the loyalist sympathies of many of the organisation's Protestant members. Secondly, the first all-Ireland cycling body to emerge, the National Cycling and Athletics Federation (NCAF) developed under the control of the GAA. The nationalist overtones of the GAA ensured the alienation of Ulster's Protestant cyclists, particularly during the years leading up to and immediately following the partition of Ireland in 1921. Competitive cycling in Ireland during the inter-war years suffered because of a series of official and unofficial disputes between the two rival governing bodies. A compromise was reached in 1949 whereby the Federation of Irish Cyclists (FCI) and the NICF adopted joint powers and responsibilities for cycling in the Irish Republic and Northern Ireland. However, this was never a harmonious relationship and the sport was riven with political controversy throughout the 1950s and 1960s, both in Ireland and overseas. Rival factions scuffled during races and equipment was sabotaged. In 1955 the start of World Amateur Cycling Championships in Rome was delayed because two teams turned up to represent Ireland. Jointly licensed by the ICF and the NICF, an official Irish team lined up alongside an unofficial, pro-nationalist team. The latter refused to withdraw and, in order to start the race, the organisers were forced to let down the tyres of the unofficial team.

A change in international rules has resurrected the issue of national affiliation and has led to a split within the ranks of the NICF. In the late 1970s a working party called the Irish Tripartite Cycling Committee was formed in an attempt to resolve the sport's organisational crisis. The group recommended that a unified Irish cycling federation should be formed, but this was rejected by the majority of the Protestant membership of the NICF. After a High Court battle, a splinter group, representing nationalist interests and affiliated to the Dublin-based all-Ireland body, broke away from the NICF and formed the Ulster Cycling Federation (UCF). In an attempt to resolve their differences, the NICF and the UCF brought in George Glasgow, the former Director of the Northern Ireland Sports Council, as a mediator, but despite his considerable skills as a diplomat, he was unable to forge an agreement between the two sides. Speaking on BBC Television Northern Ireland's Spotlight programme, Glasgow[6] confessed that while he had solved a multitude of sporting problems he would never be able to solve

Northern Irelands' cyclists' conflict so long as it remained bound up with Ireland's political crisis.

Another team sport worthy of mention is cricket, which is particularly interesting because, despite its quintessential Englishness, it continues to be played in both parts of Ireland and not merely in that part which remains within the United Kingdom. Indeed, the existence of the border has made no difference to the all-Irish character of Ireland's international cricketing selections. Although club competitions are organised at provincial and district levels, the international eleven is chosen from players throughout Ireland and, in addition, a knock-out competition is contested by clubs from both parts of Ireland each season. Although international fixtures against Scotland, Wales, visiting touring sides, English counties and so forth attract little attention, there is no doubt that people throughout Ireland, regardless of political or religious affiliation would favour an Irish victory. None of this, however, is to suggest that the game of cricket plays a significant role in the formation of an all-Irish political consciousness which transcends religious and cultural differences.

The game's origins in Ireland would alone militate against such an achievement. While there have been suggestions that a form of cricket was played in Ireland before the British arrived, it is generally argued that the game, like rugby, was an English import. According to Stanley Bergin and Derek Scott, 'to gain a true picture of the history of cricket in Ireland it is necessary to relate the game to the political and social life of the country in the 18th century.'[7] In terms of politics, this meant British rule and, as Bergin and Scott point out, 'whatever cricket was played in Ireland was confined essentially to the military, the gentry and members of the viceregal or Chief Secretary's staff and household'.[8]

The first recorded cricket match in Ireland took place in 1792 in Phoenix Park, Dublin, the Garrison defeating an All-Ireland selection by an innings and 94 runs to win the wager of 1000 guineas. According to W. P. Hone, the leading historian of Irish cricket, it is almost certain that the future Duke of Wellington represented the all-Ireland side on this momentous occasion.[9] The captain of the Garrison, Colonel Lennox, was one of the chief founders of the MCC and he helped to popularise cricket in Scotland and in various parts of England as well as in Ireland. In his political life, he was to become Viceroy of Ireland and a figure of hatred for the Catholic party.[10] Ironically, his opposite number in the Phoenix Park match, Major Hobbart, was given the task in 1792 of steering the Catholic Relief Bill through the Irish Parliament, for which he received little admiration from nationalists including Wolfe Tone who described Hobbart as 'a monkey' and 'a fluttering English jay'.[11] The top scorer in the All-Ireland side was Secretary Cooke, later to become one of the functionaries employed by Castlereagh and Fitzgibbon to bribe members of the Irish Parliament to vote for the Act of Union.[12]

It is evident, therefore, that from the very outset cricket in Ireland was bound up with the politics of the day and was intimately connected to the British presence in the country. With that in mind, it is rather curious to note that some of the earliest clubs to be established in Ireland, during the 1820s, were in Ballinasloe, Carlow and Kilkenny, all of which were to become strongholds of Gaelic games in the years that followed.[13] On closer inspection, however, it becomes clear that the English influence was again crucial. As Hone surmises, 'it may be that boys coming home by coach and ship from their English schools lamented that their favourite games could not be enjoyed during their summer holidays and that their fox-hunting parents, themselves hard put to know how to pass the summer months, saw in cricket a means of gratifying their gregarious instincts'.[14] As a result of similar influences, former pupils of the English public schools ensured that cricket was played at Dublin University from as early as 1827 and a club was formed there in 1842, approximately ten years after the establishment of the Phoenix Club with its strong military connections.

Ironically, in view of the subsequent development of Ireland's constitutional history, cricket took hold more quickly in what was later to become the Irish Republic than in the north-east corner of the island. As Hone expresses it, 'no doubt the game was played in Ulster almost as early as in the South, but it seems to have been of slower growth.'[15] Lisburn Cricket Club was founded in 1836 but it was not until the 1860s that the game began to spread rapidly in Ulster, following the formation in November 1859, of the North of Ireland Cricket Club under the patronage of the Lord Lieutenant of Ireland and the visit to Belfast, in 1861, of an All-Ireland team led by Charles Lawrence, a professional player who had been engaged by the Phoenix Club. From then onwards, cricket made even greater progress in Ulster than in other parts of Ireland, not least because of the continued dependence elsewhere on participation by the military and the influence of the English public school system.

How then did Irish nationalists respond to the emergence and growth of the game of cricket? Some surprising facts are to be uncovered in the history of Irish cricket. For example, the game was introduced into Co. Wicklow by John Henry Parnell, father of the Nationalist leader Charles Stewart Parnell. According to Hone, 'the great Parnell ... inherited his father's taste for the English game ... and he captained the Wicklow team for many years before entering nationalist politics'.[16] In one season C. S. Parnell averaged 35 with the bat. This naturally involved Parnell in matches against members of the British administration and garrison. By a bitter twist of fate, however, after his adoption of the nationalist cause, his favourite game was to be affected adversely at his own hands and those of his followers inasmuch as the growth of the Land League and the resultant deterioration in relations between landlords and their tenants brought about the demise of most of the small cricket clubs which had been situated outside of Ulster, Dublin and the Anglo-Irish Pale.[17]

Nevertheless, during the intervening period, a number of Catholic schools had taken up the game of cricket, amonst them Clongowes Wood where a game crudely resembling cricket was first played as early as 1820 and the game in its proper form had become well established by the 1870s. It was at Clongowes Wood that another future Irish Nationalist leader acquired a love of cricket.

> John Redmond and his brother Willie were at Clongowes in these years, and it is curious to find that he, like his predecessor in the leadership of the Nationalist Party, Parnell, was also a bit of a cricketer.[18]

One of Redmond's closest political allies, Tom Kettle, was yet another nationalist with a great affection for the sport.[19]

During the 1840s and 1850s the most prominent cricketing school in Ireland had been the Church of Ireland's St Columba's. Even there, however, the game had flourished in a nationalist environment, albeit cultural rather than overtly political. The founder and headmaster of St Columba's, the Reverend William Sewell, a Fellow of Exeter College, Oxford, was a cultural nationalist who ensured that the Irish language was taught in his school and who expressed concern that 'in the English Public Schools to which the wealthier Irish Church people were already sending their sons, nothing would be taught of Irish Antiquity, and the boys would return to live their lives in Ireland as strangers to their country'.[20] Clearly this concern did not lead Sewell to the conclusion that an appreciation of cricket was alien to Irishness.

The 1860s and 1870s witnessed the rapid growth of cricket in Ireland but this trend was halted to some extent, at least outside Ulster, both as an indirect consequence of Land League activities and as a direct result of the emergence of the GAA with its avowed policy to usurp such 'foreign' games as cricket. It should not go unnoticed, however, that many of those who supported the GAA and some of those who were active in its foundation had learned an appreciation of organised sports through participation in British games like cricket.

Nevertheless, it is no accident that since the turn of the century cricket has been disproportionately more popular in Ulster, along with the Dublin area, than elsewhere in Ireland – that is to say, in those regions where anglophile sympathies were sufficiently strong to withstand the nationalist onslaught. To this day cricket is played in the Irish Republic in only 3 per cent of vocational schools (the overwhelming majority of schools) and 25 per cent of fee-paying private schools.[21] One strange anomaly, however, is the fact that it was only after the partition of Ireland that cricket became properly organised on an island-wide basis. The Irish Cricket Union came into existence in 1923 after a meeting between representatives of the Leinster Union and the Ulster Union in July of that year. The existence of the ICU further facilitated contacts between cricketers from throughout Ireland and the relationships between cricketers from the Irish Republic and Northern Ireland have remained strong and friendly regardless of the vicissitudes in Ireland's political life, particularly since the onset of the Troubles. That cricket does have a quasi-political image, nevertheless, is best seen if one considers the character of the sport in contemporary Northern Ireland. Who plays cricket and what is the game's function in Northern Irish political culture?

Currently, it is convenient to employ four categories in order to classify Northern Irish cricket clubs. Firstly, there are the old boys' clubs, traditionally linked with certain schools, notably in Belfast. Secondly, there are clubs specifically tied to particular institutions such as the Royal Ulster Constabulary, the Civil Service or the

Universities. Thirdly, there are the clubs which serve the major urban areas of the Province. And, finally, there are numerous clubs scattered throughout Northern Ireland serving villages, small towns or particular districts of the larger towns and cities. Other categories of clubs did exist such as those specifically associated with landlords, parks departments and factories, but these have either disappeared or been subsumed within the structure outlined above. Also vanished from the Ulster scene are the large number of military cricket clubs which were influential in the game's early development, but which, for security reasons, had to abandon a regular commitment to sporting engagements with external leagues and organisations. In addition there is an administrative distinction, resulting in separate competitions, between the north-west of the Province and the remainder. It is immediately clear from the number of clubs and players that cricket is a popular sport (at least in terms of participation if not spectating). But a superficial appraisal of the widespread distribution of cricket clubs throughout Ulster should not be taken as evidence that the game is popular with both communities. On the contrary the great majority of club members are Protestants and most of the clubs are located in predominantly Unionist areas, including those small towns and villages which are Protestant enclaves in largely nationalist regions such as West Tyrone and South Derry. Given the game's English heritage and its historical association with British rule, this should not come as any major surprise. However, in the light of the amicable relations between cricketers, north and south, it demands some investigation if only to discover whether or not cricket is a game which could ever serve an integrative function in Northern Ireland's recreational life.

Since cricket is not a spectator sport to any great extent in Ireland, clubs can easily avoid sectarian attachments. Furthermore, since the majority of Northern Irish cricketers possess a deep love for the game, only a small minority would regard religious affiliation as a cause for denial of club membership. So why do so few Catholics play?

A similar picture emerges as with Rugby Union. First there is the cultural symbolism of cricket. It came to Ireland as a British game and it has failed to become so universally played that its 'foreignness' can ever be forgotten. As a result, it is far easier for the spokesmen of Gaelic games to dissuade young men from playing cricket than to lure them from association football. A second factor, however, related in part, reveals why so few Catholics would opt for cricket even if it could be freed from its pro-British connotations. Cricket is seldom played in Northern Ireland's Catholic schools or colleges. Football, on the other hand, is played in an even higher proportion of Catholic grammar schools than Protestant ones. The results are there for all to see. A third and final factor is the location of cricket clubs, particularly the smaller ones. A great many grew up in communities which were, and have remained, almost exclusively Protestant, sponsored by local aristocrats and factory and mill owners, either English by birth or educated in England. Thus, a tradition of playing cricket was established which has persisted to the present day. In these communities it is doubtful if Catholic incomers would be actively encouraged or would show any inclination to join the local cricket club.

On the basis of the foregoing analysis and in spite of the all-Ireland identity of cricket and the camaraderie which abounds it is unlikely that cricket could ever play a part in helping in the process of integration through sport. On the contrary, because of its anglophile connotations, cricket has already been a casualty of sectarian politics in Northern Ireland. Cliftonville Cricket Club was burned out of its premises in north Belfast in 1972, two years after the club's centenary. As a consequence of demographic polarisation following the serious rioting of the early 1970s, this area of north Belfast was transformed from neutral to predominantly Catholic. The presence of one of the Province's oldest cricket clubs in the neighbourhood was unacceptable to local nationalists. According to its souvenir brochure, Cliftonville Cricket Club 'fell victim to elements who were hostile to the club and what it represented in the area'.[22] The Club opted to relocate in Greenisland, an area on the outskirts of the city which was largely Protestant. Ironically, because in certain Protestant circles, the name Cliftonville was associated with the football club and connoted Catholic territory, a number of Greenisland loyalists mistakenly assumed that the cricket club was Catholic and anti-Catholic slogans were daubed on its new premises!

In many ways the political currents which operate beneath the surface of rugby and cricket are more clearly visible in the world of Irish hockey. The roots of hockey in Ireland are virtually indistinguishable from those of cricket and rugby. Indeed, the three sports often co-exist within the same clubs. As a game involving stick and ball hockey can be viewed as the English alternative to the native Irish sport of hurling and as one of a range of anglophile recreations which were in competition with traditional forms of Gaelic sport in the later half of the nineteenth century. The men's Irish Hockey Union (IHU) was established in Dublin in 1893 and this was followed shortly by the establishment of the Irish Ladies Hockey Union (ILHU). Indicative of the sport's heritage, the first men's president was the Reverend Canon Gibson, the headmaster of King's Hospital Public School. Soon afterwards, the Provinces of Leinster, Munster and Ulster set up their own regional governing bodies, meaning that the Union was in fact a federation with each Province being partially autonomous. However, the strongholds of hockey, and the main Provincial rivals, were in the east and north of Ireland, in Leinster, the centre of British administration and influence at that time, and in Ulster, the heartland of Protestantism and Unionism. Illustrative of the demography of British influence in Ireland, Connaught, the island's most westerly Province, did not embrace hockey, preferring instead to concentrate on the Gaelic games of hurling and camogie. Even today Connacht does not participate in senior inter-Provincial hockey.

Like rugby, hockey operates both within and between Provinces and Ireland is represented in the sport by players drawn from both sides of the border. In this sense, hockey can be described as an all-Ireland sport. In order to avoid political problems, traditionally, when the all-Ireland team play they do so under the flag of the Irish Hockey Union, which consists of the crests of all four Provinces, in preference to the Tricolour. Furthermore, players and officials stand to the 'Londonderry Air' at the start of internationals, rather than to the 'Soldier's Song', the national anthem of the Republic. However, relationships are not always so harmonious and neither are resolutions always so pragmatic.

Unlike the situation in rugby, whereby players from Northern Ireland are classified as Irish and can only play for the Irish national rugby team, to date hockey players have been able to play either for Ireland or for Great Britain, or indeed, in the case of the men's game, both. This tradition of dual nationality has led to serious controversy in ladies' hockey and is beginning to have an impact upon the administration of the men's game. In 1980, two of Ulster's top senior ladies were banned from playing hockey for six years by the ILHU because, after being selected to play both for Great Britain and for Ireland, Jenny Redpath and Violet McBride elected to play for the former. The case of Redpath was particularly controversial as, at the time the ban was imposed, she was captain of the Irish team. For her, the decision to play for Great Britain was made for a combination of sporting and political reasons. The Great Britain team is of a much higher standard than the Irish and would be expected to achieve greater success on the international stage. Thus, in terms of her hockey career it was a sensible decision. In addition, however, despite being the captain of the Irish team, she felt more British than Irish and experienced a greater sense of national pride when playing for Great Britain. Likewise, in 1991, Ulster players Joanne Menown and Jackie Burns, who were established as members of the Irish ladies' hockey team, elected to play for Great Britain, a decision which upset many senior administrators in the ILHU, particularly since Ireland were drawn to play against Great Britain in the Olympic qualifying tournament.

These developments have been echoed by events taking place within the men's game. Up until 1990, unlike the ladies' team, the All-Ireland men's team had never competed for a place in the Olympic Games, places for which were by invitation only. Furthermore, the Great Britain men's hockey team was constituted only every four years in order to take up the challenge of participation in the Olympic Games. For the rest of the time, as in Rugby Union, England, Scotland, Wales and Ireland have fielded individual teams and, in the absence of a Northern Ireland team, the best Ulster players have played for Ireland. However, rule changes by the International Olympic Committee meant that for the 1992 Games in Barcelona, the tradition of 'invitation only' was abandoned in favour of holding a qualifying tournament.

The participation of Ireland in this qualifying tournament has had two political side-effects. In the first place, the rules of the IOC state that participating countries must march in the opening ceremony under their respective national flags and, if they win a medal, that flag should be raised at the medal ceremony and, in the case of the gold medal, accompanied by the appropriate national anthem. This means that the flag of the Irish Hockey Union and 'Londonderry Air' would have to be replaced by the Tricolour and the 'Soldier's Song'. This scenario has proven to be unacceptable to some of the game's senior administrators, particularly those from Ulster, who feel that it is disloyal to have a team which consists mostly of British citizens from Northern Ireland competing under the flag and anthem of the Irish Republic. Secondly, the Irish men's participation in the Olympic qualifying tournament would mean that Northern Ireland's better male players would be confronted by the same difficult choice faced by Violet McBride and Jenny Redpath in 1980. Stephen Martin is an Ulsterman who has won silver and gold Olympic medals with Great Britain's men's hockey team. Speaking on BBC Television Northern Ireland's Spotlight programme, he revealed how complex the question of sports participation and national identity can be in the prevailing circumstances:

> It is a great honour to play for Ireland, but no one ever feels that you are playing for your country as such because of the political situation here. When you play for Great Britain and Northern Ireland, as the team is described in the Olympic Games, then you feel you are playing for your country as such, but then it's one of those political dilemmas.[23]

The whole issue of whether or not to compete went to a vote, with Munster and Leinster voting in favour of entry, but with Ulster voting against, albeit by the narrowest of margins. However, the Ulster branch is bound by the majority decision and reluctantly agreed to bow to the Union's ruling, but not before the Chairman of the Irish selectors, Ulsterman Francis Baird, resigned in protest.

The fact that both Great Britain and Ireland continue to lay claim on the allegiances of hockey players from Northern Ireland means that the political dimension of sport in the Province has a more obvious impact on top hockey players than it does on their counterparts in other sports such as association football and rugby. In the case of the latter, because Northern Ireland does not enter a separate team in the annual five nations championship series and because Ireland as a whole contributes players to the British Lions, questions of national identity are not usually raised when players from Northern Ireland are selected for either Ireland or the Lions. Although, in deference to sensitive issues of national sovereignty, in the Republic of Ireland there is a tendency among rugby writers to drop the national adjective and refer to the composite team as 'the Lions'. The situation in hockey is different and in many ways encapsulates the national question in general, particularly as it confronts Ulster Protestants. The written constitution of the Irish Republic effectively ignores the Partition of 1921 by claiming statehood over the six counties of Northern Ireland which have remained part of the United Kingdom. Nevertheless, even though the people of Northern Ireland can legitimately claim to be British, because they are born in the island of Ireland, they have an equal claim on Irish citizenship. Indeed, some people in the Province hold two passports. Not surprisingly, however, the majority of Ulster Protestants choose to consider themselves British rather than Irish, while many Catholics consider themselves to be Irish rather than British. This explains the logic of the arguments put forward by both Redpath and Martin. However, when British selection is not on offer and in the absence of a Northern Ireland hockey team, both players are willing and eager to play for Ireland, just like their counterparts in rugby. This reasoning involves a further consideration.

Notwithstanding relations with the Irish Republic, within the United Kingdom itself there is a high degree of national rivalry, particularly between England, the main political power and the remaining countries of Scotland, Wales and Northern Ireland. Nowhere does this rivalry find clearer expression than in the world of sport wherein beating the English generates great emotion and celebration among the non-English British. This is as true of the Northern Irish as it is of the Welsh and the Scots. As we have argued, the Province's soccer team provides a clearly defined outlet for the intra-United Kingdom nationalism of the Northern Irish. Alternatively, in sports for which the Province does not have national representative status, as is the case with rugby and hockey, most people in Northern Ireland, including many Protestants and Unionists, are happy to play for and/or support an all-Ireland team. However, for these Protestants, this display of cultural affiliation to Ireland does not translate into a political preference and is quickly abandoned in favour of support for combined United Kingdom teams and organisations when the focus of sporting competition is altered to include Great Britain as an entity, as is the case with the Olympic Games. In this way, it can be argued that the Northern Irish Protestants are Irish in the same sense that the Welsh are Welsh and the Scots are Scottish: that is at the level of culture they preserve a strong separate national identity while generally accepting the political authority of the British state. On the other hand, for many Northern Irish Catholics, sporting expressions of Irish nationalism are manifestations of a deeper seated feeling of identification with the Irish Republic and the desire for a united Ireland.

Organised sport is not alone in in being entangled with Ulster's political crisis. We have argued elsewhere that the current and extensive pattern of public leisure provision in Belfast was, to a large extent, determined by the Province's political crisis.[24] Specifically we believe that while in recent years the question of municipal leisure provision in deprived urban areas has gained ground on the political agenda throughout the UK, in the late 1960s and early 1970s, in Belfast, because of the serious and widespread social unrest which accompanied the Troubles, getting young people off the streets and into leisure and recreation centres was seen as a matter of particular urgency by the authorities at Westminster.

Initially, the hypothesis that the British state had developed public leisure in Belfast as an instrument of social control was supported by a high correlation between the upsurge in civil unrest and sectarian violence between 1969 and the present and significant increases in central government spending on leisure and recreation services over the same period. In this context, within approximately ten years Belfast went from being one of the UK's most under-provided cities to becoming one of the most well endowed in western Europe. In support of our argument we pointed out that the development of fourteen leisure centres in Belfast is far in excess of Sports Council recommendations for a city of no more than 400,000 people. In addition, in most cases these leisure facilities had been located pro-rata, 'tit for tat', in the most deprived inner-city areas which had notorious reputations as sectarian ghettos. In conclusion we argued that because of the unique and deeply divided character of Northern Ireland and the changing nature of the Troubles from mass civil unrest to polarised conspiracy and terrorist violence the state's strategy of using leisure as an instrument of social control for the most part has been an expensive failure, particularly for Belfast's ratepayers. Since their publication the above arguments have been subjected to criticism, particularly from within Northern Ireland where those professionally engaged in public leisure provision fiercely resist the accusation that they are involved in some form of soft policing on behalf of the British state. We intend briefly to answer some of these criticisms by taking a more detailed look at the problematic role which the state has played in the development and administration of leisure in Belfast.

The extensiveness of the provision of leisure in Belfast is not open to question. It is the original rationale for provision, its day-to-day operation and its impact on the social and political character of the community which raise controversial questions about the nature of the state. From the perspective of those responsible for running the city's leisure services, such provision is justified as a response to the recreational needs of civil society, particularly in areas of social deprivation. This replicates the broader UK-wide official rationale for public support for leisure as an appendage of an expanded welfare state. This argument has been dismissed by Marxists as liberal-democratic rhetoric. They argue that historically the interest of the state in popular culture has been to undermine the potential for class struggle through diversion, ideological penetration and spacial and physical control. The co-opting of leisure and recreation in their modern forms merely extends this function. The clearest statement of this position is provided by Jean-Marie Brohm in *Sport: a Prison of Measured Time*.[25] When applied to the impact of a public leisure facility in the largely untroubled shires of southern England the latter argument seems rather absurd and the pluralist position more tenable. However, the situation in Belfast is markedly different from that of southern England and as an explanatory framework the balance is tipped in favour of the Marxists, but with certain important qualifications.

There is no public record of the discussions which surrounded the decision making process through which Northern Ireland received and implemented its leisure windfall. However, in 1988, during a televised interview, Dr Brian Mawhinney, the minister then responsible for the public funding of sport and leisure in Northern Ireland, admitted that, in the past, attempts had been made by the state to use leisure as a means of channelling the energies of young people away from direct involvement in political violence. While carrying out research for Workers' Playtime, a documentary on leisure for BBC Radio Northern Ireland, David Huntley uncovered evidence which clearly suggests that the Troubles were the catalyst for the rapid expansion of Belfast's leisure services and that the political will and material wherewithal for such development originated from Westminster.[26] Huntley interviewed a number of politicians, senior civil servants and local government officials who had been key players in the establishment of Belfast's leisure services in the 1970s. John Saulters, Assistant Secretary at the Department of Education for Northern Ireland (DENI) until 1983, saw a clear connection between the efforts of the British government to pacify the Province in the 1970s and the extensive leisure centre building programme for Belfast during the same period. This view was shared by Jim Hull, Deputy Principal Officer at the Department, who made the 'control' factor explicit when he said:

> In the 1970s, money was running out of our ears. The Government saw that it was extremely important to provide facilities in Belfast, because if you got them there at ten in the morning and kept them there until late afternoon, then they weren't dragging up stones and slabs to throw at the police at night.[27]

Alan Moneypenny, the Director of the Antrim Forum, Northern Ireland's first major leisure centre, agrees that at least in part the expanded volume of provision in Belfast was a consequence of the city's civil disturbances. In the 1970s Paddy Devlin was a local councillor and an influential member of the Leisure Services Committee, the body which planned the structure of provision in Belfast. While recognising a genuine community need for increased provision, he believes that it was really to prevent young people rioting that such an extensive programme was financed by central government:

> We set up 14 not 8, because the Sports Council in England who drew up the figures hadn't the problems we had – they didn't have the population massacring themselves. In order to stop the rioting it was agreed that 14 would be needed.[28]

Thus, there is evidence to suggest that at all levels of the delivery system – central and local government and professional leisure administration – there was an awareness that Belfast's leisure windfall was to some extent caused by the state's desire to harness this aspect of civil society to a broader strategy of social control in Northern Ireland. There is also evidence in support of another aspect of our argument: that rather than promoting cross-community integration, the actual pattern of public leisure provision established in the city has reinforced sectarian polarisation.

Policy may have been decided at Westminster, but its implementation was enacted through a series of offices and agencies which towards the planning and building stages came progressively closer to the divisive currents which are indigenous to the Province. Central government, through the Department of Education, provided the bulk of the money for the capital building programme and in consultation with the Sports Council (for England and for Northern Ireland) and the local Leisure Services Committee, dictated broadly what the design and contents of Belfast's leisure centres should be. However, it was to be the ratepayers who would finance the day-to-day running of the centres and as such city councillors had a large say in determining local demand and identifying the areas within which these facilities would be located. Research by both Huntley and Knox[29] indicates that the issue of leisure provision was seen by many local councillors as one of us versus them (Protestant versus Catholic; Loyalist versus Nationalist) and in council chambers the map of provision was clearly influenced by a balance of cross-community claims. Out of a total of fourteen leisure centres only two occupy neutral sites with seven situated within the heartland of Protestant Belfast and five located in Catholic enclaves, and this is an accurate reflection of the size and distribution of the two communities in Belfast's inner city. To underline the separate community possession of these facilities, the respective schedules of summer opening and closing are dictated by the different calendar of Protestant and Catholic religious/political holidays and street festivals.

This pattern is a reflection of two things: sectarianism and pragmatism. It is sectarian in the sense that it has been influenced by local politicians who have sought to maximise their constituents' interests. In any other UK context this could be applauded as a civic duty, but in Belfast local council constituencies are almost exclusively either Nationalist/Catholic or Loyalist/Protestant. Once in place leisure centres do become an important community resource, but for one community and not the other, and this adds to sectarian polarisation in the city.

At the Department of Education Jim Hull is critical of what central government funding has led to:

> It would have been much better to site the centres on a more widespread basis. A lot of the community centres and some of the leisure centres throughout the Province are being virtually run by paramilitaries, and the decent citizen is just not welcome. If they were situated in more neutral areas of the city, then people who wanted to use the facilities could have travelled to them, and I think that would have been a much better idea. Now, everybody is just becoming further entrenched in their own wee corners and can't get out.[30]

Knox's latest research shows that local councillors understand the political sentiments behind central government's original reasons for funding an expanded programme of leisure centre provision, but dismiss notions of integration through leisure as unrealistic. In this regard they are probably correct. Jim Hull's suggestion of siting leisure centres in 'neutral areas of the city' has been tried, but without significant success. The separate communities have become increasingly suspicious of one another in Belfast and this is clearly reflected in the ghettoisation of housing along sectarian lines, particularly in working-class areas. It is naive to suggest that in Belfast a leisure centre in no man's land would attract otherwise opposite and entrenched communities and facilitate the suspension of hostilities in the name of recreation. People in Belfast are much more likely to use leisure centres if they are within walking distance and in the heart of their own territory. As such they are incorporated within the localised network of communication and surveillance through which all routine activities are kept secure. Siting them outside of either enclave encourages obsolescence. Thus, the 'tit for tat' pattern of provision ends up being a pragmatic and realistic response to the city's uniquely divided community structure. Within this framework, those entrusted with running Belfast's public leisure facilities are instrumentally apolitical and concentrate upon providing the best service possible for those on both sides of the peace line.

A recent study commissioned by the Sports Council (London), the Sports Council for Northern Ireland and Belfast City Council and carried out under the guidance of Ken Roberts of Liverpool University claims that the people of Belfast have been well served by the city's leisure provision.[31] However, a study carried out by government auditors concludes that through subsidising the city's leisure services to the tune of £26 per head Belfast's ratepayers (the poll tax has not been introduced to Northern Ireland) are not getting value for money.[32] Local voters are unlikely to continue to support council subsidies to leisure, especially if this contributes to rate increases. Colin Knox[33] has evaluated both reports and is particularly critical of Roberts's document because of its lack of quantitative breadth and qualititative depth. He is also suspicious of any evaluative process which concludes by praising those organisations which commissioned and paid for the research in the first place. However, in our view, a more damaging criticism of Roberts is his failure to locate his research in the context of a deeply divided urban landscape and to account for the impact of Belfast's expansive leisure provision on the socio-political contours which sustain those divisions.

O'Dowd *et al.* have argued that, regardless of individual beliefs and intentions, administrators in Northern Ireland are bound by the sectarian nature of the structures within which they operate.[34] It is the Province's institutional order which perpetuates division. Thus, despite the professed neutrality and demonstrated professionalism of public leisure officials, one effect of Belfast's leisure provision has been to shore up the deep and antagonistic community divisions which keep the Province close to the edge of chaos. Outside of Northern Ireland, the British state's capacity to harness sport and recreation, and through them to attempt to gain access to and control of civil society both instrumentally and structurally, can be seen to have evolved against the reality of and potential for class conflict: keeping the working classes divided and diverted through sport and leisure and undermining their capacity to act as a class for themselves. But the problem of order in Ulster is not primarily rooted in vertical class divisions. Sectarianism cuts across classes with the most bitter divisions and antagonisms being manifest between groups of working-class Catholics and Protestants. Paradoxically, by applying a British model of rational recreation to Northern Ireland the state may have helped to keep the working class divided at the expense of feeding the more potent sectarian divisions which are at the root of serious public disorder in the Province. There is even some doubt as to whether, within opposing communities, leisure centres are a significant deterrent to disruptive behaviour. One thing that is certain is that the presence of leisure centres in one community or another, whether they be green or orange, does little to deter a return to the streets, albeit by leaner and fitter young men, should the latest episode of the Troubles demand it. This is a further example of how consequences do not necessarily follow intentions when the state seeks to extend its influence into civil society.

By the end of the 1980s it became clear that the provison of large, lavish and expensive leisure facilities had achieved little in terms of community reconciliation. At the same time the British government, through the Department of Education for Northern Ireland, became committed to a new, people-centred and ground-upwards approach to community relations. Almost by definition, community relations work means involving people in situations which require a certain level of interpersonal interaction among those elements of a given community which are experiencing tension and conflict. In the context of Northern Ireland this amounts to discovering ways of bringing together people from the different traditions in non-threatening environments wherein they can engage in collective activities in the hope that co-operation will lead to shared understanding, mutual respect and, eventually, community reconciliation.

In recognition of the importance of cultural institutions in forming separate political identities and preventing the development of a harmonious relationship between state and civil society, the Cultural Traditions Group was set up in 1988 by the newly formed Community Relations Council. The Group's intention has been to explore ways of promoting a better understanding of, and a more constructive debate about, our different cultural traditions in Northern Ireland.[35] In keeping with a long-standing academic tradition which views sport as ephemeral and trivial, sport was not on the agenda of the Group's inaugural conference held in 1989. However, a year later it had become apparent that sport could not be excluded from any discussions concerned with Northern Ireland's cultural divisions. As one of the Group commented:

> The group felt it important, firstly, to endorse the inclusion of a discussion on sport in a conference on Cultural Traditions. Many of the participants recognised sport as an important medium through which

culture is expressed and all were in agreement that sport was an agent for communication even though it could, at times, be divisive.[36]

In response, at the Group's second annual conference a seminar was convened, the main focus of which was 'the potential for both producing and reducing division through sport'.[37] At this seminar it was recognised that there are many examples of sport being used in a positive way to encourage cross-community relations. However, the group also recognised the divisive nature of sport. Indeed, sport was described as 'an important part of Northern Ireland's problem'.[38] Whilst acknowledging the valuable role played by sports in the maintenance of distinctive identities, the seminar expressed fears that the tribalism inherent in such activities as Gaelic sport and Rugby Union contribute to sectarian animosity.[39] Furthermore, it was suggested that cross-community tensions are exaggerated by association football, which although intrinsically less tribal, has proved to be fertile terrain for the cultivation of sectarian rivalry.

It was recognised that 'sport cannot opt out of the divided society within which it operates'.[40] Nevertheless, administrators of sport in the Province were criticised for their lack of sensitivity to or ignorance of the divisive nature of sport:

> They must start looking at the impact of their policies; not just is it good sport, are more people participating; but what impact is it having in a divided society? Is it sectional in its effect?[41]

Finally, the point was made that as in most societies, socio-economic status places constraints on the access of individuals to the whole range of sporting and recreational opportunities in Northern Ireland. However, access and choice is further limited by the vertical division of Northern Irish society and its unyielding sectarian geography.

The seminar concluded by making the following series of recommendations:

> 1. A curriculum for comparative sport could be developed which would maximise the advantages to be derived from diversity in sport by providing the opportunity to sample and become familiar with the full range of sports and the skills involved.
> 2. Those organisations which share responsibility for provision of sport and leisure facilities must look at ways of 'unlocking' the substantial

facilities which already exist to provide access to those who need them most.

3. The governing bodies of sport must begin to look at those aspects of their sports which are divisive and create barriers to cross-community appreciation and participation. They must also seek to maximise the cohesive potential of sport within a divided society.

4. Public agencies charged with responsibility for sport and its development must begin to look at the impact of their policies and deal with any sectional effects they may be having.[42]

While the aspirations inherent in these proposals are laudable, they are by no means all practicable. We agree wholeheartedly that those who administer sport in the Province could do more to help lessen community tension and enhance efforts designed to promote reconciliation. By refusing to acknowledge that sport is intimately bound up with the political crisis, they give tacit support to those who actively seek to use sport for the expression of sectarian sentiments. However, sport is not and can never be a panacea for social cleavages and some of the recommendations are unrealistic. The notion of a curriculum in comparative sport, for instance, is a utopian fantasy in the context of Northern Ireland's existing education system which, apart from a handful of integrated schools, operates along strict lines of sectarian division. Furthermore, the idealism of recommendations such as this contradicts the fundamental principle recognised by the Cultural Traditions Group itself, that sport cannot opt out of the divided society within which it operates. It is not sport *per se* which espouses sectarian values. Rather it is the people who play and watch sport who introduce political values into an otherwise neutral and inanimate enterprise. To expect people to affiliate to sport in any way which differs from the manner in which they affiliate to all other areas of social life in the Province is asking the impossible. This applies equally to sports administrators, physical educationalists and leisure managers who, in effect, are being asked by the Cultural Traditions Group to 'opt out' of their own divided society to provide the forum within which their fellow citizens can be freed from the constraints imposed by sectarian division.

Nevertheless, because by their very nature, many forms of sport and related forms of recreation are social activities which are especially appealing to young people, it is not surprising that they have been incorporated into what is rapidly emerging as a community relations industry in Northern Ireland. This was reinforced in 1991 by comments made by the Secretary of State for Northern Ireland, Peter Brooke in a speech on the importance of community relations:

> We must try to build on the willingness shown by local politicians from both traditions to work together to improve community relations; we must also continue with the important work of implementing the programme of cross-community contact schemes. Other areas where there is clearly scope for further action and where a number of exciting initiatives have taken place recently include the churches, sport and popular culture.[43]

Clearly, given what has already been said about the divisive impact which sport, in its native cultural setting, can have in Northern Ireland, the context of any sport-based community relations projects must be carefully managed and the outcome evaluated in some detail. Many such projects are currently being supported by DENI and other government agencies. It is worth mentioning two for illustration.

The first, which is called Belfast United, is a cross-community sports programme involving soccer and basketball. Essentially, youngsters are recruited from Catholic and Protestant areas of Belfast to be trained and coached as members of integrated basketball and soccer teams. The fact that both of these sports are already played, albeit usually separately, by both sections of the community provides an important common denominator, initially measured in terms of interest and skill in the games themselves, but also serving as an interactive medium for the underpinning community relations work. The highlight of the Belfast United project involves residential playing/coaching experiences in the United States. The youngsters are required to live with American families in mixed pairs (Catholic and Protestant). Project evaluations have shown that it is during these extended periods away from home, in the intimate company of peers from a different religious background, that the best community relations work can be done.[44] The second example is an experiment which is attempting to introduce Rugby Union into Belfast's Catholic community. In this case a number of Catholic secondary schools and non-rugby-playing Protestant secondary schools have been encouraged to send teams to Malone Rugby Club to participate in a series of tournaments using a simplified form of the game. From these tournaments three integrated rugby teams have been selected (under-18s, under-16s and under-14s) and are currently playing regular junior rugby on Saturday mornings in Belfast as well as going on tour together.[45]

The range and number of community relations programmes which use sport in the ways outlined above will continue to expand so long as government and other agencies are willing to provide the finance. It would be a mistake to make grand claims as to the impact which such programmes are having on commuity relations in the Province. Nevertheless, it is quite clear that these practical, grass-roots experiments in social engineering can have some impact on the relatively small numbers of individuals who experience them. The view taken by many of those who are involved in the development and supervision of such initiatives is that after a quarter of a century of serious sectarian violence and in the absence of any impending political panacea, this very gradual grass-roots work is the only way forward. At least it is better than doing nothing.

There is, however, another way of assessing the function of sport-based community relations work. The people involved in projects such as those outlined above make vigorous claims to have objectives which are fundamentally apolitical. Nevertheless, if Government thinking remains the same and the move away from municipally financed mass leisure continues apace, it is increasingly likely that support for these smaller-scale activities will be the favoured means through which the state seeks to use sport in the service of community stability and social control. In this sense and regardless of the motivations of those who organise and animate projects such as Belfast United and the Malone experiment, if the results of their interventions are a reduction in community conflict, then they must be counted on the state side of the contest for hegemony in Northern Ireland.

Conclusion

What then, in general, can be learned from Northern Ireland about the relationship between sport and society outlined above? Certainly, the view that sport can reflect and often exaggerate the most salient features of a given social order has been confirmed. The blighted history of the Olympic Games and the politicisation of sport in South Africa have clearly demonstrated that sport is vulnerable to political exploitation. The case study of Northern Ireland presented above leaves us in no doubt that sport can be a malleable and potent social force in the mobilisation of political sentiment. In modern history sport has developed as one of the most significant vehicles for national and regional identification and when there is conflict over the boundaries of such identification, as is the case in Northern Ireland, sport becomes engaged in at least two ways in the struggle for self-determination. Firstly, sport provides the arena for a symbolic contest for the hearts and minds of a divided population. In Northern Ireland, for instance, what games are played and which teams are supported is less a matter of individual sports preference and more a matter of collective national fidelity. Secondly, sport provides a cultural rallying point and platform upon which more formal political manifestoes are built and sustained. In this way political symbolism can be directly linked to political action. The heritage of the GAA and its current status within Northern Ireland exemplifies this relationship.

Another general point is that, as aspects of civil society, sport and leisure only reveal themselves clearly as foci for political struggle during times of protracted civil unrest. Such manifestations may well be the end results of continuous historical processes, but it is only when the co-operation and control of civil society itself is at stake, as in Northern Ireland, that the state is forced to show its hand. However, what the state has learned to its cost in the Province is that, as part of civil society, neither sport nor leisure can be mobilised automatically in support of the established forces of law and order. They are both areas deeply rooted in popular culture and as such are likely to be part and parcel of the undercurrents which fuel dissent. As such they are easy neither to penetrate nor to manipulate and, to paraphrase Ralph Miliband's argument, once the state targets sport and leisure as battle fronts in the war to establish hegemony it discovers them to be 'highly contested territory'.

The picture is further complicated by the fact that civil society in Northern Ireland is terrain contested not just between social classes, but also between Catholics and Protestants, various groupings of Nationalists and Loyalists and the multiple façades of the British state. In terms of sport and leisure, the state in Northern Ireland has at least two faces: firstly, an open and smiling countenance which supports community integration and cross-border co-operation; secondly, and closer to the scene, a scowl which accompanies coercion and force to maintain the status quo. Accordingly, on the surface a conventional British model of community recreation and sport for all is encouraged. In practice, however, this model tends to reinforce rather than ameliorate sectarian divisions and at a local level, through the activities of politically motivated pressure groups, local politicians and ultimately the security forces, sport and leisure have become part of Northern Ireland's wider cultural and political conflict. Thus, while sport and leisure may not be the Province's most important battle grounds, by no means are they the least significant.

Notes

1 J. Sugden and A. Bairner, 'Northern Ireland: sport in a divided society', in L. Allison, ed., *The Politics of Sport*, Manchester University Press, 1986, pp. 90–117.
2 C. Knox, 'Policy evaluation in leisure services – the Northern Ireland case', *Leisure Studies*, 10 (2), 1991, 105–17.
3 *Sunday Life*, 5 January 1992.
4 *Sunday Life*, 2 February 1992.
5 *Sunday Life*, 26 January 1992.
6 *Spotlight*, BBC TV, 1991.
7 S. Bergin and D. Scott, 'Ireland', in E. W. Swanton, ed., *Barclay's World of Cricket*, Collins, 1980, pp. 508–9 (p. 508).
8 *Ibid.*
9 W. P. Hone, *Cricket in Ireland*, The Kerryman Limited (Tralee), 1956, p. 3.
10 *Ibid.*, p. 5.
11 *Ibid.*
12 *Ibid.*
13 Bergin and Scott, p. 508.
14 Hone, p. 6.
15 *Ibid.*, p. 36.
16 *Ibid.*, p. 11.
17 *Ibid.*, pp. 12–13.
18 *Ibid.*, p. 23.
19 *Ibid.*
20 *Ibid.*, p. 28.
21 *Irish Times*, 14 June 1990.
22 Cliftonville Cricket Club Centenary Brochure, 1990.
23 *Spotlight*, BBC TV, 1991.
24 J. Sugden and A. Bairner, 'Northern Ireland: the politics of leisure in a divided society', *Leisure Studies*, 5, 1986, 341–52.
25 J.-M. Brohm, *Sport: A Prison of Measured Time*, Ink Links, 1978.

26 *Workers' Playtime*, BBC Radio Northern Ireland, 5 April 1987.
27 D. Huntley, *Community Interest or Political Pressure: Public Leisure Provision in Belfast*, unpublished B.A. (Hons.) dissertation, University of Ulster, 1988, p. 44.
28 *Workers' Playtime*, 5 April 1987.
29 Huntley, *Community Interest or Political Pressure*; C. Knox, 'Territorialism, leisure and community centres in Northern Ireland', *Leisure Studies*, 6, 1987, 212–37.
30 Huntley, *Community Interest or Political Pressure*, p. 50.
31 K. Roberts, S. Dench, J. Milten and C. York, *Community Response to Leisure Provision in Belfast*, Study no. 34, London, Sports Council, 1989.
32 Department of the Environment, *Value for Money Study: Leisure Facilities*, Belfast, Local Government Audit, 1989.
33 C. Knox, 'Policy evaluation in leisure service'.
34 L. O'Dowd, B. Rolston and M. Tomlinson, *Northern Ireland: Between Civil Rights and Civil War* CSE Press, 1980.
35 M. Crozier, ed., *Cultural Traditions in Northern Ireland*, Institute of Irish Studies, Queen's University, 1990, p. vi.
36 *Ibid.*, p. 107.
37 *Ibid.*
38 *Ibid.*, p. 109.
39 *Ibid.*
40 *Ibid.*, p. 108.
41 *Ibid.*, p. 106.
42 *Ibid.*, p. 116.
43 Northern Ireland Information Service, Community Relations Press Release, February 1991.
44 J. Sugden, 'Belfast United: encouraging cross-community relations through sport in Northern Ireland', *Journal of Sport and Social Issues*, 15 (1), 1991, 59–80.
45 R. Snowling, *Youth Rugby in Northern Ireland: Cross-Community Recruitment and Development*, unpublished M.A. dissertation, University of Ulster, 1992.
46 R. Miliband, *Marxism and Politics*, Oxford University Press, 1977.

10

Sport as an environmental issue

LINCOLN ALLISON

Sport is increasingly in conflict with the conservation of the environment. This essay is an analysis of the issues which arise from this conflict. These can, of course, be represented in terms of the concept of interests, as clashes between the 'tastes', 'wants' and 'demands' of different groups of people, between those, for example, who want to walk or to contemplate natural phenomena and those who want to participate in a vast range of more active or competitive pastimes, like golf, water-skiing, hang-gliding or moto-cross. But my principal interest in these issues is as conflicts of principle: both the 'environment' and 'sport' have been institutionally raised in status above the level of mere marketable commodities and assumed to consist of activities which are either ends-in-themselves or of public benefit or both. The questions of principle concern why this should be so, how the boundaries of the activities should be drawn and how their worth can be assessed against each other.

For those who want to develop a hermeneutic understanding of the structure of language and the values it carries and expresses, the general areas of sporting activity and our attachment to our environment are areas full of meaning. Both 'sport' and 'the countryside' suggest aspects of life which people care about deeply, which are locations for their senses of achievement and identity. In the more policy-oriented terms of Utilitarian political philosophy which interest me more, the experience of traditional and natural landscapes and sporting endeavour are prime candidates for what John Stuart Mill called the 'higher' pleasures – qualitatively different from ordinary pleasures and worthy of public encouragement and protection. Even if this distinction is reduced to one of degree (of the profundity of pleasure) it holds its place as a pointer to serious issues.

In more common parlance, we are dealing with extremely vague terms. In *The Politics of Sport*, I concluded that it was impossible to draw precise boundaries around what we normally mean (or would want to mean) by sport.[1] I also suggested that at the core of the modern idea of sport was an ancient idea of prowess which distinguished what sport, in its typical and undeniable instances, was about from what mere recreations, forms of exercise, pastimes and competitions (such as those of pure chance) offered. But clarifying a core idea does not necessarily help much with the drawing of boundaries. Most of the sports which raise issues about the countryside are mere leisure activities or forms of exercise, even if they also exist in a form which is undeniably sporting. This is true, for example, of walking, jogging, fishing, rowing and swimming. Where the activity is not formally organised as a sport it can, nevertheless, have sporting characteristics. Setting out to swim a lake or climb a 'Munro' which you have never swum or climbed before, represents a 'challenge', a form of competition against yourself and the elements which is sporting in character.

The investigation of sport and the countryside must tackle the question of 'What is sport?' at the outset, even if only in the rather trivial way of sketching out boundaries between sport and other forms of leisure. But that question must also be tackled at a later stage in a rather more profound way. 'What is supposed to be special and specially good about sport as a practice?' There must be a suspicion that sport is like religion, not only in the general senses in which sport is popularly conceived as being like religion, but also in the more narrowly logical sense that religion (in contemporary legal notions of blasphemy, offence and toleration, for example) and sport both have a privileged status without it being clear what they are or whether all those activities currently included really share the advantages supposed to accrue to the general practice. 'Which, if any, form of paganism is a religion?' is a question like 'Which, if any, card game is a sport?' and has the same practical significance once we embody 'sport' and 'religion' into important policy principles. In Britain this raises interesting questions about the definition of sport operated by the government's principal agent in the matter, the Sports Council.

At least with sport there are existing boundaries for the activity, even if they are not, ultimately, justifiable. With the question of what it is to preserve 'the environment', or a particular environment such as the English 'countryside' we move to a yet higher form of mysticism. The rhetoric of ordinary language has it that landscapes are 'preserved' or 'destroyed'. But a more serious consideration of the meaning of words tells us that neither of these words is even remotely appropriate except in a tiny fraction of cases. Landscapes change, in different ways and to different degrees. Human beings are responsible for many of the changes, but not for all of them. The changes can be evaluated as good or bad according to a wide variety of standards. The environment does not set its own standards. Ecology has no moral substance: 'harmony' and 'balance' of nature are artistic ideals rather than objective states of equilibrium. Most professional ecologists, including Ernst Haeckel, who first published the term and James Lovelock, who has become a contemporary ecological guru, are quite clear that the science of ecology gives us neither rules nor goals for controlling the environment.[2] We are left to debate and resolve our own values and must reject pseudo-objectivity. We do value the status quo. We think we value nature, but there can be no value placed on nature as such, only on established nature, our ideal of nature or on diversity of nature. A conflict of values between sport and conservation is something like a clash of ghosts, a battle between the mystical and the ethereal. But it is important, nevertheless.

The conflict between sport and conservation often occurs in heavily disguised forms. The sports involved here are non-urban sports. The nature and variety of terrain (and of water) are very much part of the sport: knowing and dealing with a variety of conditions is an important part of demonstrating prowess and achieving satisfaction (as it is, to a lesser degree, in such predominantly urban sports as cricket and football). Participants feel part of their sporting environment and protective of it; they are instinctively hostile to any idea that they are intrusive and inappropriate. The most perceptible conflicts of interest (as opposed to principle) are between sports and not between sport and any other value. Goodall and Whittow, in a study for the Forestry Commission, looked at twenty-four country activities, twenty of which were sports to some degree. Of the 552 possible relationships between sports, there were 61 'empty sets', in that the sports could not use the same kind of terrain. Of the 491 remaining, 153 were considered wholly incompatible in that they could not take place on the same area, even at different times, 272 could not take place at the same time and only 66 were fully compatible. Their figures for thirteen aquatic sports were: 156 theoretically possible relations, 4 'empty sets', 18 completely incompatible, 20 completely compatible and 114 simultaneously incompatible.[3]

Of course, for all the self-image of the English as living in a 'small and densely-populated country', recreational land is not so scarce that most of these theoretical incompatibilities become real conflicts. Some of them do, however: the resentment by pedestrians of all sorts against horse and motorised transport which tears up green lanes and bridleways is widespread as is the emnity between freshwater fishermen of all kinds and canoeists. Even some of the empty sets can cause pain: anglers are not in direct competition for space with the land forms of motor sport, but if what you like about the river or canal bank is its calm, you are likely to be fairly aggrieved by motorbikes on the towpath or any form of racing which involves engines taking place within half a mile.

Traditionally, the issue about recreation in the countryside has concentrated on the problem of access and this has tended to distort and undervalue the importance of what is at stake between conservationists and sportsmen. For most of the history of recreation in the countryside the central issue has been thought to be the demands made by the townsman upon space belonging to landowners, a source of conflict which has often been seen, simplistically, as an issue between rich and poor. In the legislation passed by the Attlee government in the 1940s, particularly the National Parks and Access to the Countryside Act of 1949, access and conservation are seen as not only compatible, but allied objectives and this assumption has remained the established idea of the problem since. Farmers have helped maintain this framework by expressing resentment of all access to private land at least in principle. According to research commissioned by the Countryside Commission and Sports Council, 82 per cent of farmers have rights of way across their land and 87 per cent would oppose any further increase in public access; 71 per cent of farmers claim their land is used illegally and 94 per cent allow some recreational use of their land.[4]

My own impressions are compatible with the survey though do not constitute the only possible interpretation of the figures. The overwhelming majority of farmers tolerate public access to their land, provided it is in forms they regard as harmless or which they can control, but they are very jealous of any increased rights to encroach on their land. Walkers, picnickers and naturalists have little conflict with farmers. I find the desire to maintain a generalised issue of access at the forefront of the rural debate to be self-interested and out-dated. The appeal to one's user solidarity which comes from many of the organisations of many different sports and which pervades the ethos of Sports Council research, may fit the paradigms of traditional left/right politics, but it does not represent the real and deep divisions in the contemporary country-side. Walkers, who still outnumber by far all other country visitors, have far more to fear from war-gamers, motor-sports enthusiasts or riders changing the atmosphere of their favourite stretch of country than they do from farmers restricting access to it. In any case, it is clear by now that the old access coalition, as one might call it, has broken and that many individuals and organisations who regard themselves as conservationists now believe it is important to restrict many kinds of access to the countryside.

A range of examples

In the area with which I am most familiar, Warwick District, at the time of writing, sporting issues have taken over the planning agenda to an unprecedented degree. The political sticker (in the broad sense of political) seen most often in Leamington Spa expresses opposition to a plan to build an indoor bowling facility in one of the chain of parks which runs through the town. For its proponents, this facility is necessary not only to meet demand, but to the town's campaign to assure and increase its status in the world of bowls. (Leamington already hosts the English Women's Bowls Association championships and there is a campaign to attract further events.) To its opponents, this proposal represents a major breach of the green corridor which runs through the town. The current issue is parallel, and a sequel, to an earlier conflict in which a major swimming facility was constructed on Newbold Comyn, the large park to the east of the town.

Newbold Comyn is a remarkable park; it is over 300 acres in extent, has a river and a reservoir and is able to accommodate almost all the recreational activities which can normally be pur-sued in lowland England. (The figure of 300 acres for the area of Newbold Comyn does not include the water surfaces nor a number of adjoining public open spaces – recreation grounds, flood meadows and river banks – which amount to about a hundred acres. The Comyn is part of a roughly contiguous chain of parks and public open spaces which make up the bulk of Warwick District Council's publicly owned open space. Of the 300 acres, 150 acres are currently devoted to golf facilities and 40 acres to playing fields for team games.) Beyond it, further east and on privately owned land, is a well-known equestrian cross-country course. The Comyn is still remarkably rural in character having, in my judgement, a larger range of wildlife and of landscape features than most agricultural land in Warwickshire. An important dimension of its recent history has been a succession of issues in which sports organisations and the Amenities Department have pressed for more and more modern facilities, including car parks, and conservationists and the Planning Department have sought to preserve the character of the area. Currently, there is a proposal for a further golf course to add to the existing full-scale and 'pitch and put' courses, which would encroach on land previously allocated for afforestation and a nature reserve.

Golf is by far the biggest single environmental issue in sport in the locality. Nationally, the best known of the issues in the area I am describing is the proposal to construct two new golf courses and a hotel in the parkland of Warwick Castle. The park was designed by Lancelot 'Capability' Brown and is now separately owned from the castle. The planning application was 'called-in' by the Secretary of State for the Environment and a public inquiry held. Conservationists took their stand principally on the historic interest of the landscape. The owners argued that it had already deteriorated and that they could not be expected to finance its restoration unless they could derive income from it. Elsewhere in the District, Lord Leigh's estate, north of Leamington, already has one newly constructed golf course and a proposal for a second, while the Arkwright estate in Hatton is proceeding with the construction of a course.

Many of these proposals have been dogged by controversy. By contrast, there is a belt of land around the north of Leamington whose development has been a non-issue, though conservationists are concerned by it in retrospect and planners concede that it has only stayed off the agenda because of its slow, incremental nature.

This belt consists of horse-jumping paddocks, a football club and two rugby clubs. Its development is very largely a consequence of Green Belt policy which has severely limited the space available for housing. Thus recreational space within the existing urban area, including school playing fields and sports clubs, has come under severe market pressure to become residential development. A displacement effect occurs in which the sports facilities retreat to the Green Belt. But modern sports facilities, requiring car parks, advertising hoardings, floodlights, all-weather pitches and extensive buildings, are in many respects an extension of the urban area. Green Belt policy, unlike other rural designations such as Areas of Outstanding Natural Beauty, has always encouraged recreational uses. But this policy was conceived in a period when the range and nature of sports facilities was rather different from what it has become. One sporting project which has not been able to find a site in Warwick District is Leamington Football Club (formerly A. P. Leamington and before that Lockheed Leamington) which ran the town's semi-professional team. Since the parent company sold the land for housing, the club (now consisting of a committee and a bank account) has looked in vain for a ground, only to meet with virulent opposition in each case. The story is similar to that of other football clubs, such as Maidstone United and Oxford United, which have tried to relocate in south-east England and the Midlands. Leamington F C have not kicked a ball since 1987.

So far I have been discussing the problems of one English district, whose problems and policies would be considered fairly 'typical' of the Midlands or south-east of England, though it is marginally more prosperous and has a great many more tourists than the average. Its countryside is pleasant and distinctively English, though it lacks any kind of wildness or great diversity of scenery: it has been described as an 'area of outstanding natural mediocrity'. In more spectacular and distinctive areas, the tensions between sport, recreation and conservation are much more obvious though no less complex. The South Downs, for example, are designated as an 'Area of Outstanding Natural Beauty', a hybrid and ambiguous category which arose out of the implementation of the National Parks Act of 1949. AONBs have generally been interpreted as places in which design and development are controlled and no facilities provided. But the South Downs have over $2^{1}/_{2}$ million visitors a year (as compared with only a million in the Northumberland

National Park): many of these visitors want to pursue specific recreations such as horse riding, 'all-terrain' cycling, ballooning and hang-gliding. The area has edged towards National Park status without quite getting there. It has an inter-authority 'Conservation Board', a ranger service and a Conservation Project Officer who reports that reconciling sport and leisure activities with each other and with conservation is now a far more important problem than agriculture or development. As a tragi-comic symbol of the need to reconcile activities he points out that a hang-glider was killed in 1990 when a line was cut by the propellor of a model aircraft.[5]

The Norfolk Broads have approached the status of a National Park much more closely so that their current status is almost deliberately ambiguous. The area consists of the valleys of the Bure, Ant, Thurne, Yare and Waveney, including a total of forty-two shallow lakes created by the digging of peat, a practice almost certainly initiated by the Danes. The Norfolk and Suffolk Broads Act of 1988 set up a Broads Authority with all the powers of a National Park and more. The Act did not designate a National Park, but the Board it established does refer to itself as 'our newest and very special national park'. Paradoxically, more powers than a National Park may effectively mean fewer, because the Authority has navigation powers and a powerful Navigation Committee dominated by boating interests and committed to the principle of free access to most of the area for boats.

To deal with the tensions between sport, recreation and conservation, the Board has evolved a zoning policy. Some areas, including Hickling Broad, the largest of the true broads, have ample opportunities for such sports as yachting and water-skiing. Others are cut off from traffic altogether, like Cockshoot Broad which has been 'restored' to its ecological condition at the beginning of the century, before mass tourism and modern farming began to have effect, and is now one of six broads in this condition. These ares of strict conservation complement the nature reserves established in the area by the Nature Conservancy before 1988. In between, a majority of the area is dominated by recreational navigation, though with strict control of speeds and moorings.

A zoning policy of this kind looks fairly logical from the Authority's offices in Norwich, though it can have some distinctly odd consequences. In 1991 Norfolk Friends of the Earth found themselves without allies in their attempts to protect Whitlingham

Marsh, on the south bank of the Yare, about three miles from Norwich, from the incursions of gravel extraction by Crown Point Estates. The 'marsh' is an attractive water meadow of about a hundred acres, traditionally used by Norwich people for casual recreation. It was odd to discover the lack of opposition from the Authority, and from their Conservation Officer in particular, to these activities. But part of their perception was that the extraction would create substantial and accessible new areas of water suitable for competitive sports, which would make it possible for them to pursue more conservationist policies elsewhere.[6]

Most of the designated National Parks of England and Wales consist of moor, mountain and 'rough grazing'; they are degraded environments with simple and resilient eco-systems. They have been relatively little threatened by agricultural change and protecting them from development has proved fairly straightforward. Increasingly, their most serious problems have been the inter-relations and impact of mass recreation: in the extreme case, the Lake District has 13 million visitors annually. Even walking causes 'people erosion': typically, broadly worn paths become water-channels, forcing walkers to take an even wider berth and creating linear swathes of bare earth across the hills. The only solution is restriction of access and careful restoration, often accompanied by the construction of a suitably durable artificial path. But there are also more specifically sporting problems arising out of the popularity of motor sports and the 1980s vogue for 'all-terrain' bicycles. Increased people-erosion comes from the growth in popularity of fell running, which remained a purely Cumbrian sport until the 1960s, but has now spread throughout the Pennines and beyond.

I have taken a fairly intuitive idea of environmental and ecological quality in talking about these problems. The research done by Roger Sidaway for the Sports Council concentrates on much more specific ideas of environmental damage, usually in relation to the habitats of particular species.[7] He looked at the impact of caving in south Wales, the problems caused by climbers to cliff-nesting birds in north Wales, the consequences of upland access for ground-nesting birds in the Peak District, the impact of orienteering on woodlands in the East Midlands, that of sub-squa diving on marine reserves around Skomer Island, off Pembrokeshire, and the relation between watersports and over-wintering wildfowl in the Solent and the East Midlands. His general conclusions are that there are few conservation problems caused by recreation and that the most serious, concerning over-wintering wildfowl, can be solved by the imposition of strict regulations at certain times. This is important research, but I will be arguing later that the narrowness of its focus can be highly misleading if one wants a broad and true picture of the environmental problems caused by sport.

This survey, and the essay generally, have been confined to England and Wales. People who study environmental problems in England and Wales are often in the position to claim that their study is of special interest because the problems represent a prototype and these issues are no exception. Britain has gone through processes of industrialisation, urbanisation and disurbanisation before any other and there have been lessons to learn from its experience at each stage. Levels of density and of value (in both senses) in relation to land have been reached in advance of other countries. However, the 'prototype' model must always be set against the 'cultural difference' model: some differences between societies are not related to the stage of development, but to differences of values and meanings between cultures. Hunting, for example, is an entirely different range of activities in continental Europe when compared with the British Isles: it is on a different scale and has a much greater impact (many would say a more adverse impact) on the environment.

Even so, some sort of comparative perspective is important here, even if it is only to point out that sport creates environmental tensions in most societies, though they tend to be different from our own and less generally important than those found here. In continental Europe, apart from hunting, the biggest issue is skiing, a sport operating on an unrivalled geographical and commercial scale. (The parallel in England must be golf.) The skiing industry has caused enormous social and environmental disruption in many mountainous areas. Beyond Europe, hunting is an issue almost everywhere, but, in principle at least, the most common experience is that hunting seasons and licences can be operated in such a way that hunting complements ecological control more than it hinders. It is only in social and political circumstances in which such regulations cannot be enforced (and it is unlikely that any environmental regulations could be effectively enforced) that hunting (or fishing) causes insoluble problems. In North American and Australian national parks there has always been intense debate about the balance to be struck between recreation and conservation and this has further intensified in recent years with greater mobility and the arrival, in often fragile ecological systems, of the all-terrain bicycle.

An historical perspective

A quarter of a century ago I was an undergraduate in an Oxford college, very few of whose students were from the north of England. I used to tell my contemporaries that I came from Burnley, a place they were far more likely to have heard of, and have an image of, than Colne, my real home. With variable amounts of polite, benign and genuine curiosity, they asked what sort of place it was. My favourite, stage northerner, reply was that it was the sort of place where, on a Saturday morning, I could walk across Pendle, among the clouds, alone with the skylarks and curlews and on a Saturday afternoon I could be part of a packed, emotional crowd of 25,000 people watching Burnley play football.

I could not possibly make these claims now. In the 1980s crowds at Turf Moor, the home of Burnley Football Club, slumped to 2500 on occasions, in a stadium that had once held more than 54,000 people. I continued to climb Pendle regularly, but was rarely alone: usually there were dozens of people, sometimes hundreds, and they included fell-runners, mountain bikers, motor-bikers and hang-gliders as well as walkers. The Pendle local authority used government-subsidised youth labour to turn the traditional main path up the hill into a set of steps, in order to prevent erosion. This is my personal version of the transition from the predominance of a model of 'modern sport' to one of 'post-industrial sport', to use the terms we employed in *The Politics of Sport*. Modern sport is typified by being a mass activity, highly organised, taking place in the limited and well-defined segments of time and space available in a manufacturing society. Post-industrial sport is more diverse and participatory, requires much more time and space and typically reverts to pre-industrial traditions and values. The post-industrial sportsman is not a 'townsman' who finds the country alien, but would claim to feel at home in it.

In many respects, post-industrial sport is a return to the mass occupation of land and rural leisure that we called 'traditional sport', which used the great spaces and many holidays of an agricultural society. (In 1761 there were 47 'bank holidays' defined as the Bank of England closing on a day other than Sunday; in 1834 there were four![8] Seen from another point of view, it represents a 'fourth wave' of land-use planning problems which have arisen since industrialisation. Michael Dower's graphic and influential image was constructed at the same time that I was describing, to my fellow undergraduates, the last stages of an overwhelmingly industrial society:

> Three great waves have broken across the face of Britain since 1800. First, the sudden growth of dark industrial towns. Second, the movement along far-flung railways. Third, the sprawl of car-based suburbs. Now we see, under the guise of a modest word, the surge of a fourth wave which could be more powerful than all the others. The modest word is *leisure*.[9]

The 'leisure' society offers important analogs to the traditional society. In neither are the masses incarcerated in the urban-industrial milieu, but tend to penetrate the whole land surface, bringing themselves into conflict with each other and with landowners, creating issues with dimensions of conflict involving class and alternative principles of property rights. In 1831 a sixth of all prosecutions were still under the gaming laws and the opinions held by landowners of the incursions on their land were broadly similar to those expressed by contemporary farmers, especially on the urban fringe.[10]

But those similarities amount to analogy, not homology. The context of power, class and property which relates modern leisure seekers to farmers is entirely different from the relationship between landowners and landless labourers in traditional society. Despite these differences, there were two brilliant premonitions of our contemporary problems in the 1840s. William Wordsworth campaigned against the coming of the railway to Windermere and condemned, among other things, the growing practice of Lancashire manufacturers organising trips for their workers to the Lakes.[11] John Stuart Mill wrote of the need for society to arrive at a 'stationary state' without economic or demographic growth lest the lack of opportunities for such experiences as the 'solitary contemplation of natural grandeur' should irredeemably reduce what we would call the quality of life for future generations.[12] Mill's concern that our experience of wild and spectacular landscape should not seem too crowded or commonplace seems extraordinarily in advance of its time. Wordsworth, too, was concerned with the quality of the outsider's experience of the wild but he was also concerned with the values of an existing rural society in a way that Mill was not.

In this context what is important about Wordsworth and Mill is *not* that they stand at the beginning of a long debate about the tensions between access and conservation, it is that theirs were exceptional premonitions quite different from most perceptions of environmental problems. During the Victorian period there came into existence a coalition of thought which linked the conservation of the countryside with the campaign for public access to it against the interests of developers and landowners. Lord Bryce's campaign for access to mountains, the establishment of the National Trust by Octavia Hill *et al.* and the purchase of Burnham Beeches by London County Council were Victorian manifestations of this access–conservation coalition. It was maintained by the movement for the preservation of the countryside which grew powerful in the interwar period, which gave rise, in 1926, to the Council for the (then) Preservation of Rural England and to ideas which influenced the Scott Report on Land Utilisation in Rural Areas in 1942 and the legislation of the Attlee government after the war. The leading figure of this movement was the architect Clough Williams-Ellis. Although he did have some interesting comments on the impact of golf courses on the countryside, nearly all of his influential output can be classified as being within the access–conservation coalition.[13] Even more remarkably (to my mind) these assumptions have informed most postwar thinking within the relevant policy-sectors up to the present day, including research done for the Sports Council and the Countryside Commission and by the Countryside Recreation Research Advisory Group.[14]

But, before returning to these crucial conflicts and ambiguities of principle, it is necessary to examine more closely the idea of a leisure age and its correspondence to the facts of contemporary life.

Myths and realities of a leisure age

An age of leisure, a condition in which the great majority of people, and not just a leisure class, would have large and increasing amounts of free time, has been the subject of speculation and expectation for many decades. In the 1920s and 1930s automation was expected to bring the leisure age into being; by the 1970s, it was expectations of under-employment and job-sharing. The brute fact is that the leisure age has never arrived. In 1989, full-time manual employees still worked an average of nearly 44 hours a week, under two hours less than in 1961.[15] Roughly 40 per cent of the adult residents of Great Britain did not take a holiday of four nights or more, exactly the same proportion as in 1971.[16] If those facts are put alongside the phenomenon of steadily rising female employment and the perception in the 1980s that salaried professionals were working harder and putting in longer hours, the inference must be that we have been moving towards an era of harder work rather than one of leisure. Several modern economic theories have undermined any possibility of a leisure age. Fred Hirsch suggested that, even in an age of material abundance, our thinking would still be dominated by perceptions of the need to acquire 'positional goods' which are scarce by definition.[17] Tibor Scitovsky portrayed the *volkgeist* of the USA as a 'puritan ghost' which turned the instrumentalities of work into ends-in-themselves and made work the true meaning of life and many commentators have alleged an Americanisation of western Europe in this sense as in others.[18]

But, if the leisure age has proved something of a myth, some of the changes in social life do combine to create the effects of a leisured society. There has been an expansion of the leisure class: in the same period (1971–89) that the number of people not taking a holiday remained constant, the number taking three or more holidays increased by around 150 per cent and the number taking two or more increased by around 50 per cent.[19] If work time scarcely decreased, the time needed for what I would describe as private instrumental time was decreased by domestic automation and fast and convenience foods, among other things. In 1989, men in full-time employment had 44 hours of leisure time per week and women 33 hours.[20] Geographical mobility has been increasing for most of the period. There was, of course, a great leap in petrol prices in 1973–4 but, despite this, the real price of petrol is still lower than in 1972. More importantly, perhaps, expectations of mobility have increased dramatically. Sociologically, in narrow terms, there has been considerable net upward mobility. Corresponding to this has been a shift from the classic industrial recreations to the post-industrial.

Thus the leisure economy grew in the 1980s. In cash terms 'leisure items' increased from £16.82 per household per week to £35.01 between 1981 and 1989; as a percentage of household expenditure this was an increase from 13.4 per cent to 15.6 per cent.[21] Looking at figures for particular activities, it is noticeable that the only things that were in decline were associated with traditional working-class life. Of the ten most popular tourist attractions with free admission, Blackpool Pleasure Beach was alone in having fewer visitors in 1989 than in 1981, though it remained, in absolute numbers, the most popular.[22] Of the ten most popular sports, only football, cricket and greyhound racing lost spectators during this period.[23]

By contrast, the General Household survey shows quite remarkable increases in the percentage of the population participating in sports between 1977 and 1987, though at least some of these are attributable to changing techniques and timing in the conduct of the survey (Table 10.1).[24]

Table 10.1

	1977	1987
Walking	17.1	37.9
Swimming	6.7	13.1
Cycling	0.8	8.4
Golf	2.3	3.9
Activity in general	39.0	61.0

Just as remarkable, and perhaps more reliable, were the figures reported by Roger Sidaway relating to the percentage increases in membership of outdoor sporting organisations in the 1970s, the only period when the real cost of travel was going up (Table 10.2).[25]

Table 10.2

Angling	26
Canoeing	67
Yachting	85
Surfing	263
Sub-Aqua	100
Water-skiing	119
Horse riding	59
Skiing	29
Field sports	125
Cycling	58

It may be dubious and ambiguous to talk of a 'leisure age', but there can be no doubting the reality of a sustained boom in

post-industrial sports and recreations which make great demands
on the countryside and create conflicts with a range of values which
focus on the countryside.

The golf boom

I suggested earlier that, in the densely populated regions of south-
east and Midlands England the expansion of golf courses is not only
the prime case of sport and conservation being in conflict, it is one of
the most important planning issues of any kind. Golf raises complex
issues and is worthy of far more detailed study than can be offered
here. But even a preliminary survey of the nature of the conflicts
created by the expansion of golf and the possible compromises will
be suggestive.

Golf is not a typical issue, however, if there is such a thing.
Golf courses are almost sole occupiers of land, though they do
leave some room for walking, nature study and the enjoyment
of scenery. The game can hold its own on the market, not
only because it is popular, but also because it can be effectively
controlled and sold. There are four main forms of golf course: the
private club, owned by its members, the hotel or 'leisure complex',
the 'pay-as-you-play' private course and the municipal course. All
of them have proven financial viability; in the public sector, golf
courses have everywhere been the most remunerative of amenity
departments' activities, having a potential, given the right price
structure, to show a healthy profit.[26]

The potential for the expansion of golf is almost unlimited. It is
a game that can be played by people of any age and both genders.
What is more, drama and satisfaction can occur at any standard
and the handicapping and 'Sunningdale' systems can assure competition between individuals of different standards. Thus, unlike
their messianic rivals preaching the gospels of cricket and rugby,
golfers can argue, not only that all the world's problems would be
solved if everybody played golf, but also that everybody *could* play
golf. And unlike (say) skateboarding or marathon running, a boom
in golf is not automatically undermined by the experience of injury
or athletic incompetence. Almost everything about contemporary
society – an ageing population, upward social mobility and a more
geographically mobile population, for example – is favourable to
the expansion of golf. Rates of participation in golf have expanded

steadily and by 1987 it was the seventh or eighth most popular activity for men (depending on the time stipulated in the survey) and the most popular outdoor game.[27] At that time courses had not begun to expand on scale with the expansion in players. Elspeth Burnside commented more recently in *Golf Monthly* that 'Not so long ago, golfers in Britain would raise a smile at the notion of Japanese golfers swinging away on tiered driving ranges, while never having the chance to venture out on a golf course. It will not be so funny if a similar situation occurs in this country.'[28]

A potential land hunger for golf courses developed in the 1980s against the background of an increasing extent of and commitment to such designations as Green Belts and Areas of Outstanding Natural Beauty and a decline in the agricultural value and importance of land. The 1981 Wildlife and Countryside Act contained no real acknowledgement of agricultural over-production and its environmental consequences, but by 1984 the first major real cuts (in dairying) were occurring and by 1987 the government was producing its ALURE ('Alternative Land Use in the Rural Economy') package of incentives to encourage farmers into forestry, tourism and 'valued added' industries like cheese and yoghurt. Successive Department of Environment directives devalued the importance to be attributed to agricultural value as such in planning decisions and the orthodoxy came to be established that England had between 3000 and 6000 too many square miles of land in agricultural production. The supply of land reciprocated the demand for golf.

In 1989 the Royal and Ancient Golf Club of St Andrews published a report, *The Demand for Golf*, which suggested a 'need' for seven hundred new courses by the end of the century.[29] It was alleged that these would cover that familiar giant unit of land-use, 'an area roughly the size of the Isle of Wight', or about 85,000 acres. The projected increases in the Midlands (75 per cent), the south-west (64 per cent) and London and the south-east (43 per cent) were greatly in excess of those in other regions.[30] A general standard of one course for every 25,000 people was stipulated, though it is difficult to translate this into practical planning arguments because this norm looks very different when interpreted within different boundaries. For example, Warwick District would require only five courses on this basis, which it already has. But what about the hundreds of thousands of people who visit Stratford and Warwick as tourists? Or the two-and-a-half million who live immediately to tbe north in the Coventry and Birmingham conurbations?

The threat of the golf course boom has produced a reaction and something of a switch in policy on the part of major conservation organisations, particularly the Council for the Protection of Rural England and English Heritage.[31] Generally speaking, their reaction was fairly favourable to golf at an earlier period: golf courses, after all, generally have more landscape features and more wildlife than the equivalent acreage in arable farmland. They took their cue from Clough Williams-Ellis who had written in 1928: 'Golf courses are really specialised parks, often very beautiful parks, and as such they are most welcome, particularly in or near large towns.'[32]

The argument against modern golf courses is not against golf as such, but against the 'Trojan Horse effect' as the CPRE has called it, which uses a general presumption in favour of golf to introduce developments which urbanise the landscape or destroy its local character. The conservationist position can be seen most clearly as a contrast between the environmentally sympathetic golf course and the Trojan Horse (Table 10.3).

Table 10.3

	Sympathetic	Trojan Horse
Location	Green Belt/Urban fringe/Derelict land	Area of Outstanding Natural Beauty or other sensitive landscape
Access	Existing roads	New roads
Building	Existing building (e.g. country house) or modest vernacular clubhouse	Major hotel/chalet development
Design	Emphasis on using character of local landscape. Unfussy sand and water features	'Augusta syndrome': imitation of US or Scottish models
Wildlife/ecology	Minimal disturbance	Imported trees and grasses requiring high input of fertilisers and control chemicals
Clientele	Local people	Wealthy tourists
Additional features	Planning gain from screening by woods/nature reserves	Floodlit driving range, squash courts, etc.

It is clear that compromise is possible. It is becoming clear that compromise is being implemented in those counties (like Warwickshire and West Sussex) which are inundated by golf course applications. Such compromise can be reached because of the faith in clear planning policies revived by the 1990 Town and Country Planning Act and the status now accorded to district-wide local plans. There is, in this case, a reasonable spirit of compromise on both sides. Planners and conservationists (even Friends of the Earth) have stated that there is no objection to golf as such, but only to those developers who want to use golf as a loophole in planning controls. Many spokespeople for golf reciprocate this spirit and believe that courses should fit into the broad design criteria suggested by the CPRE and the more specifically ecological criteria recommended by the Nature Conservancy Council.[33]

There are, of course, economic problems. Some projections suggest that the target for 2000 AD may be achieved by 1995! Golf may currently have created its own version of the classical economists' pig cycle: high prices attract investors who, acting simultaneously and after an unavoidable time-lag, create a glut. In which case they will find it very difficult to forgo profitable extras such as floodlit driving ranges and luxury hotel accommodation. Certainly, the potential developers of Warwick Castle Park were not prepared to compromise their 'unsuitable' proposals and may have cost themselves a right to any course development because of this failure.

But most golfers, as opposed to developers, want to fit in with nature and to be part of nature. Golf depends on landscape as a background and as a challenge and the more attractive golf courses are those which are part of, and live easily with, their established environment. A compromise will cost some facilities but for a greater overall benefit. That model might serve for the relationship between sport and conservation generally.

A conflict of values

My own interest in this subject arises from a clash of values in society in which I have sympathy, though perhaps not the same depth of sympathy, with both sides of the argument. I believe that sport and the conservation of environmental quality both make large contributions to human well-being, but I must confess that when I see remote and beautiful countryside assailed by motor sport my intuitive reaction is that something profoundly important is being sacrificed for something relatively trivial. My reaction, in short, is rather like the horror Wordsworth had of the industrial workers arriving at Windermere in coaches drawn by a loud and dirty machine. It might be objected that this is a mere personal taste of mine, a piece of snobbery, an illicit distinction between hierarchies of pleasure. But this argument takes us down the intellectual cul-de-sac inhabited by Jeremy Bentham and diverse economists in which all tastes, needs, pleasures and satisfactions are ranked on the same scale (an apparently psychological scale for Bentham, a financial one for the economists) and there is no possibility of arguing that the 'solitary contemplation of natural grandeur' (to use Mill's phrase) is a more profound pleasure, more in tune with a deep and ineradicable form of human desire, than is car racing. Of course, this is a personal opinion, but it can be argued: my intellectual opposition here is not to people who have different opinions, but to that tradition of thought which says that nothing can be said about desires except in terms of a one-dimensional relation of magnitude to other desires ('more pleasure' for Bentham, 'exchangeable for more money' to the economists).

This narrow economic view appears to have been absorbed into 'official' ideas of sport and to inform the research produced for the Sports Council and the Countryside Recreation Resarch Advisory Group. The effective assumptions of such research are that all sports have equal claim to consideration and to some form of public assistance and that access to land (including all forms of sporting access) has a common cause with conservation. They are, I think, philosophically, banal and bizarre assumptions, but they do have their political advantages: they appeal to the solidarity of a broad coalition and they avoid the ideological difficulties of evaluating the worth of different activities.

In dealing with conservation, those who argue from these assumptions have a tendency to dismiss the problem by reducing it to narrow ecological criteria. Thus, Sidaway sees the problems of sport and nature conservation purely in terms of the population of species and Charles Arthur asserts that 'Playing golf is unlikely to kill Scandinavian fish or pine trees by causing acid rain. Golf doesn't create nuclear waste and (19th hole stories apart) it doesn't kill whales.'[34] But during the time I was writing this section I cycled past the brand new golf course on (what was) Lord Leigh's estate. The design has been commended by planners and retains most of the habitats on the land, including many ancient oak trees. But as I rode past on a winter afternoon the lights were on along the drive to the new clubhouse; what had been a dense and rather mysterious little corner of the English countryside had lost its charm and intrigue. It was a reminder that it is quite wrong to see those forms of 'environment' known as the English countryside in ecological terms. As ecology, they are a complex, layered degradation of nature. But as culture they are our sole source of powerful images which relate ourselves to the earth, our past and each other.

It is an implication of most research in this field that something called 'sport' is of profound social value, which is an odd proposition given the range of activities which might be called sport and the vagueness of the concept's boundaries. Historically, the acceptance that sport is good and worthy of public subsidy through state education and Sports Council and local authority activity, comes from the acceptance of some quite different ideas. It is generally agreed that the Victorian approval of sport was because it was character-building. The idea of a physically fit population (so powerful in Germany and, later, the Soviet Union) came afterwards and was more intermittently invoked. Official statements of it were usually connected with war (for example the Inter-departmental Committee on Physical Deterioration after the Boer War and the Physical Training and Recreation Act of 1937 in anticipation of renewed war with Germany). The Sports Council has both denied that it is a fitness council and acted as if it were. We can add to these reasons a low-level approach to market failure, an assumption that states should provide sport facilities, as they provide trains and doctors, simply because the market was not very good at meeting demand in this sphere of activity.

The Sports Council's own statement of the benefits of sport for all seems suspiciously promiscuous in the range of arguments it is prepared to consider.[35] Sport teaches moral standards; it encourages human vitality: it creates a fitter public; people like it, anyway; it *does* develop the personality; it helps incorporate potential disaffection and makes people more conservative. There is even some flirtation, in a different section, with the idea that sport is an 'end-in-itself' rather than of demonstrable benefit in broad Utilitarian terms.[36] This is a real hotch-potch: some of these arguments would suggest a free market in sports facilities rather than public sponsorship and subsidy, while the argument about conservatism presumably appeals only to conservatives. It is 'typically British', as the late John Mackintosh used to say, to have a policy or institution for lots of different reasons, which contradict each other and which could be used to justify quite different alternatives.[37] Watching football does create or preserve communities, of a sort; marathon running gets people fit. What motor-cycle scrambling achieves is less clear. The Sport-for-All report does honestly admit that it is socially divisive to encourage sport in the countryside. The major participants, it says, 'have all been at odds with each other ... in a crowded country, such as Britain is, Sport for All has brought as much division as unification and will continue to do so'.[38]

Conclusion: the nature of conflict, the possibility of compromise

For some people the ethos of sport and the ethos of environmental-ism are in conflict as fundamentally as sin and virtue or capitalism and socialism. A long tradition of ecologically-oriented thought, ranging from John Massingham and the Earl of Portsmouth and their intellectual peers before the war to the feminist greens, the German 'fundis' and Jonathan Porritt at the time of writing, have expressed a hostility to sport in general, at least as far as it is competitive or commercial. To writers in this tradition, sport is a corollary of, and a metaphor for, the worst of industrial capitalism and represents values which are debased, trivial and destructive of possible harmony between people and nature. There are important strains of this perspective even in such (superficially) orthodox figures as Kipling and Baden-Powell.[39]

But, although there may be undertones of this fundamental hostility in the conflicts between sporting and environmental values, the mainstream of the debate, certainly at the higher levels of the administrative culture, takes the form of two positive sets of values competing for scarce resources. But the conflict does go beyond the normal sense in which major clusters of values compete within government. It is not quite like the relationship in which 'health' and 'education' compete for scarce resources. In principle, such a competition could be resolved by increasing expenditure on both at the expense of (say) defence or by increasing public expenditure generally. Sport and environmental quality are in competition for a resource, land, which is virtually fixed in general supply and for particular pieces of land which are unique and irreplaceable so far as many of the political actors are concerned. In short, land is limited in general supply and particular pieces of land are non-substitutable, which makes competition over land politically different in kind from other resource conflicts. A further complication is that the conflict takes at least two basic forms. It can be a conflict between two general public objectives where a broad value and market failure are assumed or it can be a conflict between private market mechanisms and public regulations: the resolution of golfing issues takes both forms.

I have not attempted to give a 'balanced' account of the conflict of values between sport and conservation, at least in the sense of balance which is supported by the Benthamite administrative culture. This insists that all possible tastes and demands are of equal status and are to be measured and compared rigorously on the same scale, so that we can compare the amount and frequency of the demand to see the view from the top of a mountain with that to motorcycle up it. That sort of balance is an imbalance, even to a moderate environmentalist, being heavily biased towards demonstrable, marketable and immediate goods and against the subtle, the long-term and the spiritual because it insists in measuring value in demonstrable, marketable and immediate terms. In fairness, though, it must be added that many sports organisations (those concerned with motor sport, for instance) which are accused of being 'environmentally unfriendly', regard the system as biased against *them*, asserting that the ramblers and nature organisations are 'insider' groups, better organised and with better access to policy-making ears. There is almost certainly some truth in this and the implication must be that, if administrative Benthamism is a prevailing ideology, its prevalence is at the overt, and perhaps superficial level, and there are deeper biases against some of its implications.

In many cases sport and environment require their own space: some places should be zoned as 'environmental totems', as I have called them elsewhere, protected from specific sporting activity and from the intensification of access as from development.[40] In orthodox economic terms the justification for this would have to be expressed in terms of 'existence' and 'option' values vested in a diversity of landscape and species, but those concepts cannot really be stretched far enough to incorporate the senses of wonder and mystery in landscape and the satisfaction of knowing its diversity and permanence (irrespective of any direct experience or act of consumption). I believe these senses are massive contributors to human well-being.

The compromises evolved in golf and in the Norfolk Broads are suggestive of a general approach. This involves a system of zoning, incorporating areas of totemistic tranquility and areas of intense use. This would necessarily have some paradoxical consequences from the environmentalists' point of view. For a supporter of this sort of policy what is happening to Whitlingham Marsh outside Norwich, in the case I discussed earlier, has to be regarded as unpleasant but necessary. In many cases, of course, the very demand for sporting activity incorporates a totemistic valuation of the place and the 'naturalness' of its context and challenges. What people seek in the pursuit of post-industrial sports is a sense of involvement and prowess which relates them to nature and tradition. If such sport were allowed to be environmentally destructive we would be guilty of throwing out the baby with the bath water.

Notes

1 Lincoln Allison, ed., *The Politics of Sport*, Manchester University Press, 1986, pp. 4–6.

2 Their best-known works are Ernst Haeckel, *The Evolution of Man*, translated from the Fifth (enlarged) Edition by Joseph McCabe, Watts, 1910, and J. E. Lovelock, *Gaia: A New Look at Life on Earth*, Oxford University Press, 1979.

3 B. Goodall and J. B. Whittow, *The Recreational Potential of Forestry Commission Holdings: A Report to the Forestry Commission*, Department of Geography, University of Reading, 1973, tables 2.3 and 2.4. Quoted in J. Allen Patmore, *Recreation and Resources, Leisure Patterns and Leisure Places*, Blackwell, 1983, pp. 220–21.

4 R. M. Sidaway, J. A. Coalter, I. M. Rennick and P. G. Scott, *Access Study*, Summary report, Countryside Commission and Sports Council, 1986, p. 12.

5 Thanks to Phil Belden, the West Sussex County Council Conservation Project Officer for supplying me with the relevant ephemera and for agreeing to be interviewed. He is, of course, not responsible for any of the errors or opinions here.

6 Thanks for information, ephemera and interviews to the following: Professor Timothy O'Riordan of the Department of Environmental Sciences at the University of East Anglia; Jane Madgwick, Conservation Officer of the Broads Authority; John Alloway of Norfolk Friends of the Earth; Martin George, former Regional Officer of the (then) Nature Conservancy Council; David Court, Managing Director of the holiday firm, Blake's. The opinions and errors are my own. See Lincoln Allison, 'A Broads view of politics', *The Countryman*, 96 (4), 1991.

7 Roger Sidaway, *Sport, Recreation and Nature Conservation*, Sports Council Study 32, Sports Council and Countryside Commission, 1988.

8 J. A. R. Pimlott, *Recreations*, Studio Vista, 1968, p. 39.

9 M. Dower, *The Challenge of Leisure*, Civic Trust, 1965, p. 5.

10 E. W. Bovill, *English Country Life 1780–1830*, Oxford University Press, 1962, p. 196.

11 William Wordsworth, *Guide to the Lakes*, Frowde, 1906, includes the prosaic and poetic expressions of his opposition.

12 John Stuart Mill, *The Principles of Political Economy*, Book IV, chapter 6, 'Of the stationary state', *Collected Works*, Routledge, 1965, vol. 3, p. 753.

13 See, especially, Clough Williams-Ellis, ed., *Britain and the Beast*, Dent, 1938.

14 For example, Hilary Talbot-Ponsonby, *New Approaches to Access in the Countryside*, Countryside Recreation Research Advisory Group, 1986, is a record of a conference held in Sheffield on that theme and contains my first protest against an all-embracing sports access principle, especially against Martin Elson's, 'A better deal for motor sports'.

15 Central Statistical Office, ed. Tom Griffin, *Social Trends 21*, HMSO, 1991, Chart 10.3, p. 170.

16 *Ibid.*, Table 10.20, p. 180.

17 See Fred Hirsch, *Social Limits to Growth*, Harvard University Press, 1976.

18 Tibor Scitovsky, *The Joyless Economy: An Inquiry into Consumer Satisfaction and Human Dissatisfaction*, Oxford University Press, 1976.

19 CSO, *op. cit.*, Table 10.20, p. 180.

20 *Ibid.*, Table 10.2, p. 170.

21 *Ibid.*, Table 10.24, p. 181.

22 *Ibid.*, Table 10.16, p. 177.

23 *Ibid.*, Table 10.18, p. 179.

24 Jill Matheson, 'Participation in sport', *General Household Survey 1987*, HMSO, 1991, Table 2, p. 9.

25 Interpolated from figures given in Peter McIntosh and Valerie Charlton, *The Impact of Sport for All Policy 1966–84*, Sports Council, Study 26, Table 14, pp. 125–6.

26 Chartered Institute of Public Finance and Accounting, *Leisure and Recreation Statistics, 1980–81, Estimates*, quoted in Patmore, *op. cit.*, p. 25. Confirmed in conversations with officials of Warwick District Council Amenities Department.

27 CSO, *op. cit.*, Table 10.17, p. 178 and Matheson, *op. cit.*, Figure D, p. 12.

28 Elspeth Burnside, 'Course crisis', *Golf Monthly*, December 1990, 10.

29 The Royal and Ancient Golf Club of St Andrews, *The Demand for Golf, 1989*.

30 The percentages were interpolated by the author.

31 Council for the Protection of Rural England, *Briefing Paper – Golf Courses*, September 1991; English Heritage, *Golf Course Proposals in Historic Landscapes*, 1991. See also Nature Conservancy Council, *On Course Conservation – Managing Golf's Natural Heritage*, 1990.

32 From *England and the Octopus*, quoted in CPRE, *op. cit.*, p. 1.

33 See for example, Charles Arthur, 'Environmentally friendly?', *Golf Monthly*, February 1991, 14–19.

34 Sidaway, *Sport, Recreation and Nature Conservation*; Arthur, *op. cit.*, p. 14.
35 McIntosh and Charlton, *op. cit.*, pp. 103–12.
36 *Ibid.*, pp. 192–3.
37 See, for instance, J. P. Mackintosh, *The Devolution of Power*, Penguin, 1968, p. 39.
38 McIntosh and Charlton, *op. cit.*, p. 107.
39 See Lincoln Allison, *Ecology and Utility: The Philosophical Dilemmas of Planetary Management*, Pinter/Leicester University Press, 1991, pp. 137–8 for a (slightly) fuller account of this antithesis.
40 *Ibid.*, esp. pp. 166–9.

Index